12 STEP

WISDOM

AT WORK

TRANSFORMING YOUR LIFE AND YOUR ORGANIZATION

12 STEP WISDOM AT WORK

TRANSFORMING YOUR LIFE AND YOUR ORGANIZATION

HAZELDEN FOUNDATION

Edited by William C. Hammond III

Foreword by Ian I. Mitroff

Introduction by Jerry Spicer

KOGAN
PAGE

Kogan Page Limited
120 Pentonville Road
London N1 9JN, UK

Kogan Page U.S.
163 Central Avenue, Suite 2
Dover, NH 03820, USA

© The Hazelden Foundation, 2001

The right of the Hazelden Foundation to be identified as the authors of this work has been asserted by them in accordance with the Copyright, Designs and Patents Act 1988.

British Library Cataloguing in Publication Data

A CIP record for this book is available from the British Library.

ISBN 0 7494 344 06

Typeset by Eliot House Productions
Printed and bound in United States

Contents

P A R T   I I I

Foreword

$\mathcal{T}$he chapters in this book serve as a powerful testimony to one of the most important ideas ever invented by humans—the Twelve Steps of Alcoholics Anonymous. The book represents an important step forward in extending the Twelve Steps (which originally were intended to address recovery from alcoholism) to business organizations.

If one scrutinizes the Twelve Steps, it becomes apparent that there is nothing in them that cannot be applied to business organizations. Indeed, every chapter in this book demonstrates the extent to which the Steps can and should be applied in this way.

I find the concept of extending the Twelve Steps to business organizations immensely appealing and exciting. Organizations are no more capable of quick, easy changes than are individuals. Indeed, organizations suffer from many of the same dysfunctions as individuals; for example, organizations are prone to deny engaging in unethical practices, such as cheating, lying, or physical and sexual harassment that may occur within their walls.

We accept the fact that organizations have a culture or a "group mind." In this sense, there is no conceptual difference between attributing a psyche to organizations and to individuals. What is problematic is knowing where individuals leave off and organizations begin. The "brain" may reside inside of every individual, but surely the "mind" does not. Indeed, the "mind" is a complex social phenomenon and is shared by many others, as within an organization.

The most important reason why it is appealing and necessary to extend the principles of AA to business organizations is due to the extreme difficulties of securing permanent change in complex business environments. To put it in philosophical terms, very few good ideas can be self-implemented. That is, the goodness or the truth of an idea alone rarely if ever leads to its implementation.

We are beginning to realize why implementation and change are so hard to achieve: Most propositions for improving the life of an individual or a business organization require a commitment to making massive changes in fundamental lifestyles. This is precisely where the Twelve Steps enter in.

As one works through and understands each of the various Steps, one comes to understand that collectively they constitute a *system* for affecting change at every level and aspect of a person's life. The Steps are not only designed to improve a person's life, they are suggestions for overcoming the massive resistance and denial that blocks true change from happening. In other words, the Twelve Steps can be viewed as an ethical system for the purpose of helping one design a set of principles by which to achieve and lead a better life.

I cannot overemphasize the word *design* in relation to the Twelve Steps. Since AA places such a high value on each individual's interpretation of the Steps, the Steps are a direct invitation to redesign one's entire life so that it will be more ethical and in concert with that of others, or the community.

Another reason why I find the application of Twelve Step principles to business organizations so appealing is that they follow the progression of psychological and social development of the last century. A moment's reflection on the last century shows that it steadily moved from treating individuals to larger and larger social groups. In the 1900s psychoanalysts, such as Freud and Jung, treated deeply disturbed individuals. Thirty of forty years later, the ideas of Freud and others were extended to the treatment of whole family systems. At the end of the twentieth century and the beginning of the twenty-first, we perceive that this progression can be extended to the treatment of whole organizations. We are beginning to understand that human systems must be transformed at all levels simultaneously if any of the sub-systems are to have hope of changing. In short, there is no hope of affecting profound change *within individuals* unless there are also profound changes occurring simultaneously within organizations and society as a whole.

This book is to be applauded for its use of personal stories to illustrate how Twelve Step principles have deeply affected the lives of individuals and organizations. Such stories are immensely important, for they reveal the strong presence of the authors in their work as consultants and spiritual advisors to business leaders. The results of their work validate the principles they seek to apply. Indeed, they are consultants/practitioners/ therapists/healers in the highest sense.

There is one aspect of the present volume that I believe needs further reinforcement. Hopefully, this volume points to and encourages enacting the next step forward: We need many more empirical studies of the use of Twelve Step principles for achieving large-scale change in organizations. While the present volume undoubtedly demonstrates the strengths and the shortcomings of the present approaches to studying business organizations and to achieving substantial change, unless we produce more studies that are grounded in the actual experiences of exec-utives and organizations, the Twelve Step principles will not have the influence on the world of business that they deserve. We need many more case studies of the application and adapta-tion of Twelve Step principles to organizations. For a start, we need to do more in-depth case studies, which this volume is to be celebrated for initiating.

We need to go forward from here to catalogue and to compare the various interpretations that executives and organizations give to the Steps. We need to understand better why certain Steps are more readily to be adapted by organizations than oth-ers. We need to understand more how each of the Steps can be translated into day-to-day operational "rules" for running organizations. Of course, by "rules" I do not mean narrow guidelines or prescriptions. If this were the case, the cure could indeed be worse than the disease.

Twelve Step Wisdom at Work provides a solid foundation for tak-ing a great leap forward. The approach it ushers in will allow organizations to be better designed and more successful. The spirit it purveys will allow leaders and followers alike to achieve a healthy, meaningful existence.

—*Ian I. Mitroff,*
Harold Quinton Distinguished Professor
of Business Policy
Marshall School of Business
University of Southern California
Los Angeles, California

Preface

$\mathcal{T}$he concept for this book was born in October 1997. At that time I was publisher at the Hazelden Foundation, an international leader in the research, education, and treatment of alcohol and other drug addiction. Hazelden was launching a new strategic initiative: to apply its fifty years of innovation in the holistic treatment of addiction to other illnesses.

The setting was an off-campus meeting of middle and senior managers. Jerry Spicer, President of Hazelden, challenged us to think "out of the box" in projecting the core competencies of Hazelden and the principles that historically have sustained these competencies: the Twelve Steps of Alcoholics Anonymous. He asked, "If the Twelve Steps are so effective in transforming the lives of people cursed with addiction, might not the Steps also serve as a successful model for change in other environments?"

His question sparked intense discussions. A number of avenues were explored, until one stalwart manager wondered out loud if the corporate world might not serve as an ideal testing ground for this hypothesis.

Jerry turned to me. "Well, Bill," he asked, in a tone of one who has finally received the answer he had surreptitiously been seeking. "What about it? Can we do a book on this subject?"

I left Hazelden soon thereafter to return to my previous vocation of business consultant to the publishing industry. Hazelden remained a client, and over dinner in New York the following summer Jerry again broached the subject of the book. With little hesitation, but with no clear understanding of how the work would ultimately evolve, I agreed to serve as project manager and editor in this initiative. After all, I had witnessed firsthand during my time at Hazelden the power of the Twelve Steps and the many miracles they inspire. Though not in recovery myself, I am and forever will remain an apostle of Twelve Step principles.

In many successful business ventures luck seems to play a hand. It certainly did in this initiative. I was able to recruit several excellent writers from Hazelden's staff and board, as well as some of the premier leaders in the burgeoning—and increasingly interconnected—fields of organizational change, leadership development, and spirituality in the workplace. Although only a few of these business professionals could recite the Twelve Steps with any degree of accuracy, all of them intuitively understood the principles of the Steps and realized they had actively applied them to their daily life and work.

The authors and I were together on the learning curve to more fully understand the differences between our proposed book and those already available in the marketplace. We met regularly as a team to work at the "big picture" as well as the myriad details that resulted from sewing threads of common theme and voice through the tapestry of an anthology. Our respect for each other grew as our excitement over the project intensified. So did our sense that we were describing a powerful tool for corporate change—one that is neglected in existing business literature, yet one that has a proven efficacy and a potential to encompass the common wisdom underlying many currently accepted methodologies.

It has been a year since our first author meeting. So much has transpired in the last twelve months that it is difficult to recall those early days of wonder. Suffice it to say that for me this past year has been one steeped in insight and privilege. I applaud both the input and the contribution of all the authors. I appreciate beyond measure their enthusiastic commitment to this project. Working with them, and getting to know them on both a personal and professional level, has truly made this project, for me, a career milestone. I can only stress that I believe both business and the Twelve Steps have been well served by the authors' collective effort.

I hope you enjoy reading this book. More importantly, I hope that what you read in this book will have a profound and long-lasting influence on both your life and the health of your organization.

—*William C. Hammond, III*
Minneapolis, Minnesota
March 2000

Introduction

In 1949 a unique journey began in Center City, Minnesota. It was a journey that combined the wisdom of personal growth and the knowledge embodied in Alcoholics Anonymous with a holistic view of change, encompassing mind, spirit, body, and community. This book brings together the ideas of a number of thoughtful experts, each of whom, having unique and diverse experiences, offers insights into personal and organizational transformation.

The idea for this publication came from a group of Hazelden managers who attended a leadership development meeting and suggested that Hazelden's fifty years of experience in empowering personal change could serve a broader educational purpose for other organizations and business leaders. My personal experience at Hazelden began in 1978 when, as a candidate for a research position, I was struck with a clinical outcome measurement system that considered more than the amount of alcohol or other drugs a person used before and after treatment. Rather,

Hazelden assessed a broader range of outcomes—relationships, self-awareness, quality of life, spiritual growth, engagement in a community of support, and overall physical and mental health. I knew then that Hazelden was a unique place, committed to removing addiction as a barrier to a holistic change process. When Hazelden leaders suggested that we bring this knowledge to others, I knew they were right, and with help from our contributing authors, I believe this book can help you, and your organization, achieve your vision.

As you read through the different concepts expressed by the authors in the pages that follow, keep in mind a few general principles that can be found in all the chapters, namely that all people and organizations have the potential to change, grow, and improve. To begin this journey we must have a vision of where we can be in the future. We form this vision through self-reflection as well as seeing positive change and growth in others. With our vision for the future in hand, we can determine a starting point through a candid, honest understanding of our current situation and our strengths and weaknesses. Much like our vision for the future, we gain understanding of our current reality through personal introspection and the information others give us. The gap between where we are and where we want to be creates a sense of organizational and personal purpose. When the gap is too big, we despair; if the gap is too small, we are unfilled. Consequently, a first critical step in a change process is to set challenging but not overwhelming goals.

Continuous change results from raising our vision as our reality improves. At Hazelden, patients may arrive intending to learn how to be "controlled drinkers," but hopefully at the end of their treatment stay they will leave Hazelden committed to an alcohol-free life and to the pursuit of holistic growth. Similarly, moving from our current situation to our personal or corporate vision requires work and action. Empowering ourselves and our employees to engage in this journey is the difference between an unfilled dream and continuous change and improvement.

This model for change I've been describing contains a final element that is often overlooked: Creating a support system that gives people, such as your employees, a sense of assurance that if they reach for the next trapeze and miss, there's a safety net below that provides them a chance to try again. Employers provide employees a variety of formal safety nets through policies and practices. Perhaps the most significant safety net, however, is the support of other people. Our communities and social support networks not only provide inspiration for our vision and assistance in change, but our friends and colleagues hold the net that catches us when we slip (we all will slip, sooner or later) and help us climb back on board to start the journey again.

An examination of the steps and writings of Alcoholics Anonymous, in a general sense, speak to these same principles: We begin with honest self-appraisal and take steps to engage others in our change process; we then commit to action; and in the end we understand that the ultimate measure of recovery is when we reach out to others, giving support and sharing our own learning.

With these perspectives in mind, each of the contributing authors have provided their insights into change, transformation, and applying the wisdom of the world's largest grass-roots social movement, Alcoholics Anonymous, to achieving personal and organizational visions.

—*Jerry Spicer*

The book is dedicated to the employees of the Hazelden Foundation. These professionals are both followers and leaders in helping Hazelden fulfill its mission of helping individuals, families, and communities achieve a transformation beyond their initial expectations as patients and clients. To those who have preceded us, for our colleagues, and for the next generation, we dedicate the ideas and hope in these pages.

—*Jerry Spicer*
President/CEO
Hazelden Foundation
Center City, Minnesota

PART I

Chapters 1 and 2 lay the foundation for this book. Pat has worked with the Hazelden Foundation for over twenty years and is well versed on Twelve Step philosophy and principles. She is also a leading authority on the Twelve Steps as a model for change and on the dynamics of change in one's personal and professional life. In this chapter Pat presents the theories behind the change process. In addition, she describes the process we encounter when we make major changes in our lives, and offers fundamental reasons why people may decide not to seek change in their lives and other reasons why they may. All future chapters are based in this first chapter, as change is the catalyst that drives what is described and recommended by the other authors beginning with Chapter 3.

—Editor

Why We Change, Why We Don't

Patricia Owen, Ph.D.

*C*hange cannot be willed. Or, to be more exact, change cannot be created by will alone.

Contrary to all of the messages we receive, toddlerhood to adulthood, our conscious will alone has little effect in producing and maintaining most of the truly significant changes in our lives. In fact, the more concretely we can point to something we have changed simply by mandating it, the more likely it is that it is limited or superficial. Or, we are taking credit for change that has occurred beyond our willing. For example, we can change how many hours we read and study current events, but for most of us, this will not put us in line for the next ambassadorship. We can change the number of hours we work on a project, but we cannot ensure that this will propel us to a higher position. We can go to school for many years, but this doesn't mean we will be the head of a company, at the top of our profession, or even that we will end up successful or happy in the career to which it leads us. So why should we even think about changing? Is it ever possible?

Change occurs on many levels; the more we understand and allow ourselves to be open to change, the more likely that change will occur. The changes that occur may be beyond our wildest dreams.

As human beings, we have a natural inclination toward change. On a cellular level, our body is dying continuously, and new cells are created to take their places. During our first year on earth, we change tremendously, increasing our physical size, social awareness, and basic knowledge about the world many times over. Yet somehow as adults, we find change more difficult. We are less satisfied simply to let ourselves develop, and are more likely to have an end goal in mind. We fail to make the changes we dream of not because we are lazy or unintelligent. Usually the reasons are far more complex.

Change theorists can describe the five-step process we go through when we make major changes in our lives.

1. **Precontemplation phase.** During this phase we may be dissatisfied or conflicted, but not yet thinking about change. We might think our dissatisfaction is a passing phenomenon, attributable to someone or something else. For whatever reason, the idea of accepting personal responsibility for change has not yet occurred to us.

   For example, Bob has been a realtor for two years and making only a few sales despite a booming housing market. He wakes up in the morning with a knot in his stomach, dreading the idea of glad-handing and selling. But he thinks if he sticks with it long enough, the fun will begin. After all, his brother-in-law is a top salesman in residential real estate and clearly loves his job.

2. **Contemplation phase.**
   "What do you plan to do with your one wild and precious life?"
   —Mary Oliver
   Our consciousness was raised during this phase, and we begin thinking things like, "How would my life be different

if . . .?" Imagination plays a significant role in the actual change process.

For instance, Carol became a teacher because it seemed like the logical thing to do when she was in college and planning her life. Her real dream, though, since she was a little girl was to be a forest ranger. Now she's wondering, "What does a forest ranger really do? Is that something I'd still like? How does a person become a forest ranger?"

3. **Preparation phase.**
   "There is at bottom only one problem in the world and this is its name. How does one break through? How does one get into the open? How does one burst the cocoon and become a butterfly?"

   −Thomas Mann, Doctor Faustus

   Now we are actually making moves toward our goal. We might call a friend who has changed careers and ask, "How was that for you?" We might pick up a book at a library about the new career in which we are interested. This might be the time we talk to our family and discuss ways the change would affect them, and how everyone could help make it possible. We might check out training programs or associations where we could make connections with others. This is the time to explore and plan.

   For example, Josh was working as a social worker, but he was seriously considering starting a new career in the computer field. He got a catalogue from the local technical school and read the course descriptions to help him narrow down his area of interest. He bought a home computer and learned everything he could about it. He met a few people who did computer graphics work, and after talking with them, he knew that this was the direction he wanted to go.

4. **Action phase.** This is when the leap occurs. If the previous three stages have been done thoroughly, we're ready, and the disconnection between our old life and our new life need not be huge or painful.

Until one is committed,
There is hesitancy, the chance to draw back,
Always ineffectiveness.
The moment one definitely commits oneself,
Then Providence moves to.
All sorts of things occur to help one
That would otherwise have never occurred.
Whatever you can do, or dream you can, begin it.
Boldness has genius, power and magic in it.
Begin it now.

–Goethe

Now we begin to take classes, to network with others, to send out our résumé, do exploratory interviews, and keep the imagination alive. Some people do daily mediation and journal specifically about their new career ideas. You might find ways to take on small parts of the job you'd ultimately like to have—through consultation contracts, volunteer work, extra assignments on your current job, or class projects.

For instance, Sally's job is in retail, selling home furnishings. But she knew she wanted a new career, teaching English as a second language to immigrants. She did her preparation work and knew the training she needed and where she might be able to get a job in her new field. She had never done any teaching before, however, and did not have much experience with people from other cultures. But she put her plan into action: She asked her boss if she could help teach the next class on interior decorating that the store often offered to the public; she began tutoring one evening a week at an after-school program for inner-city youth; and she signed up for her first class at the local college that would give her credits toward a teaching certificate. She found out that after three classes, she could begin working as an assistant teacher at an international learning center and made arrangements to do that the following summer.

5. **Maintenance phase.** Now comes the hard part—sustaining the motivation and the dream. This is when we keep doing the things we started doing during the action phase that will help us stay on track. If the first flurry of activity—résumés, meetings with others, classes—has not produced the immediate results we are aiming for, we don't stop. This is the time to surround ourselves with people and things that help keep us motivated. It might be an inspirational quote taped to the refrigerator, a weekly lunch with a supportive friend or mentor, or treating ourselves to a new book about the new career interest we are targeting.

James, for instance, was an accountant, aiming for a new career buying and selling antiques. He was diligently taking community courses on starting and running a small business, going to trade shows and doing some buying and selling on a small scale, and working with a financial planner to save up enough money to launch his own store. He knew his dream would take two or three years to come true. But there were things that kept him going—he checked out books at the library about biographies of people who had had a passion for antiques. He found small antiques for friends' birthday presents, knowing that this would give them a special part of himself and would be a good excuse to buy an antique. On business trips he made a point of visiting small antiques stores and photographing them to help him continue to imagine what his own store might look like. He slowly started to build his own collection, knowing that someday these would be among the first items for sale in his new store.

Change generally occurs in a spiral fashion, rather than in a linear way. As we move through the stages, we may find ourselves circling back to previous phases. For example, as we reach the action phase and new doors open to us, we may find ourselves doing some more work in the contemplation phase, adding to our understanding about our direction and ourselves. Each time we circle back our journey becomes richer and the foundation more solid.

If change can occur in such a neat, predictable way, what happens to derail it? Why doesn't it always happen the way we want or plan?

The following is a top nine list of why we don't succeed in making the changes we strive for.

Why We Don't Change

1. *The idea of change is someone else's more than it is our own.* Sometimes we seek change out of a vague belief that we should. But the new career, the advancement to the next level, the grand achievement may be someone else's dream for us and not our own. Joseph Campbell, the mythologist and philosopher, says, "If there is a path, it is someone else's path and you are not on the adventure." The someone else may be a parent, friend, or boss; more likely it is our own internalized view of what society in general values.

   In our postmodern era, change is billed as inherently better. What sells is "new and improved," implying that "same as always" is not good enough. We are the first generation to have several careers in a single lifetime; in our parents' generation, it was common for people (generally men) to stay in the same career—in fact, the same company—for thirty to forty years until retirement. The implication now is that if you are not advancing, you are falling behind. Expert computer programmers are encouraged to take on large-scale systems and projects; compassionate clinicians are moved into supervisory and administrative positions; fantastic one-on-one salespeople are given regions with staffs, budgets, and annual goals. The typical response of any of these people is generally, "Great! I'm appreciated!" They get new titles and raises and celebrate with friends and families. For many of these people, the change fits them well, and they adapt. Others feel further and further removed from both their heart and expertise.

For instance, Jim was an ace cereal and grain salesman for a large company. In time, his company recognized his abilities and hard work and gave him a large western US region. Instead of being on the road selling, he worked in an office. He no longer built up relationships with customers, closed sales, or worked toward his own individual goals. Instead, he coached others and kept his eye on regional results. He was making double his previous salary but becoming increasingly unhappy. After his marriage fell apart he decided the changes he had accepted were the wrong ones, and he quit his job. He decided to spend the summer working as a bicycle taxi driver in New Mexico and catch on to the job market again in the fall—but this time as a salesman and not as a regional vice president. "The salary was great, but the job wasn't me."

In this case, Jim made the changes expected of him, found they did not fit, and was willing to backtrack to find the career he truly loved.

Britt is another example. She eyed the supervisory job posted. She was an excellent teacher and wondered about the new responsibilities the new job might give her. She was wise enough to acknowledge that just getting the job—the promotion, the acclaim from her peers—would feel good. But she decided against applying for the job. "I think it'd be a great wedding but a disastrous marriage," she joked.

Britt contemplated a change but decided against it because she saw it fed her need for recognition and appreciation from others but would not feed her heart.

Sometimes we don't change because we see that it is not a change we really want to make. This is a wise reason not to make a change.

2. *The thing we're trying to change is connected to something bigger or that is immutable.* Some people decide to make a career change when in fact another aspect of their life is the source of the problem. For example, a person who

experiences conflict in the workplace with other people may think, "I'll get a different job and then things will be different!" Someone else may think, "I don't get along with authority figures; I want to do things my own way," and on the basis of that decide to start his or her own business. Another person may consistently take on too many projects and become overwhelmed and may decide a different line of work would be better. For these people, the problems with others and themselves will follow them wherever they go. While another career may indeed suit them better, they will not be happier unless they also resolve the more basic work issues about themselves.

A related misstep occurs when people try to ameliorate non-work-related personal or relationship problems by changing external trappings, such as their career. This is like thinking you are improving a house by painting it, when in fact the foundation is rotting. For example, people with an addiction, chronic low self-esteem, or excessive power and achievement needs may be looking for something outside themselves—a new career, a new position—to fill up what is lacking inside. Most likely any success in the new position will be fleeting or fraught with problems, and these people will not be any happier.

In both these cases, there is a mismatch between the problem and the solution. The person identifies the problem ("I'm unhappy with other people" or "I'm unhappy with myself") and seeks a solution that may not solve the problem ("I'll get a new job").

3. *A major leap is needed. Some changes seem so big or complex that we shy away from them.* For example, if a person wants to switch careers from teaching English to computer programming, the thought of going to months or years of technical school in the evening may seem overwhelming. Or a person in a technical field may dream of going to art school and becoming a costume designer but cannot face the idea of starting over. Some career changes require a large-scale

sacrifice. Emotional and financial security may need to be sacrificed. A person may use energy wishing and dreaming instead of taking the big leap that is needed.

4. *Change takes time and the results aren't obvious or immediately rewarding.* It is hard to maintain change when the novelty wears off. Using the change model presented above, we often think of change as being what occurs in the action phase. In fact, change occurs in at least seven phases in a nonlinear fashion. In other words, change is not something that happens all at once; it is a process. But when we are in the midst of that process, it can seem like we are going nowhere, we have failed, or that the end is so far down the line that it is no use to continue. We might feel embarrassed to tell others that we have not made the big career move yet, but we are still working on it. We ourselves may wonder whether we really have it in us to accomplish our dreams. Giving up on ourselves is probably the biggest reason change does not occur.

5. *Lack of imagining.* A team of researchers followed forty-six female valedictorians from Illinois high schools in the graduating class of 1981. Ten years later, researchers found that the early career levels of these young women varied greatly. A key to success was what the researchers called tacit knowledge. This differs from academic or intellectual knowledge. It is a kind of practical intelligence, an understanding (in this case) of how to build one's career. Specifically, many women could not imagine themselves in the high-level careers to which they aspired. They could imagine themselves being good students and top performers, or accomplishing and achieving more of the same. They could not, however, imagine themselves at the next level. For example, one woman acknowledged that she liked math and did well in it but "I'm not a mathematician." After looking at all the variables that might predict success, the researchers concluded that tacit knowledge played a critical role: "Even high achievers cannot realistically aspire to what they cannot imagine."

We have plenty of time for imagination—all the spare moments running errands, commuting, waiting in line or for someone to meet us—but we often fill this otherwise empty time listening to background music, perusing old magazines, watching TV or listening to the radio, or doing busywork. Letting our imagination run free, placing ourselves in important new roles can be anxiety provoking. It may take conscious practice and willingness to allow our minds to imagine. Without imagination even our most intelligent choices and best efforts may fail.

6. *Lack of knowledge.* If we have our sights set on a career path that is totally foreign to us, we might not know where to begin. The new job may seem unobtainable, either because the people in these careers seem perfect or godlike to us, or because the career itself is so undefined.

7. *We believe it is too late and we're too old.* Even though we once could believe that we were bright and promising, we might be all too willing to give up that view of ourselves as we grow older. We live in a culture that values youth. After all, most of us who are now in the baby boomer age group had the rallying cry of "don't trust anyone over thirty," assuming that anyone "that old" was intolerant and inflexible. By sheer mass, the millions of us born in the post-World War II era set the standard that young was best. Now that we are growing older ourselves, we may find ourselves denigrating our own wisdom and believing our own jokes about aging.

The fact is, our intelligence continues to increase until we are well into our fifties, and there is little intellectual decline until we are in our late sixties. A team of researchers conducted a study that lasted twenty-one years, testing people between the ages of twenty-one and eighty-one. The researchers found that verbal meaning—comprehension and the ability to use and understand language—actually increases until the age of fifty-three, and then does not decline until after age sixty-three. Spatial intelligence—

sequencing, piecing together the whole from parts, imagining and manipulating figures in three dimensions—peaks at age forty-six and does not significantly decline until age sixty-seven. Finally, reasoning—our ability to analyze complex problems and come to logical conclusions—remains steady until after age sixty. These researchers also found that when declines did occur, they could often be reversed by training. In other words, most of us can expect to maintain or improve our intellectual abilities well into our later years. Doubts about our ability to learn need not block us from embarking on change.

Some older adults give up the hope of change because they believe their time is past. They imagine what their life might have been like if they'd taken that career path when they were just starting out and think now, "I missed my opportunity." If a person dreams of being a musician and equates that with going to Juilliard, studying in Europe, and taking the world by storm at the age of twenty-seven, it is true that that time is past. If, on the other hand, the person can imagine a new scenario to go with the goal, he or she may find it entirely possible. Instead of Juilliard, it might be the local university or lessons from a neighborhood teacher. Instead of performing at Lincoln Center, it might be at the community orchestra, with a church choir, or with a group of other late bloomers who love music and performance. While it may take some humility to accept and foster the new dream, if the passion is there, the manifestation of it will take its own appointed shape—and will matter less.

Sometimes being older has advantages that can actually help us make changes. Francis Crick, codiscoverer of the molecular structure of DNA and Nobel Prizewinner, wrote how making a career move comparatively later in life made his scientific achievement possible:

> When the war finally came to an end, I was at a loss
> as to what to do... I took stock of my qualifications.

A not-very-good degree, redeemed somewhat by my achievements at the Admiralty. A knowledge of certain restricted parts of magnetism and hydrodynamics, neither of them subjects for which I felt the least bit of enthusiasm. No published papers at all... Only gradually did I realize that this lack of qualification could be an advantage. By the time most scientists have reached age thirty they are trapped by their own expertise. They have invested so much effort in one particular field that it is often extremely difficult, at that time in their careers, to make a radical change. I, on the other hand, knew nothing, except for a basic training in somewhat old-fashioned physics and mathematics and an ability to turn my hand to new things... Since I essentially knew nothing, I had an almost completely free choice.

8. *We don't make choices.* It can be a good thing to keep all options open until we are certain in which direction we want to go. This approach has advantages and disadvantages; it may, however, mean a person will stay at one level, rather than moving forward. For instance, there is the college major who waits until the very last moment to declare a major (and then declares at least two!); the generalist who keeps taking lower-level positions in several career paths to check them out; or the employee who takes on a wide range of projects rather than focusing on one type. These people have something in common: They are uncertain or unwilling to claim just one area as their passion or interest. It takes energy to sustain interest in a wide range of topics, which is energy that might otherwise go toward moving forward in one area.

9. *Fear.* The biggest reason for not changing, and the umbrella over many of the reasons we've discussed thus far, is fear. We may have many reasons why we believe change is not possible—we are not sure how, maybe we're too old, we can't imagine ourselves in a new role, we have

difficulty making major commitments—but fear is the common denominator.

Despite the myriad obstacles we manage to create for ourselves, people do find ways to make important changes in their lives. Let's turn our attention now to the opposite side of the coin and take a look at the top reasons why people do and can change.

Why We Change

1. *External forces propel us.* We may want to keep our world unchanged, but outside events may force us to make new choices. Many of these forces come initially as a tragedy or an unhappy event such as the death of a partner or parent, job loss, or serious illness. Suddenly the security of our old ways is gone. When this kind of change happens to us, we are usually propelled back to the beginning of the change process. Any plans we had for ourselves are often shattered. At first we may be so preoccupied by the event that we cannot focus on our own responsibility for moving forward. Over time, however, we sometimes find that the change that happened, actually gave us the reason or opportunity to try a new direction. Sometimes the new direction turns out far better than the path we were on.

2. *Internal factors push us toward change.* Our biological time clock and societal expectations about it nudges us. When we turn thirty, forty, or fifty, we are often reminded that life is finite and passing quickly. When we are younger, we may be content to leave our options open, or to follow someone else's path. As we grow older, we realize that the time to try out our own ideas is limited.

3. *We change as changes unfold.* Sometimes we do not change intentionally, but we instead leave ourselves open to changes. As our talents are appreciated or as others see things about us that they believe will benefit them, we may

be offered new positions. Depending on our personal goals, this type of change may bring us closer to or farther from where we intended to be. Or we may be pleasantly surprised that we were able to test all the career paths we did simply by following where the path seemed to be going. (In entrepreneurship, this phenomenon is call the corridor principle.)

4. *Others encourage us.* Some people say the best way to determine where your talents lie is to listen to what others tell you. Indeed, other people can influence us tremendously. In the study of valedictorians cited previously, the researchers found that other people played a key role: "The most successful women in the valedictorian study were unusual in having received special opportunities and attention from faculty." Sometimes the special recognition or validation comes from unexpected places.

For example, when asked what made her decide to become a prevention specialist working with youth, Mary answered, "Why, it was Sally Mae Jenson!" She went on to explain: years earlier, she completed college with a degree in English, but she had no clear goals or career path. She worked in a series of office jobs, but was ill suited for most of them. One Sunday she helped with a short worship service for the children. Another member, Sally Mae Jenson, caught Mary as she was leaving church and said, "You're really great with kids!" This simple comment fell on fertile ground; Mary knew right then that this was a good direction for her to take.

We all have the opportunity to receive input from other people, but it takes a special willingness to be open to guidance and direction to act upon the words we hear.

9. *Unexpected opportunities present themselves.* Though we may think that some people are just extraordinarily lucky, the real truth is that "luck" is simply being prepared for opportunity. When we nurture and grow what we love, we are likely to be graced with remarkable new possibilities.

For example, Mark was an artist, but his day job was working in an office. He noticed that an elderly neighbor was having trouble with chores and began to shovel his sidewalk after snowstorms. Over time, they engaged in conversation, and his neighbor asked, "If you could do anything with your art, what would it be?" Mark said that he would love to be an artist-in-residence at the local conservatory and start an art education program for kids. Little did Mark know that his neighbor was wealthy, and that when he died he would leave a provision in his will to get Mark started in his dream.

As another example, Michael Crichton, the author of *Jurassic Park*, and director of the movie The Great Train Robbery and the popular TV show ER, intended to become a physician and attended Harvard medical school. But while a medical student, he wrote a book about germ warfare and submitted it to a publisher. *The Andromeda Strain* became an instant best-seller and a movie. He left medicine and pursued a career of writing.

Victor Bonomo, for a third example, helped his father in a small candy business on Coney Island, New York, which his father began in 1897. After World War II sugar rationing was lifted, the cooks at the candy factory came up with a new recipe, and the public was clamoring for sweets as never before. The popular drugstore Woolworth's became the distributor for their new candy bar: Bonomo's Turkish Taffy. The company sold eighty to one hundred million bars a year for decades until it was bought by Tootsie Roll Industries and discontinued in 1989. Bonomo died in 1999 at the age of 100, a wealthy man.

5. *We are in an emotionally and spiritually safe environment.* After years of trying to prove ourselves to others or to satisfy our need to feel important through achievement, we may be ready to listen to our heart, to what we really wish to do. This is most likely to occur when we feel loved for who we are. Until then, we may be too filled with fear or

low self-esteem even to claim our passion, much less to follow it. When we finally reach the point where we are willing to claim our unique gifts and talents, it is usually because we have come to a place—within ourselves—where we realize the object of life is to become more of who we are, rather than less. At this point, fear dissipates and nothing can stop us from what may be nothing short of our true calling. This will not necessarily be a shining career path or lofty goal of changing the world.

As an example, John was an insurance executive, but all his life he loved the romance of airplanes and flight. He kept model planes in his office and looked forward to vacation or business trips that required cross-country flights. But he stuck to his duty of succeeding in his career and supporting his family. After thirty years, he retired early to do what he knew he really loved. The first thing on his list was to take flying lessons.

As a second instance, Laura started her career in the ballet in New York City. After several years of advanced training and practice and a few brief jobs, she decided to be more practical and went back to school to become a city planner. She worked in the city office on several important projects and over the years become proficient and well respected. But after facing a severe stress-related illness, she knew she needed to find her way back to her heart. She realized she cared deeply about the body, how it worked, and how to take care of it. She went to massage school and is now helping dancers, athletes, and performers maintain their conditioning.

When we are living close to our heart, previously repressed ideals can come to the surface. We may come full circle and reclaim them.

7. *Willingness to do things that we fear.* When we are secure within ourselves, we become willing to take risks. We know that even if we fail, we will not lose our center.

And, in doing the scary things—going back to school, learning public speaking, beginning to speak about our dream job—we find that we grow in strength and self-esteem. Each confidence becomes a bridge that leads us to the next hard thing, until before we know it, we have crossed the great divide between our old self and our new self.

8. *Others inspire us.* We may have no particular aspirations ourselves, but as we see others taking risks and reaching for more, we may find ourselves doing the same.

Gordon, for example, was working in construction, as his father and grandfather had done before him. He was reasonably happy. When the lease was up in his apartment, he decided to move to a small apartment building nearby. When he moved in and started to meet his new neighbors, he learned they were all going to college or starting new careers. He never thought of himself as smart enough to go to college and in high school hung out with all the "bad kids." But now, older and more settled, he could see that he was as smart and capable as anyone else. He had always secretly dreamed of becoming a civil engineer; now he began to think it could be possible.

Another individual now at the age of 70 a partner in a prestigious New York law firm, retired from his job and went to law school at the age of 65.

9. *We change because we are changers.* The more we change, the more we are willing to change again. Sometimes we think of change as a big undertaking, a large-scale event. In actuality, even the smallest change can propel bigger changes, like a pebble in a pond, or a small snowball rolling down from the top of a hill. Any activity that you help initiate to modify your thinking, feeling, or behavior is a change process. This is what change experts say. Any of us can do one small thing to change how we think, feel, or act.

How We Can Make our Lives a Fertile Ground for Change?

While change itself cannot be created, change can occur in leaps and bounds when we "announce" that we are ready for it. The Twelve Steps are sometimes called a blueprint for change or a design for living. Their simplicity and wisdom is universal and can be easily applied to the points in this chapter. Our lives will be open to change when we:

- Are honest about our current situation (First Step)

- Are willing to truly hear and trust the input of others who love us and can see us for who we really are. Some people know this as a Higher Power. (Second and Third Steps)

- Have examined our own patterns of thinking, feeling and behaving, to see where fear is blocking us or where images of external achievement rather than our own unique gifts and passion lead us (Fourth and Fifth Steps)

- Have faced the realization that we need to change these patterns and have made a heartfelt commitment to do so (Sixth and Seventh Steps)

- Have examined how we have treated other people along the way of our own seeking, making note of when we have used them for our own gain—and making amends when possible (Eighth and Ninth Steps); people who have been driven by external achievements alone and are now reconsidering their career path may especially recognize the importance of this work.

- Daily review our own behavior to see when fear or other negative emotions have blocked even small potential for growth; and—just as important—where acting in love or commitment to our heart has brought us closer to our dream (Tenth Step)

- Have used tools like imagining or meditation to slow us down, stop the busy-ness, and hear what our heart is saying instead of trying to control all the outcomes (Eleventh Step)

- Take time out of our own self-centered search to reach out to someone else who may be struggling with career choices, failure, or confusion (Twelfth Step); in doing so, we may help someone else, but we most certainly will be reminded of our own fallibility and dreams.

Will we get the career of a lifetime when we do these Steps? Not necessarily. The book *Alcoholics Anonymous* describes these Steps and also lists a series of promises of new things that will occur even halfway through this journey:

> We are going to know a new freedom and a new happiness. We will not regret the past nor wish to shut the door on it. We will comprehend the word serenity and we will know peace. No matter how far down the scale we have gone, we will see how our experience can benefit others. That feeling of uselessness and self-pity will disappear. We will lose interest in selfish things and gain interest in our fellows. Self-seeking will slip away. Our whole attitude and outlook upon life will change. Fear of people and of economic insecurity will leave us. We will intuitively know how to handle situations which used to baffle us. We will suddenly realize that God is doing for us what we could not do for ourselves.

As we stand poised, ready for change, we may not be able to fathom the possibilities that lie in wait for us. If we are willing to lead a life that is open to change, we will most likely find ourselves traveling down paths that we never expected but that lead us to places we have always wanted to be.

References

Arnold, K.D. "Academically talented women in the 1980s: The Illinois Valedictorian Project," In K.D. Hulbert and D.T. Schuster (Eds.), *Women's Lives through Time: Educated American Women of the Twentieth Century*, San Francisco: Jossey Bass, 1993.

Crick, F. *What Mad Pursuit*, New York: Basic Books, 1988, pp 15–16.

Prochaska, J.O., J.C. Norcross, and C.C. DiClemente. *Changing for Good.* New York: Avon, 1994, p 25.

Tennant, M., and P. Pogson. *Learning and Change in the Adult Years: A Developmental Perspective*, San Francisco: Jossey Bass, 1995, pp 12–13.

Patricia Owen, Ph.D.

Patricia Owen is Vice President, Research and Development, for the Hazelden Foundation. She has been employed at Hazelden for twenty years, as a Unit Psychologist, Director of the Butler Center for Research and Learning, and as Executive Director of Quality Outcomes. She also currently serves as Clinical Assistant Professor in the Department of Psychiatry at the University of Minnesota.

Patricia has written for a number of publications including *The New Yorker, Addictive Behaviors, Journal of Drug Education,* and *Employee Assistance Quarterly.* Her book *I Can See Tomorrow* (Hazelden, 1995) has sold over 10,000 copies. In addition, she has co-authored several books, including *Addiction: A Guidebook for Professionals* (Oxford University Press) and *Handbook of Group Therapy* (Wiley, 1994).

Patricia is a Licensed Psychologists with the State of Minnesota. She is a member of the American Psychological Association, Minnesota Psychological Association and the American Association for the Advancement of Science.

CHAPTER TWO

Like Pat Owen, Jane is a recognized international authority on the Twelve Steps and the power inherent in both their philosophy and application. In this chapter Jane moves beyond the general theory of the Twelve Steps as a model for change and begins to apply this theory to the work of and within a business organization. Definition is given to each of the Twelve Steps, both as they appear in the Big Book of Alcoholics Anonymous and as they may be employed as a vehicle for organizational and personal change. This chapter also contains information on how the Twelve Step model contrasts with, corrects, and enriches other organizational change models.

—Editor

The Twelve Step Principles: Tools for Organizational Change

Jane M. Nakken

*W*hich is easier to change: an organization or an alcoholic?

As a manager in a large organization that provides treatment for alcoholics, it's an interesting question to me. Could the most successful program known for changing alcoholics—the Twelve Steps of Alcoholics Anonymous—hold lessons that can help us change organizations?

To answer the question, I have done three things. First, I have tried to find within the Twelve Steps a process that might apply to organizations. Second, I have read the work of others that discusses the possibilities. Third, I have compared these Steps to three respected models of organizational change. What I found is powerful: the change process in the Twelve Steps contains all the elements in the change models written for organizations, and four additional elements that make it radical, transformational, and supercharged. Could it be that these extra elements are the ones that could make big, hard changes successful?

There is another reason to look at the Twelve Steps in relation to changing and leading organizations. Many members of Alcoholics Anonymous (AA) find themselves in leadership positions and situations as a result of the character they develop in living these Steps and as a result of others recognizing the wisdom, love, and service of such individuals. AA's book *Twelve Steps and Twelve Traditions* says that when leadership is bestowed, it is to be worn humbly, as a simple exercise of the Higher Power's will for the alcoholic. The program also asks recovering alcoholics to practice Twelve Step principles in all their affairs. For leaders, a natural and pressing question is, How do I apply the Twelve Steps to the tasks of running my organization? In this chapter, we'll look at how the change process in the Twelve Steps can be applied to help organizations move beyond current models to bring about transformation.

The Need for Better Change Models

Leaders and managers in today's organizations see that the fast-paced rate of change in today's world challenges organizations to change to survive. James O'Toole notes in *Leading Change,* "Corporations must not simply change, they must be transformed effectively. Executives say that nothing could be harder." We struggle in our jobs because an organizational change is notoriously difficult to envision, implement, and sustain. Yet our efforts for change continue as we consider one fad after another to manage change, noticing that each fad seems to disappear more quickly than the last.

We are not alone in our frustrations. Fifty to 70 percent of all organizational change interventions fail to achieve or sustain their desired goals. On one hand, nothing is particularly surprising about this; the phenomenon of homeostasis in organizations and groups describes the tendency of systems to maintain the status quo. Translation: It's darn hard to make change stick! While change may be instituted and maintained for a period of time, it is usually only a matter of time until things return to the way they were before the change.

Why Look to AA for a Model of Organizational Change?

Helping individuals make significant life changes and make them stick, in the face of one of the most hopeless diseases known, has been my profession for twenty-six years. The best tool for helping alcoholics is AA.

Alcoholics Anonymous is a tremendously successful program for bringing about change in individuals once considered hopeless: those with the disease of addiction. How successful is AA? While the membership is anonymous and therefore any count is inexact, estimates put AA membership at almost two million in 141 countries. There are 96,000 active AA groups throughout the world. In addition, fifteen million Americans attend 500,000 Twelve Step meetings each week—Narcotics Anonymous, Overeaters Anonymous, Gamblers Anonymous, and many more—modeled after the AA program.

The people in all these groups practice this program of recovery for one simple reason: it works. The rewards for AA membership are intrinsic. People attend AA and become members because by following its program, they make and sustain changes that transform their lives. AA's 1997 membership survey reports that 27 percent of its members have been sober less than one year, 28 percent have been sober for one to five years, and 45 percent have more than five years' sobriety.

Organizational change efforts would be proud to boast results as good as AA's. In fact, a few experts in the field of change management have begun to look at AA as a model, and a new and growing body of literature seeks to apply principles of Alcoholics Anonymous to organizations.

AA's Twelve Step Model

In 1935 two alcoholic men started the program of recovery fr⸍ alcoholism. The program later became known as Alcoh⸍

Anonymous. One of the men, a New York stockbroker, had achieved sobriety through a spiritual conversion. The other, an Ohio physician, achieved it through the intervention and support of the first man. These men initially modeled their group after the Oxford Group, a popular spiritual movement of the 1920s and 1930s.

Alcoholics Anonymous provides a multidimensional and richly textured approach to recovery from addiction. In addition to the Twelve Steps, AA offers a set of written and unwritten advice, tradition, and culture that supports the recovery process. At the core of AA's program of alcoholism recovery, however, are the Twelve Steps. Everything else is a way of actualizing or protecting these Steps. AA meetings, sponsorship, literature, and all the other dimensions of AA structure and experience evolved as ways of helping people live and work the Twelve Steps.

These Twelve Steps first appeared in 1939 in the text *Alcoholics Anonymous,* from which the fledgling group took its name. Publication of this text, known as the Big Book, speeded the growth of AA and allowed replication of its program across widely separate locations. Page 58 of the third edition says:

> Here are the steps we took, which are suggested as a program of recovery:
>
> 1. We admitted we were powerless over alcohol—that our lives had become unmanageable.
>
> 2. Came to believe that a Power greater than ourselves could restore us to sanity.
>
> 3. Made a decision to turn our will and our lives over to the care of God as we understood Him.
>
> 4. Made a searching and fearless moral inventory of ourselves.
>
> 5. Admitted to God, to ourselves, and to another human being the exact nature of our wrongs.

6. Were entirely ready to have God remove all these defects of character.

7. Humbly asked Him to remove our shortcomings.

8. Made a list of all persons we had harmed, and became willing to make amends to them all.

9. Made direct amends to such people wherever possible, except when to do so would injure them or others.

10. Continued to take personal inventory and when we were wrong promptly admitted it.

11. Sought through prayer and meditation to improve our conscious contact with God as we understood Him, praying only for knowledge of His will for us and the power to carry that out.

12. Having had a spiritual awakening as the result of those steps, we tried to carry this message to alcoholics, and to practice these principles in all our affairs.

These steps, written to describe the actions of the alcoholics who had achieved and sustained sobriety in AA, defined a model for personal change that clearly both *describes* and *prescribes* a sequenced set of activities. For many alcoholics, performing these activities results in change. Embedded in these Steps we can find the key elements of change that form the framework for comparison to existing models of organizational change.

Elements of Change in the Twelve Steps

The AA book *Twelve Steps and Twelve Traditions*, written in 1953, provides the official AA explanation of the Steps. Ian Mitroff, writing with Richard Mason and Christine Pearson in *Framebreak: The Radical Redesign of American Business* and with Elizabeth Denton in *A Spiritual Audit of Corporate America*—in addition to writing the Foreword to this book—provides powerful insight on using AA's Twelve Steps to guide the ethical and spiritual transformation of American business. Kermit Dahlen, writing for addictions treatment professionals, succinctly advises that the Twelve Steps outline is an excellent management strategy, as well as outlining an effective program for personal recovery from addiction. Denise Breton and Christopher Largent in *The Paradigm Conspiracy* prescribe a Twelve Step process to transform society and its institutions into a new and yet unknown form for the coming millennium.

Diagnosing the Problem and Facing the Need for Change

In describing the Steps as they apply to alcoholics, the Big Book says that accepting defeat over a problem is absolutely necessary for recovery; in fact, it is Step One toward recovery. The authors of *Twelve Steps and Twelve Traditions* state, "The principle that we shall find no enduring strength until we first admit complete defeat is the main taproot from which our whole Society has sprung and flowered." The authors further say about the First Step that alcoholics almost never recover on their own resources; they do it with the company and assistance of others—thus the first word of the Steps is "we." Third, the authors state that over the years of AA's existence, members have learned to help alcoholics who are in less dire straits than the early members, who were almost without exception destitute and personally bankrupt.

Similarly, Step One can be applied to organizations to address or prevent crisis, depending on the foresight with which leaders act. It's difficult to face the problems and limitations of our organizations and to admit that our old ways of doing things aren't working any longer—especially if we've been successful in the past. Mitroff, Mason, and Pearson describe Step One in the crisis mode:

> By whatever path management has traveled to reach the enlightened realization that they and their organization are out of control—most likely through the experience of a repeated series of major crises—management is finally able to admit that the principles they have

used in the past to guarantee success are now responsible for imminent failure. Continued reliance on the
old guarantors of success will in all probability lead to
the organization's demise . . . It is not an exaggeration
to say that it is an act of extreme courage and heroism
to admit that one is suffering from the failure of success—that what worked so well in the past is now
responsible for failure.

But there is also a way leaders can live daily with Step One,
without the press of impending crisis. We can identify those
important factors over which we have no power—customers,
markets, the impact of new technology and research, natural disaster, even the behavior of our employees or bosses—so that we
can construct management systems based upon fact and reality
rather than arrogance and control. When we understand unman-
ageability, we can better allocate resources and create an environment where mistakes and problems don't result in crisis.

Taking it a step further into a bigger picture, Step One invites us
to think hard about the ways we do things. When the old ways
don't work any more—even though we're doing our best—it's
time to look at what we are doing and why. Step One means we
face the fact that, for whatever reasons, our paradigm isn't working any more. We must look at change.

Principles from Step One that help us with change are that
change happens when we admit and diagnose our limitations
and problems, face the necessity of change, and accept that we
are not alone with either the problem or the solution. This Step
requires frankness and an unusual degree of courage.

Opening Up to New
Possibilities and Influences

The alcoholic in crisis must believe that there is help and must
identify a source of help outside self. AA addresses this concept
in Step Two by suggesting that new members develop a belief

in a Higher Power that can restore them to sanity—someone or something whose advice they are willing to take to find their balance.

Leaders need faith to find balance too. They need to believe that there is a path for our organizations and that they can find it if they open up to it. They need a new vision, model, or mentor to help find and follow this new perspective or path.

Many people work in organizations that expect them to produce short-term gain, profit for the sake of profit. While we all know the bills and salaries have to be paid, Step Two says sanity—balance and meaning—are important. When we define our organization's mission, philosophy, and values, we begin to build a framework for sanity, balance, and health in our organizations. A simple example of an approach to Step Two might be to decide that the organization will follow the Golden Rule and treat its stakeholders—customers, shareholders, constituency groups, employees, and neighbors—as the organization would want to be treated.

Principles we find in Step Two that support change are faith, trust in some new source of help, and vision of a better future.

Making the Commitment to Change

Step Three is to be willing to accept the help and make a commitment to change. This is a particularly courageous Step because it requires us to decide to follow a process that will change our organizations—perhaps a little, perhaps a lot—without knowing the exact outcome. An example of putting these Steps into action is simply to believe that following the Twelve Step suggestions will work and to decide to practice them.

Running our organizations with new guiding principles means being willing to respond to different rules, letting go of roles and assumptions we have held. It sounds simple but think for a minute how American business would change if corporations decided to treat others the way they would like to be treated: they might tell the truth, sell only high-quality, useful products, charge fair prices, protect employees and the environment from toxic chemicals—you get the idea!

Key principles of change in Step Three are making a decision, surrendering the attachment to old ways to move ahead, and to be guided by care.

Auditing the Organization's Operations

Conducting our organizational Fourth Step is our first really concrete action toward change. We're asked to be analyzing and fearless in honestly assessing our organization's strengths and weaknesses. It also requires that we examine all areas of the company's strategy and operations in relation to our stated values. This audit forms the basis for a redesign of the organization, one that will place mission and values at the core. Key elements are a thorough inventory of the organization's intentional behavior (strategic action, risk management decisions, systems and processes), unintentional behavior (industrial accidents, shipping defective products), and set of values and standards that we will use to evaluate our behavior.

In Step Four we attempt to learn more about who we really are. We try to learn more about ourselves and our organizations by taking a hard look at what we do and what consequences result from our actions. We are asked to look at the rules, roles, and strategies that define our current situation—the one that isn't working. This is hard to do because our awareness, our viewpoint, is located within our prevailing paradigm; it isn't a viewpoint or paradigm to us, it's simply the way things are.

Opening the System and Inviting Feedback

Step Five of the Twelve Steps tells us to share the findings of our fearless organization audit with someone who is likely to have a different, more objective point of view about what the problems are and how to change them. This event creates the opportunity for gaining new insights and understandings, and seeing things from a different perspective. An often-heard AA warning is, "You're only as sick as the secrets you keep."

Step Five asks us to expose our paradigm—to talk about the assumptions we make about rules, roles and strategies. Exposing ourselves in this way, explaining our reasoning, and opening it to discussion, is threatening because we are afraid of being judged or questioned. Therefore, most individuals and many organization leaders keep their thinking to themselves. This is a good way to make sure it does not change—cloak it in invisibility. Opening our paradigms, our mental models, to examination helps us to see them as tools to be used, which we are free to choose and change.

Step Five is also about ego deflation and development of realistic humility as we begin to see our responsibility to be a healthy contributor to our society. Just as alcoholics must let go of secrecy and isolation, sharing their view of self to get feedback and about how to be healthier people, leaders of organizations must also ask for input about how their organizations can be more effective members of society. Organizational change experts refer to this as opening the system and participative planning.

Key change elements are sharing secrets, getting another view, entering a relationship, and opening our viewpoints to feedback. Step Five acknowledges that more heads are better than one. It invites others to participate actively in planning the new design for the organization, in which the concept of a Higher Power, the principles, values, and faith that have been explored and clarified, become a foundation.

Getting Ready for Change

Becoming entirely ready to change means being willing to give up our old ways of doing things. This is an extremely difficult thing to do, especially when the old ways of doing things have reaped rewards for us in the past. The Twelve Steps devote Step Six to the process of getting ready for change. An important part of becoming ready for change is to anticipate, recognize, and come to terms with the trade-offs involved. The Sixth Step of AA incorporates this awareness and acceptance of trade-offs as one kind of preparation for change.

Awareness is not enough to bring about desired changes. Leaders of organizations must analyze their readiness and capabilities before the organization acts to implement change. We must plan and design the agenda for change, the structure to manage transition, and the vision of the operations for the organization. Often, we must reallocate resources, provide education and training for leaders and employees, and conduct a thorough analysis of the subsystems involved and the best intervention points into them. We must think through the process and anticipate the intended and unintended consequences of the changes before we implement them. Finally, we must make sure we have the critical mass of support we need from within the organization.

Beyond readiness, we have to be sure top management will support the new plan, and that means they place no road blocks. Anyone who has ever worked with individuals or organizations in trouble knows that even though they have all kinds of good plans and intentions, few of them are ever implemented or realized. The more well thought out and well communicated the plan, the more we can trust the support of those whose support is needed. Preparation should minimize surprises.

Watch for Resistance and Deal with It

Step Six, the idea of becoming entirely ready for change, also addresses the inertia that sabotages change. There are various kinds of resistance to changes: personal loss of momentum, doubt, loss of the sense of urgency, road blocks from outside forces. We find ourselves slipping back into the old way. While still intending to pursue transformation, it just doesn't happen. Denise Breton and Christopher Largent, authors of *The Paradigm Conspiracy*, say we need five kinds of strategies to help us move though resistance:

1. *Technique strategies.* These operate on the level of specific circumstances, helping us fix the problem, compensate for it, pay for it, or counteract it. These reactive strategies are good in emergencies, but they don't solve the system creating the problems.

2. *Strategies that change patterns of behavior.* These are harder to implement because others expect and anticipate our patterns of behavior. We tend not to change our behavior because of social patterns in which we play a part; we are not alone, and others play by the old rules.

3. *Strategies that change systems, rules, and structures.* We can work to change the structures directly by rewriting rules, expanding roles, trying new methods, and implementing new policies and procedures. For a time, things seem different. Then the old patterns reassert themselves.

4. *Strategies that shift paradigms.* The breakthrough comes when we realize that social systems are our systems. We can change them. But what can guide us in developing new paradigms so we don't end up worse than we started?

5. *Strategies that build on soul-connectedness.* Fifth-level transformation strategies tackle change by demanding that our paradigm, and therefore also our social structures, answer to us—to our core identity, our souls. We must demand a paradigm that supports our life's processes. Soul-level change strategies continually check the fit: Are our souls, paradigm, and social structures pulling together or against each other?

Key change elements in Step Six are preparation for change, giving up defenses, and learning new ways to act.

Ask for Help in Implementing Change

Step Seven of the Twelve Steps suggests finding the best source of help available and asking for and accepting help. This implies that our own agenda for change must be flexible. We are advised to trust the process. No matter how well we as leaders have studied the problem we face, or how thorough our audits and planning have been, doubt always persists about whether the new plan is the right course of action. Step Seven says that we must move ahead and implement our new plan, remembering to keep our egos in check, to stay attentive and responsive to the change process, and to be willing to make modifications as we proceed.

The humility occurs as we realize and accept that we cannot control all aspects of implementing our change plans. We must ask for and trust the help of many people to make change work. Change doesn't always follow our plan, and sometimes that's good. AA recommends that alcoholics trust the process and let go of the outcomes. That's a tough order for individuals and an even tougher one for leaders in today's organizations.

Key change elements are asking for help, being sincere, honest, patient, and cooperative about the change process, and accepting that the process and its outcomes can't be precisely controlled.

Step Boldly Forward into Change Implementation

Step Seven is the AA version of, "Just do it." The transition from getting ready in Step Six to stepping into it in Step Seven is a bold move. This phase of change may mean making big moves such as acquisitions, investments, or divestitures. It may mean changing the organization's structure and processes significantly. These are clearly big actions that signal change is happening. This is where the effort in preparing the organization for change and enlisting support from within pays off by reducing fear and resistance and empowering employees to understand what is happening and help with the implementation.

Recognize and Take Responsibility for the Organization's Effect on Stakeholders

Making a list of people they have harmed is Step Eight for alcoholics. It requires truly facing that the actions of the individual do affect others. Organizations, too, affect others and must take responsibility for this. This principle requires examining our organizations as parts of larger systems—our field, our community, our society. We can do this in part by taking an inventory of the stakeholders whom the past actions of our organization have harmed. Management's willingness to make amends is the beginning of a process of reestablishing or rebuilding relationships with others that have deteriorated as a result of the organization's dysfunction. Step Eight acknowledges that every plan, every action, no matter how good it appears, holds the potential for harm. It forces management to look at the potentially harmful effects of new plans and to try to anticipate and remove them.

Next, "...the readiness to take the full consequences of our past acts, and to take responsibility for the well-being of others at the same time, is the very spirit of Step Nine," according to Alcoholics Anonymous.

The change principles in Step Nine are: Acting to mend the damage that has been done, learning from the process, rebalancing relationships, and regaining pride. These are radical notions for organizations. None of the organizational change models studied recommend, as AA does for individuals, that a company purposefully examine its own past behavior in the light of its values and assess the damage or harm it has done through intentional or unintentional actions. Neither do they address the importance of rebalancing the organization within its open systems environment by paying what is owed, cleaning up its own messes and fixing mistakes, settling disputes fairly, and delivering fair value.

Steps Eight and Nine teach us that our organizations are important members of larger systems to which we are responsible, and we must use our power to benefit the systems and society in which we live, work, and raise our families.

Making the Change Stick

The first nine Steps lead us as individuals or leaders of organizations through a process of transformation. We are now different. How do we maintain the progress we have made? How do we continue to grow and improve?

Continuous Monitoring for Continuous Learning

Step Ten of AA signals entry into the stage of maintaining the changes. It calls for consistent vigilance, honesty, responsibility, and action. It creates a values-driven learning loop that identifies setbacks, new problems, and the need for additional change.

Step Ten requires a commitment to continuous improvement of performance. We commit ourselves to this by regularly monitoring the organization's performance and the intended and unintended effects of its actions. The Twelve Steps suggest paying a great deal of attention to building systems for feedback and monitoring and to structuring the management system to reinforce the values of the organization.

The monitoring process results in continuous learning loops for the organization. We create a plan in the early steps, then we implement the plan. We check regularly how it is working and make necessary changes. This practice is a conscious choice to evolve and improve.

The change principle in Step Ten is to make a regular habit of monitoring performance, to admit and accept what is found, and persistently try to correct what is wrong. A key challenge as we develop our monitoring systems is to measure meaningful aspects of performance that support the organization's mission and values. As managers, we see every day that our employees pay attention to the goals we set for them, and we express these most concretely in the monitoring systems we design. The things we measure are likely to become our values.

Stay Awake and Open to Learning

Step Eleven says, "I'm awake and aware!" It is a realization of the need for continual creativity and openness to learning. We are ready to go into the unknowable, to accept new truth and viewpoints that don't fit our current thinking. Our attitude toward the possibilities of change becomes positive. We look for opportunities. We make a commitment to keep learning, stretching our thinking, and looking to the sources of values and principles that have guided our change process.

Prayer and meditation are two powerful examples of ways that human beings have developed and exercised their receptivity and creativity. Step Eleven directs the alcoholic toward the sense of belonging and peace that results from seeking conscious contact with a Higher Power and spiritual help to carry out the will of that Higher Power. Key change elements are faith, intentional listening for direction from outside, development of conscience, trust in this process, and willingness to accept grace—energy and power from outside ourselves.

Claim and Celebrate the Changes

"The joy of living is the theme of AA's Twelfth Step, and action is its key word." The spiritual awakening mentioned in this Step is a personal transformation that affects the way alcoholics live their lives in all regards. Alcoholics who have matured into the AA way of life find they have been restored to "something like their true purpose and direction." It seems that organizations, too, can find their true purpose and direction by following the principles outlined in the Twelve Steps.

Members of AA strengthen their new identities by telling their stories of what their lives used to be like before their transformation, what happened (to change them), and what their new life is like now. Organizations, too, can strengthen their new identities and create loyalty to the changes by telling the stories of what the organization used to be like, what changed, and especially what it's like now. This is a key to positioning the changes as part of a new identity, carving a fit into the organization's culture. It also helps people in the organization realize why they may feel some stress—change is hard, and they have done a lot of work to make it successful. And, because change is never complete, it takes special effort to recognize our progress and claim our triumphs. Telling our stories helps.

Key change elements are acceptance that change has happened through the subordination of ego to a process of change led by principles and values, acceptance of leadership responsibility, accountability to work at the process, and to apply the process to all areas of life.

Model the Change

Finally, mentor others. Change is, after all, not something we do alone. We all need mentors, and we need to integrate our own learning by providing leadership and support to others. We must remember that without willing mentors, we would not have succeeded. Now it is our turn to help others.

Elements of Change Found in the Twelve Steps of AA and Related Generalized Change Concepts

AA Twelve Steps Elements of change in the Twelve Steps Generalized change concepts

1. We admitted we were powerless over alcohol—that our lives had become unmanageable. We

   - Admitted limits of power
   - Powerless over alcohol
   - Current life is unmanageable. Identification with others, coalition/community
   - Create motivation for change
   - Diagnosis, clarity regarding problems, limitations

Not to change is dangerous

2. Came to believe that a Power greater than ourselves could restore us to sanity. Faith that there is help

   - Movement out of self
   - Current state not sane Open to a new vision, direction, model, outside mentor
   - Opens the system

Sense of urgency

3. Made a decision to turn our will and our lives over to the care of God as *we understood Him.* Decide

   - To surrender to care, help, values
   - Commit to move forward
   - To be ready to endure fear and uncertainty
   - To trust

Guided, centered by values, care

4. Made a searching and fearless moral inventory of ourselves. Inventory intentional and unintentional behavior

- Recognize and acknowledge right, wrong, and values
- Weigh behavior against values Internal audits and SWOT
- Recognize, acknowledge and weigh organization's values

Weigh behavior, intentional and unintentional, against values

5. Admitted to God, to ourselves, and to another human being the exact nature of our wrongs. Share the secrets

- Get another view
- Enter relationship
- What's underlying? Share information, allow outside evaluation
- Create participative process for analysis, solicit input

Continue to analyze sources of problems, examine systems

6. Became entirely ready to have God remove all these defects of character. Prepare for the changes our decision necessitates

- Give up defenses
- Continue willingness to surrender ego to value-based action Enlist and ready the system for change
- Give up defenses and turf
- Share vision of desired state, conditions
- Provide necessary resources, training
- Recognize and come to terms with trade-offs

Watch for and meet resistance, find ways through it

7. Humbly asked Him to remove our shortcomings. Acknowledge the need and desire for help

- Be sincere, honest, open, flexible, patient, cooperative

- Accept that change isn't a process that can be controlled exactly. Ask for participation from others in making change work

- Be sincere, honest, open, flexible, patient, cooperative

Accept that change doesn't follow plans exactly

8. Made a list of all persons we had harmed, and became willing to make amends to them all. Counters "I only hurt myself" and "I never hurt anybody else"

- Examine responsibility for personal power and how one uses it

- What I do matters—I matter! Open-systems audit: Recognize organization's effect on stakeholders

- List damage done knowingly or accidentally

- Decide how and to whom to make amends. Make action plan

Build damage check into strategic business planning process

9. Made direct amends to such persons wherever possible except when to do so would injure them or others. Clean up our wrongs and mistakes

- Continued learning from others' responses

- Work to rebalance relationships

- We're clean: no longer have to avoid people from our past Settle disputes fairly

- Make reparations where due

- Rebalance organization within its systems

Let go of the past and move on

10. Continued to take personal inventory and when we were wrong promptly admitted it. Suggest routine daily review of events, behavior, feelings, check against values

- Fix mistakes

- Stay in touch with value system Monitor performance in accordance with values—regularly and often

- Monitor intended and unintended consequences of behavior

- Recognize high performance

- Fix mistakes

Act responsibly in relationships

11. Sought through prayer and meditation to improve our conscious contact with God *as we understood Him,* praying only for knowledge of His will for us and the power to carry that out. Intentional listening to spirit

   - Develop voice of conscience

   - Trust and surrender

   - Grace = Energy, momentum, power from Higher Power Ongoing focus on mission and values, align culture around them

   - Cultivate agility, readiness to accept change

Invite and attend to inputs from outside

12. Having had a spiritual awakening as the result of these steps, we tried to carry this message to alcoholics, and to practice these principles in all our affairs. I have been changed through this process, not by my own control

   - Be model/resource for others.

   - Work continually at these principles.

   - Apply to all areas of life. Change has happened through this process and the actions the organization has taken through it

   - Model the change, accept leadership, serve

   - Strive for integration, apply same concepts across the organization

A Super-Charged Model for
Creating Change in Organizations

Organization leaders are not lacking for advice on how to bring about changes in their companies. One can find many books on change in the Business and Management section of almost any bookstore or library. So what can be gained by adding one more, based on the Twelve Steps? The answer is this: a new formula for higher-level change, even transformation, in organizations.

Let's look first at how the Twelve Step principles compare to those books about changing organizations that already published. I compared the Steps to three popular and classic organization change models: Kurt Lewin's (1958) *Three Step Procedure of Change Model*; Beckhard and Harris' (1987) *Change Process Model*; and Elise Walton's (1998) *Stages of Planned Change Efforts*. Nearly all the thousands of change consultants working with organizations around the world use these models, or variations of them. The Twelve Steps fit with these models very well. In fact, they include every important idea and principle found in the organization change models. All of the models pretty much agree that the prescription for successfully changing an organization is to follow the steps I've listed in the table on the next page.

The course of action outlined in the table is powerful. If current models of organization change already have such great advice, what can one more model add?

The Twelve Steps Supercharge Change

The Twelve Steps add four very significant principles that are not found in the change models already used in business. They are difficult, radical in today's business climate, and require great courage. They are strong medicine for desperate situations in which "half measures availed us nothing," to use A.A.'s

Twelve Step Change Concepts also Found in Organization Change Models

1. Recognize that change is accomplished with others, not alone.

2. Create motivation and a sense of urgency for change.

3. Diagnose the core problems. Get clarity about the problems and limitations.

4. Open to a new vision, direction, model or mentor.

5. Open the system. Get advice and feedback.

6. Audit the present system so you know what you have to work with.

7. Enlist and ready the system for change.

8. Approach the change process with humility and flexibility.

9. Watch for and meet resistance. Find ways through it.

10. Ask for help from others in making change work. Be flexible.

11. Monitor performance and intended and unintended effects of actions in accordance to values—regularly and often.

12. Admit and fix mistakes, learn from them and move on responsibly.

13. Invite and attend to advice and feedback. Deepen the top team's commitment to knowledge and right action.

14. Recognize that change has happened. Talk about it. Spread the word.

15. Sustain and model the change. Make it part of the organization's internal and external identity.

description of the motivation it takes to go to the core of the problem and fundamentally change it. These are the four additional change concepts found only in the Twelve Steps:

1. Recognize and take responsibility for the organization's effect on stakeholders. Whenever possible, make restitution wherever the organization has wronged others or the environment.

2. Openly declare the change actions being taken. Prepare for them, act deliberately, and respond to the consequences. Act in the open.

3. Values must be the primary drivers of action. Acting in accordance with the organization's values must be more important than reaching the end vision or intermediate goals.

4. Have faith in the guide(s) you have chosen and in the change process. Be willing to leave the old behind and to step into a new direction filled with uncertainty.

Adding these four principles to the fifteen listed earlier results in the appropriate level and kind of change needed, whether that is incremental or transformational change. When we bring this much faith and courage to the process of changing organizations, the right results –but not always the originally envisioned results— happen. The organization becomes what it is meant to be.

What These Principles Might Look Like in Organizations

What might these concepts look like in organizations? The first, accountability to all stakeholders and restitution for harm done holds the possibility of big changes in the operating practices of American business. Restitution for causing pollution, for example, might involve not only stopping the polluting practice, but also cleaning up the environment, restoring decimated wildlife populations and compensating victims and families who became ill or whose property was damaged—all this without being caught or sued or called to account by outside sources.

Further, the prospect of having to make amends to others for unfairness or harm might change practices within companies. For example, a company operating by this principle of accountability would not market an automobile with known dangerous features, rationalizing that lawsuits resulting from predictable deaths and injuries would cost the company less money than redesigning the car. Practices affecting internal stakeholders might change, also, as companies evaluate the anticipated harm that could be foreseen from planned changes such as downsizing, reengineering, buyouts, or unsafe or unhealthy products or workplaces. Companies would be more careful about both the intended and unintended consequences of their actions, if they held themselves to a commitment to right their wrongs and repair any damage for which they were responsible. This change concept provides a learning loop that has tremendous power to change organizational behavior.

The second new change concept, "naming and claiming" decisions and actions for change, speaks to the deliberate nature of the change work. The attention to readiness, decision-making, and communication with stakeholders and others invites input and strengthens commitment. An organization approaching change in this way would strengthen alignment and empowerment among its workforce, while decreasing employee confusion.

The third new change concept offered by the Twelve Step model for change is the primacy of values and principles over vision as a driver of change. A company implementing this concept would present to its stakeholders a vision of a desired future state, and then would clarify, define and articulate core values and operating principles to guide the change process. Integrity of the process would be seen as important, and ensured by checking actions and decisions against the company's values. Developing and sustaining alignment with the core values and operating principles would take precedence over project timetables and outcomes goals.

This concept addresses the fact that change happens in the detail of actions and decisions that occur within short-term time frames. These smaller-scale changes, made with attention to the same aligning vision, plans, values and principles, result in significant, sometimes transformational change. It is this attention to process, guided intimately by values and operating principles and headed toward a more long-term vision, that empowers employees to creatively and energetically contribute to the company's change process. They can contribute more effectively because they understand. In effect, clear values and operating principles have the potential to set up small, even daily, learning loops for employees at many levels of a company.

The fourth new change concept introduced by the Twelve Steps is faith and trust in a Higher Power. This concept is perhaps the most challenging to apply in an organization. In one sense, all organizations have a Higher Power, an ultimate driving energy that shapes the company's vision and goals and motivates its strategies. For example, employees have been heard to state their company's mission as "to make money for our shareholders." The driving energy within such a company is greed. Some would say Greed is such a company's Higher Power, and it should not be a surprise that employees individually share the motive of making money as the primary reason they work. In another company, the mission might be "to be the best, the fastest-growing in our field"; such a company's energy might come from Ambition, which could be called its Higher Power. In these hypothetical cases, the companies might do "whatever it takes" to fulfill their missions, or they might temper and guide the company according to its articulated values.

The suggestion borrowed from the Twelve Steps is that organizations consciously choose as a Higher Power some driving energy that can restore it to the organizational equivalent of "sanity"— a balanced, healthy way of operating. There are many possible levels of faith and trust in a carefully chosen organizational Higher Power. There is a wide range from a secular, values-based company whose mission might be "to transport people in safety and comfort" or "to develop new products to save lives" to a more openly spiritual organization whose mission may be "to save souls" or its equivalent.

At the organizational level, a company's Higher Power is that to which or around which it aligns. The suggestion of the Steps is that this Power be consciously and carefully chosen and nurtured. Both the character of the Power and the core values necessary to support and energize it are critical to successful change within the company.

Finding the Courage to Change

The principles for change we find in the Twelve Steps promote a powerful model for organizational transformation. A key question arises, however: Who would ever use such a model? It is radical, no doubt. It certainly doesn't fit today's business paradigm, or meet with society's current standards of "this quarter's bottom line is all that matters."

One prerequisite seems to be that only a leader who has done his or her own personal growth work will be a candidate for using the Twelve Step principles in their organization. Indeed, a common response from participating leaders in response to the question "What's missing from the Steps as a model for Organization Change?" was this: The transformed leader. There was consensus among the group that while the change elements in the Steps would be good for organizations, the model is less important than the personal influence of the transformed leader.

Next, leaders, no matter how much personal growth they have achieved, cannot change their organizations alone. They need help and support both from within and outside the organization they are leading. Development of these support and learning networks is a skill leaders must practice. It requires coming to terms with issues of power and control and allowing one's ego to be replaced by principles and values and other components of corporate welfare. It also requires a longer term approach to analyzing business solutions and financial results.

An Invitation

The Twelve Steps provide a set of change concepts that are encompassing, radical and transformational. They are not the easier, softer way to change for which the world searches.

Yet I suggest that we who are committed should develop the model, for several reasons. First, some organizations might use a transformational model, in spite of the fact that it bucks the prevailing paradigm. Some leaders already know the power of the Twelve Steps and might welcome a model to help them apply Twelve Step principles to the job of leading their organizations. Second, such a model might have a long-term effect on the thinking and conversation about organizations. And third, the current business environment, with its focus on this quarter's bottom line, can't last forever. If and when the system "breaks," perhaps through catastrophic discontinuous change such as a stock market crash or social upheaval, such a model could offer important assistance as our organizations and, indeed, our societies struggle with the tasks of survival and rebuilding. Let's not wait for an emergency. Let's build the model now.

We can't wait for someone else to do it for us. Work such as that being done by Mitroff, Denton, Mason, Pearson, and Robbins raises provocative and interesting new perspectives and philosophy for the change, leadership and management of organizations using the lessons of the Twelve Steps. Their work begs for more discussion and development. We need organizations willing to be laboratories for change. We need the perspectives of leaders and followers, managers and change agents, entrepreneurs and academics.

Finally, we need collaborative dialogue. One of the great strengths of A.A. is that its model was constructed by a group and has developed a strong supportive subculture. While the Twelve Steps provide the "basic instructions," there is a wealth of support offered in a variety of ways— through support groups, sponsorship and literature, for instance. It provides a common language, which allowed a culture of change to develop. I suggest that interested leaders and change agents join in the work of developing a new transformational model of change that incorporates Twelve Step principles.

Closing Comments

The Twelve Steps provide a set of change concepts that are encompassing, radical, and transformational. They are not the easier, softer path to change for which the world searches.

Three reasons make me believe that a lack of market readiness need not deter the development of a new model. First, some organizations might use the model, even though it bucks the prevailing paradigm. Second, it might have a long-term effect on the thinking and conversation about organizations. Third, if catastrophic change occurs, such as a stock market crash or social upheaval, such a model could offer important assistance as our organizations and, indeed, our societies struggle with the tasks of survival and rebuilding.

The early work on examining the program of Alcoholics Anonymous as a model for organizations and leadership should be continued. Work such as that being done by Mitroff, Denton, Mason, Pearson, and Robbins raises provocative and interesting new perspectives and philosophy for the change, leadership, and management of organizations. While the market as a whole may not be ready for the radical and transformational approach that this line of inquiry suggests, that market readiness is a moving and changeable phenomenon. Rather, the decisions about continuing this work should be based on the integrity and value of the model itself. When the current paradigm reaches its limits of usefulness—and many feel it already has—such innovative models as the one being explored here may provide a source of resilience, direction, and hope.

References

A.A. World Services. *Alcoholics Anonymous 1996 Membership Survey.* New York: AA World Services, 1997.

Alcoholics Anonymous. *Alcoholics Anonymous: The Story of How Many Thousands of Men and Women Have Recovered from Alcoholism.* 3d ed. New York: AA World Services, 1976.

—-. *Twelve Steps and Twelve Traditions.* New York: Alcoholics Anonymous Publishing, Inc., 1953

Breton, D., and Largent, C. *The Paradigm Conspiracy: How Our Systems of Government, Church, School, and Culture Violate Our Human Potential.* 1st ed. Center City, MN: Hazelden Educational Publishing, 1996.

Dahlen, K. "Twelve Steps Outline Excellent Management Strategy." *Visions: Journal of the National Association of Addiction Treatment Providers,* 4(6), 9, August 1998.

Judge, M. G. "Recovery's Next Step." *Common Boundary,* 16-24, January/February, 1994.

Mitroff, I. I., and Denton, E. *A Spiritual Audit of Corporate America: Multiple Designs for Fostering Spirituality in the Workplace.* San Francisco: Jossey-Bass, in press.

Mitroff, I. I., Mason, R. O., and Pearson, C. M. Framebreak: *The Radical Redesign of American Business.* San Francisco: Jossey-Bass, 1994.

Robbins, L. "Designing More Functional Organizations: The 12 Step Model." *Journal of Organizational Change Management,* 5(4), 41-58, 1992.

Robbins, L. P. *Learning in Organizations: The Effects of Interactive Planning and Twelve Step Methodologies.* Unpublished doctoral dissertation, University of Pennsylvania, Philadelphia, 1987.

Jane Nakken, M.A.

Jane Nakken has worked for the Hazelden Foundation for over twenty years. Most recently she has served as Executive Vice President of Board and National Community Relations, promoting the mission of Hazelden in the areas of Public Policy and Public Education. Her fascination with the change process began with her clinical work as a chemical dependency counselor and has led to her recently earned doctorate in Organization Change from Pepperdine University.

Jane has served on the faculty of Rutgers University Summer School on Alcohol Studies, the Florida Summer School on Addiction Studies, and has consulted and lectured internationally on the topics of addiction and treatment. She has also written extensively on the twelve steps. Selected titles include *Keep it Simple, Practical Approaches in Treating Adolescent Chemical Dependency, Step One for Young Adults* and *Enabling Change*. Over 1.5 million of her books have been sold.

PART II

CHAPTER THREE

Chapter 3 begins Part II of this book. In this section the principles of the Twelve Steps as outlined in the first two chapters begin to be applied concretely to the business world. In sharp contrast to the 1980s, which were widely viewed as freewheeling "go-go years" in American business, the 1990s have been dubbed "the values decade." Following a period of severe recession spawning such knee-jerk reactions as downsizing, rightsizing, and other crisis-related tactics, organizations of all sizes began to look internally. Some leaders even looked deeper into their "corporate souls" to find the values-based anchors that would sustain them through inevitable and necessary change. In this chapter we discover the link between a corporation's values and its culture, and the benefits of having clearly defined and consistently practiced values that are communicated throughout the organization. Much like an addict facing the first Steps toward recovery, senior executives tackle the fundamentals of what makes their organizations strong, what is holding them back, and how they can move effectively forward.

—Editor

Walking Toward the Talk

Carol Pine

$\mathcal{W}$ho can forget the free-wheeling 1980s in American business? Those were the years when people such as Carl Icahn and Michael Milken became larger-than-life symbols of corporate lust. The decade was characterized by junk bonds, hostile takeovers, and a tawdry savings and loan crisis masterminded by people who had earned—and betrayed—the public's trust. Some of those antiheroes of business even went to jail.

Movies like *Wall Street* and *Other People's Money* exposed the soft underbelly of corporate life and a good many Americans came to believe that most corporate leaders were grasping, greedy, uncaring capitalists.

But the go-go '80s came to a screeching halt in 1987 with a thundering stock market crash that rivaled the crash of 1929. A deep national recession and painful corporate downsizing followed. Few American workers were unscathed—whether they worked on assembly lines or occupied corner offices. If they did not feel the shock wave of change directly, they experienced it through friends and family.

Fresh into the decade, some observers dubbed the 1990s "the values decade." These observers believed that a percentage of corporate leaders would react to the ethical lapses of the 1980s by ferreting out their own organizational issues and taking a stand for integrity. At the same time, these corporate leaders grappled with bone-chilling competition, globalization, deregulation of many industries, monumental implications of the World Wide Web, and an accelerated rate of change.

During the final decade of the twentieth century, business leaders faced all of these forces in the searing light of public scrutiny. Customers, shareholders, employees, competitors, and future strategic allies all had unprecedented access to twenty-four-hour-a-day business news coverage, as well as the wild West of communications, the Internet.

All of these factors combined—the ethical lapses of the 1980s, monumental changes in business during the 1990s, and corporate decisions chronicled and scrutinized as never before—tested the personal values of business leaders and the corporate values of their organizations. On a more basic level, some people in business were moved to challenge, test, and even redefine their core values.

It is not surprising that a good measure of corporate soul searching emerged in the 1990s. Bill George, chairman of Medtronic, now the world's leader in medical technology, actually talked publicly about the "soul" of his company and the rough decisions Medtronic's leaders had made in placing the company's core values ahead of economics. Decisions like these were even more difficult because Medtronic, like all public companies, is hounded by analysts and portfolio managers who judge a company's worth based largely on last quarter's performance. "You're only as good as your last two minutes," singer Linda

Ronstadt said of the record business. This chilling assessment applied to companies in the 1990s as well.

It is not surprising that one of the blockbuster business books that appeared in the last decade of the century was *Built to Last*, a chronicle of case studies attributing the longevity of America's biggest and best enterprises to clearly defined values.

The Dilbert Challenge

If the cartoon strip *Dilbert* makes you laugh—and wince at the same time—the currency of these cubicle chronicles is clear. Through humor, Scott Adams, the creator of *Dilbert*, challenges the corporate soul in ways that are healthy, pointed, and close-to-the-bone. Adams, who spent seventeen years in corporate life himself, specifically chides corporate leaders and managers as he reveals the disconnect between corporate values, purpose, and day-to-day actions. He shows how flawed organizations can be because they are, after all, made up of imperfect humans. Adams urges leaders and managers to look at how well their companies' espoused values correlate with their corporate actions. He asks: How well do leaders in business walk their talk or, more realistically, walk toward their talk?

The Twelve Step Connection

As described in the previous chapter, the first Four Steps of the Twelve Step process focus on awareness, honesty, and self-assessment. They require a person—or an organization—to face hard realities and examine what is working and what is not working, and why. The Steps challenge us to ferret out the dysfunctions and disconnects, and they require us to take personal responsibility for creating chaos and pain—and for sustaining it. Most often, crisis triggers this honesty and self-assessment. Crisis is the galvanizing current that tests personal and organizational values. Crisis is often painful and unmanageable. More than a few people can be affected. Crisis forces people and organizations to return to the basics by asking such questions as: What do we stand for? What do we value? If we are to survive and thrive in this turbulence of change, what values will anchor us? How well do our values really show up in our daily decisions and actions? What is real and what is window dressing? What is well-intended but damaging in its execution?

In the last twenty years of the twentieth century, American companies had a big dose of crisis, matched with the challenge of change. In addition to ethical lapses, downsizing, and forced reengineering, there were also hostile takeovers and mergers; lower-cost, offshore, manufacturing that matched or surpassed the efficiency of American producers; an unemployment rate so low in many parts of the country that prospective employees could be picky about which company they would join—and how long they would stay. There were new ways of managing and leading people that fifty-something leaders never learned in business school. There were heightened expectations of CEOs: anyone worth his or her salt should be an overnight visionary leader—or at least conversant with the writings of Robert Greenleaf, the champion of servant leadership.

When companies tried to declare their values and walk toward their talk, intentions often backfired. Among many corporate missteps that *Dilbert* featured as cartoon fodder was the telecommunications company manager who sought to strengthen teamwork in his department. He gathered his team and told them he would carry a baseball bat with him at all times, and each team member would carry a baseball—symbols of the newly created team.

Another company's leadership chose to build a sense of ownership by not giving raises and instead awarding bonuses if five of the declared seven company goals were met. At the end of the year, employees learned they had met only four goals, so—tough luck, no bonuses. One of the goals they didn't achieve was improved employee morale.

These two examples reflect values that the leadership of both companies probably said—and believed—were important, but their implementation only spawned skepticism.

Living and Leading from the Inside Out

The Twelve Steps are an inside-out process, as is clarity about corporate values and practices. In the inside-out model, a company's values and reason for being lie, appropriately, at the core of the organization. Flowing from this core is the ripple effect that shared values and purpose have on the organization's mission and vision, strategies and goals, and finally, business practices and norms that show up in daily decisions and actions.

Just as the Twelve Steps move a person to dig deep inside and find the honesty, awareness, and self-assessment ultimately required to make changes in one's daily life, the same holds true for organizations. Corporate values must be organic and created, defined, and sustained from the inside out of an organization. To do the opposite—to let the "outside-in" of external forces and expectations define core values or organizational purpose—is folly and, at best, a short-lived exercise that only leads to organizational cynicism. To ignore the inside-out imperative or to allow an organization's behavior and business practices to shift with expedience, short-term benefits, or popular mores means the enterprise will fail or, at best, underperform.

The Power of Clear Values

A clearly defined purpose and core values are the bedrock of corporate culture. In their seminal work on corporate culture, *Corporate Cultures: The Rites and Rituals of Corporate Life*, authors Terry Deal and Allan Kennedy say:

> As the essence of a company's philosophy for achieving success, values provide a sense of common

direction for all employees and guidelines for their day-to-day behavior . . . In fact, we think that often companies succeed because their employees can identify, embrace, and act on the values of the organization.

Deal and Kennedy's book has become the "bible" on corporate culture. In their qualitative study of nearly eighty top-performing American companies including GE, DuPont, Hewlett-Packard, and Johnson & Johnson, Deal and Kennedy discovered that only eighteen companies had clearly articulated values (such as "IBM means service"), and those companies were the best performers of the eighty, by any standard, financial or otherwise. "We characterized the consistently high performers," Deal and Kennedy conclude, "as strong culture companies."

A decade later, Deal and Kennedy's work was ratified by an eleven-year statistical study of 208 American companies. The study, by John Kotter and James Heskett, led to publication of *Corporate Culture and Performance*. Kotter and Heskett found that companies with well-defined corporate values that were clearly understood and practiced were the elite performers. Compared to the others studied, this group enjoyed superior annual revenue gains, stock performance, and workforce expansion generated by growing customer demand.

In the course of researching American companies or writing about them for the business media, I have found that leaders who have examined this link between corporate culture and corporate performance agree on the three key benefits of clearly defined and consistently practiced values:

- They positively affect a company's productivity and efficiency.
- They attract the best employees and more customers.
- They attract investors.

These results have shifted the subject of corporate culture from what most called a "soft science" to a tangible, measurable corporate asset that even the most pragmatic chief financial officer can appreciate.

Corporate Culture Defined

Deal and Kennedy turned to Webster's *Tenth New Collegiate Dictionary* for a definition of *culture*: "the integrated pattern of human behavior that includes thought, speech, and artifacts and depends on man's capacity for learning and transmitting knowledge to succeeding generations." While this is a solid definition and captures the essence of corporate culture, Deal and Kennedy also shared a short-form definition coined by Marvin Bower (a former managing director of McKinsey and Company) that is powerful in its simplicity. The informal cultural elements of a business are, he said, "the way we do things around here."

Deal and Kennedy identified five elements that compose a corporate culture:

1. **Values.** These are the basic concepts and beliefs of an organization. Values define success in concrete terms for employees: If you do this, you too will be a success. "The strong culture companies that we investigated all had a rich and complex system of values that were shared with employees," say Deal and Kennedy. Leaders of those companies talk about these values "openly and without embarrassment and they didn't tolerate deviance from the company standards."

2. **Business environment.** The business environment shapes what a company must do to achieve success. "In some markets that means selling," say Deal and Kennedy, "in others, invention; in still others, management of costs. In short, the environment in which a company operates determines what it must do to be a success." This helps to explain why

the corporate cultures of Intel, Arthur Andersen, and McDonald's are markedly different.

3. **Heroes.** These people are the role models who personify the values of the company. "Some heroes are born—the visionary institution builders of American business," say Deal and Kennedy, "and some are 'made' by memorable moments that occur in day-to-day corporate life." At 3M, for example, the undisputed hero for nearly one hundred years of that company's life is William McKnight, a person with remarkable organizational vision far beyond his modest training as an accountant. McKnight went to work for $11.55 a week in 1907 (five years after the company's shaky, almost suicidal, start) and went on to become its leader. When he retired sixty years later, 3M was a billion-dollar-a-year company. Even today, the late McKnight is a 3M icon, and people refer to him with remarkable familiarity, as if he still occupies an office down the hall in this $15 billion global enterprise. Heroes don't hail from only the executive suite. They can and do come from sales, the back office, customer service, manufacturing, and security. The key is this, say Deal and Kennedy: "These achievers are known to virtually every employee with more than a few month's tenure . . . And they show every employee, 'Here's what you have to do to succeed around here."

4. **Rites and rituals.** These are often underrated in corporate life, yet they are crucial and powerful dimensions in human life. Deal and Kennedy say these are "systematic and programmed routines of day-to-day life" or "ceremonies that provide visible and potent examples of what the company stands for." They might range from the jeans-and-T-shirt business dress code of a Silicon Valley software producer to the annual holiday gathering at Medtronic, where patients who have regained their lives—thanks to a pacemaker, drug pump, or defibrillator—tell employees, often tearfully, what medical device the company invented.

5. **The cultural network.** This is the formal and informal means of communication in a company—the vehicles that carry, according to Deal and Kennedy, "the corporate values and heroic mythology." The cultural network includes employee publications, executive speeches, formal meetings, random talk at the water cooler or coffee bar, and informal chats on the Internet (or Intranet), and it even includes elevator banter.

Defining Your Corporate Culture

In Cambodia, an ancient statue carved in stone has four faces looking simultaneously in four directions. One looks forward, a second looks backward, a third looks outward, and the fourth looks inward. In my own work with companies, I have used this statue as a symbol for what I call "The Four Faces of the Future." Many companies emphasize only two views: the "outward face" that focuses on customers and the marketplace, and the "forward face" focusing on future strategy. However, without the other two perspectives, a company is handicapped and cannot realize its full potential. All views are equally important. Looking backward to understand the organization's evolution adds perspective and this understanding guides future decisions. Looking inward defines the core values that will test and support those decisions.

More specifically, the faces that look inward to values, strengths, weaknesses, and key processes and backward to history and tradition provide the foundation for understanding, defining, and sustaining a strong corporate culture. Like the Twelve Steps, the faces that look inward and backward represent an inside-out discipline that is crucial to healthy, lasting change.

Steps Five through Eight of the Twelve Steps ask people to go deeper, after they have faced reality, examined what's not working in their lives and taken responsibility for creating—and ending—their pain in these Steps. Going deeper means getting intensely personal: examining in detail the dangers of a lifestyle or current method of operating, facing the harm done or the potential for harm, and discovering how dysfunction can hold back a person—or an entire organization.

Facing the Pain

Today it is not unusual to hear people inside and outside organizations comment on what constitutes a flawed corporate culture. Words such as *dysfunctional* and *noxious* surface when a CEO like "Chain-Saw Al" Dunlap made headlines by shearing off half the jobs at Sunbeam Corporation, or when a parent company sells or closes a subsidiary simply because the subsidiary's ROI lags behind those of other more robust subsidiaries. What are the marks of a flawed culture? When asked, business leaders often identify these symptoms:

- **Shareholders first, forget the rest.** Maximizing shareholder value is the sole goal of the corporation, and financial manipulation is the means to the end. When this happens, says Bill George of Medtronic, the corporation has sold its soul.

- **A spinning compass.** This occurs when a company takes itself apart and in doing so does not transform itself but destroys itself and loses its purpose. For example, George believes ITT lost its compass bearing when it shifted from the telephone business to unknowns: casinos and hotels. One seasoned vice president of a national search firm told us that when corporate goals and strategies keep changing, employees say they feel like they are constantly in quicksand.

- **A pervasive "gotcha" mentality.** This often occurs when two different cultures are combined because of a merger. Each company's culture may have been highly effective on its own, but how the leaders of those companies make decisions, share power, and delegate may be dramatically different. Watch the sparks continue to fly as two

American banking behemoths with dramatically different corporate cultures—Norwest and Wells Fargo—combine forces and operations.

- **Me first, up the organization.** This happens when people are working for their own self-interest and self-aggrandizement rather than pulling together to advance the organization. Subgroups vie to promote their interests and personal agendas. Politics tend to prevail. "Look for a preponderance of behind-closed-doors meetings, often small and private," says Jerry Spicer, president of the Hazelden Foundation. People use such techniques to build their power base and exclude those managers and leaders perceived as "out of the loop."

- **Reward and recognition window-dressing.** This may occur in a company that espouses teamwork but rewards the lone rangers who are big producers. Another company endorses innovation but celebrates the good soldiers who control costs. When real recognition is out of sync with stated corporate values, the disconnect is obvious and destructive.

- **Corporate anorexia.** This is a marked disparity between what senior executives are paid and what others receive, especially if the pay scale is out of line compared to equivalent positions in the community or industry.

- **The good front.** "Dysfunctional organizations are like dysfunctional families," says Douglas M. Baker in Chapter 7 in this book. "There's a good front, but a lot of people are hurting behind the scenes." These are organizations with mission and values statements on their walls but, Baker says, there is little agreement on either: "People at the top try to put a good face on everything, but there isn't a lot of openness and honesty."

In its June 21, 1999, edition, *Fortune* magazine hit the issue of honesty hard (and sounded like an AA meeting) in an article entitled "CEOs in Denial." It featured five chiefs who, in the opinion of the magazine, "need to wake up—fast." The people featured with this dubious distinction included the leaders of Mattel, Polaroid, Reebok International, and Advanced Micro Devices.

"There's something in the nature of CEOs—pride, vanity, a primal need for control, an obsession with success, good old-fashioned idealism—that makes smart, well-regarded chief executives into idiots when the world turns against them," wrote journalist Patricia Sellers. "In these trying times for executives, denial is more popular than ever." Sellers quotes Chairman Andy Grove of Intel, who calls this condition "a generic disease," and he advocates the importance of facing reality: "The most vulnerable executives," Groves says in *Fortune*, "are the ones whose business models are being affected by change in fundamental ways. Which means just about everybody . . . Corporate America looks like a flotilla of boats in a stormy sea."

If the Twelve Steps ever applied to American business, it appears they are ripe for application now. Even the language of recovery and business—while seemingly distant in connection—are today intersecting with ironic accuracy and meaning.

Going Deeper to Define Your Corporate Culture

In keeping with the Fifth and Eighth Steps of Twelve Step philosophy, the two faces looking backward to history and tradition and inward to core values come into sharp focus here. Working these Steps must start with the leadership of a company going deep into its own corporate experience. There is no meaning in *time-honored values* unless the values are consistent with today's corporate beliefs and authentic in daily practices. There is no meaning in today's corporate beliefs if they are not grounded in shared reality and experience. Some companies are held back by their history and others are handicapped because they are ignorant of their history. Many companies—even the best ones—struggle because their espoused corporate values and daily practices are not aligned. It is tough enough to achieve this alignment in the U.S. market, much less with the added challenge of facing "values collisions" in other countries where business beliefs and practices can vary dramatically.

While crafting a mission and vision has become common practice in American business to clarify the purpose and values of an enterprise, too often these efforts disintegrate into superficial wordsmithing. For expedience sake, one well-respected national insurance company "borrowed" language from another company that one insider said sheepishly "seems to fit us with a little tweaking."

What does it take to identify and define your company's core values? I believe the following steps are fundamental and consistent with the deep examination of Twelve Step principles. While the decision to take these steps must come from leadership and have executive endorsement, it is wise to involve internal staff at all levels. This will ensure not only a more reliable outcome but will also build employee knowledge and support of the process.

1. **Retrieve your history.** Max DuPree, retired chair of Herman Miller and author of *Leadership Jazz* among other books, writes: "The future is turned on the lathe of the past." Becoming more aware of corporate heritage helps organizations pass accumulated wisdom from one generation to another while giving current management the insight to make decisions in authentic context. "If you don't know where the guide-signs are along the way," historian and author Joseph Campbell agrees, "you have to work it out for yourself."

   If you take this retrieval journey, the returns can be incalculable. Work to preserve your company's past and turn that knowledge into a powerful perspective tool. Search for the anecdotes and details that demonstrate your company's values over time. Identify the key decisions and external forces that have shaped your company. Explore how changes in your industry have affected your company. Know about the key people who have had a major impact on your company—and why. Seek out other heroes and role models at all levels who have embodied the core values. Look for watershed points, or "defining events," that have tested or shaped your company's value system and, ultimately, its direction. Identify the rites and rituals that have been used to mark key events in your organization's life. Examine how information has been communicated and how decisions have been made. Bring these historical explorations up to the present.

This work will enable you to preserve your company's corporate memory. In conducting research, seek out the opinions of not only leaders and valued employees, but also key customers, observers of the company, and business allies. Assure confidentiality. Approach this step with an attitude of curiosity, honesty, candor, and balance. You may be surprised how much of the same you will get back. This information will be invaluable in creating a context for understanding and defining your core values and corporate culture today. Much of the research may be for internal use only, but a good portion can also be used later in both internal and external communications to chronicle the origin and evolution of your company and its culture.

2. **Review these historical insights in view of your stated core values.** Test these values by asking yourself, your employees, and your customers how—or if—the values show up in daily decisions and actions. Identify the best practices in your company that reflect your organization's espoused values. Find the disconnects, too. Anticipate where your values collisions are—or will be. This is where the honesty and authenticity of the Twelve Step process is vital.

Create an annual review time with your strategic planning cycle that involves top management and addresses these key issues:

- Do our company's stated core values still guide our present-day decisions?

- Are these values at work in our decision-making and daily practices?

- Which "values collisions" do we confront when our beliefs are at odds with our needs and those of our key stakeholders?

- How well do employees in our organization understand and apply our company's core values in daily decisions and practices?

- How well does our company recognize people for their commitment to our core values (in performance reviews, formal and informal recognition, pay and bonus structures)?

3. **Re-envision your present.** Recognize what change has occurred and what change still needs to occur. Some of your business practices are no longer appropriate today. Understand that your core values may, in fact, have shifted. Perhaps the priority of those values has changed. In this step that takes you deep into your corporate soul, understand what you are retaining and what you are letting go with the clarity of understanding and choice. The following four questions represent four phases of change in organizations. Answering them in a spirit of honesty can help with your discovery process. These questions apply to a broad range of choices in corporate life including core business, market strategies, leadership roles, styles of working, policies and procedures, incentive, and rites and rituals:

- What has died?

- What is dying?
- What is alive and well?
- What is emerging?

These four phases are present in any organization, whatever its age—an entrepreneurial start-up or an established business of 100 years. Each of the four phases require thoughtful consideration. For example:

What has died?

- Business practices that have outlived their usefulness can be recognized as past and respectfully placed in the organization's evolving history.

What is dying?

- Policies or patterns of working that are declining in value need respect and closure as the transition to new policies and patterns begins.

What is alive and well?

- Elements of the organization that are alive and well need recognition, resources, support, and celebration.

What is emerging?

- Emerging initiatives, philosophies, and practices require nurturing, resources, and support and a more forgiving standard of evaluation in their embryonic stages.

By regularly reviewing these four phases in your own organization, you can identify and retain with respect what is still valuable and viable, and let go of what no longer fits—thus maintaining both continuity and vitality in the ongoing cycle of organizational evolution.

Sustaining Your Corporate Culture

In the final four Steps of the Twelve Step process, the work shifts from research and retrieval to making changes happen. It means acting on knowledge you have gained from self-assessment. It involves discovery of new ways of thinking and behaving. Ultimately, these Steps focus on follow-through and implementation, being open to new insights, and creating and sustaining an attitude of openness and honesty as change occurs. There are three key elements of this phase:

- Creating and sustaining a framework that supports the espoused values of your organization's culture

- Communicating clearly, often and with authenticity

- Candidly assessing yourself and testing how well your organization is walking toward its talk

Creating the Framework

Even with careful work devoted to clarifying values and defining a corporate culture, if policies and systems are not in place to support that culture, the effort will fail. More importantly, if these policies and systems in any way contradict your company's espoused values, the impact will be destructive.

Hiring and promotion practices, performance reviews, reward and recognition techniques, and criteria for mergers and acquisitions are part of this framework.

When then-CEO Bruce Atwater wrote the first draft of General Mills' values statement in the early 1980s, he emphasized community service, innovation, integrity, and financial stewardship. Soon after, the company altered its annual incentive system. Traditionally, General Mills managers had been rated on three factors: (1) meeting financial and production goals, (2) developing managers and subordinates, and (3) strategic planning. When Atwater added a fourth criterion focused on community service, some in the company balked, arguing that their performance should focus on financial targets. Atwater explained his reasoning this way: "We wanted to emphasize the importance of being a well-rounded person. If you're going to deal with upper management issues, you better have some idea about what goes on outside your cereal plant."

CEO of Norwest Banks (now merged with Wells Fargo) Dick Kovacevich says two people up the chain of responsibility and two down review performance appraisals. "These appraisals gauge how well a person has worked to instill the Norwest culture," Kovacevich says, "how they live it and teach it." Advancement at Norwest, he says, is based on "what people have done to promote our culture, not whether that person can sell more financial gizmos."

It is important to recruit people based not only on their skills and experience but also on their value system. Don Goldfus, former chairman and CEO of Apogee Enterprises, a global company specializing in fabricating, installing, and distributing glass and aluminum, has been cited in *The 100 Best Companies to Work for in America.* Goldfus used a forty-year history replete with values-based stories as a screening device when he interviewed prospective key employees. At the end of the first interview, Goldfus sent a candidate off with a copy of the book. In the next interview, he gauged the candidate's interest level based on whether his or her questions reflected a thorough understanding of Apogee's philosophy. If a candidate's values weren't in sync with Apogee's, Goldfus didn't make an offer.

Decisions to acquire another company also take cultural dimensions into consideration. Bill George of Medtronic says his company has walked away from acquisitions that looked like financial and strategic winners when the corporate values of the company and its leaders were inconsistent with those of Medtronic.

Leaders must also recognize that they are role models—and stewards—of the culture. Employees will watch what you say and, more importantly, what you do. At Norwest, for example, as the organization expanded nationwide largely through acquisition, a key plan of cultural integration was called "buddy banks and buddy bankers." The leaders of newly acquired banks were teamed up with Norwest managers, who introduced them not only to the organization's procedures but also to cultural expectations of leaders.

Communicating Clearly

Once your company has defined its core values, it is essential to communicate them clearly and often. These statements must be consistent and, most important, authentic. As part of this process, it is important to identify business practices that reflect your company's core values in action, particularly as more companies operate globally and people are put in positions of significant authority and responsibility. Consider H. B. Fuller Company, an adhesives and coatings company that has manufacturing and sales operations in thirty countries and customers in more than a hundred. "I'm convinced that the fabric that holds a company together is its culture, its values and its beliefs," said former CEO Walter Kissling, who spent many years overseeing the company's international business. "These common values will ensure that we perform successfully in this competitive, global world we're facing."

To underscore its core values and examples of key business practices that reflect these values, Fuller—at the direction of the company's chairman, Tony Andersen—created a guide to decision-making, called *The Fuller Way* for its 400 top managers around the world. It also published a synopsis in English and Spanish for all employees and a code of business conduct based on *The Fuller Way*. The company provided values training for managers and board members and incorporated this information into new employee orientation. Companies like H. B. Fuller have done this because their leadership believes it is the right thing to do as they put more decision-making into the hands of professionals beyond their own corporate backyard.

In fact, leaders who take core values seriously stand to benefit from guidelines which the U.S. Justice Department issued in 1991. These guidelines are designed to reward the presence of values-based programs and codes of conduct in American companies with reduced sentences and fines should an employee violate U.S. law anywhere in the world.

In the 1980s Levi Strauss and Company put its core values in writing and developed a series of programs designed to help employees understand and make a genuine personal connection with the organization's core values. This included a leadership program focusing on the firm's tenets, such as recognition, communication, and team building, plus separate programs on ethics and diversity.

Another powerful form of communicating core values is to publish a book that profiles an organization's values. In our work with companies, executives do not view such publications as meaningless vanity press. Instead, they see this printed chronicle as a tool for reinforcing the core values of the company. "Pure and simple," said Michael Sullivan, then president and CEO of International Dairy Queen in 1991, "we use our history to help explain why we do things the way we do."

"I personally believe," says R. L. Knowlton, chairman emeritus of Hormel Foods Corporation, "that our historic values—more than any specific product, marketing strategy or competitive price—will make all the difference in our future performance."

3M—on the eve of its centennial year in 2002—will produce a book that captures its history and examines its culture of innovation. One of the key objectives of this project is to reinforce the company's core values in a new century of accelerated innovation and intense global competition.

Storytelling to reinforce core values does not confine itself to the print medium. Earl Bakken, the founder of Medtronic, met personally with every new employee to recount the history of the company. At the end of his homespun presentation, he gave them a medallion with the Medtronic mission—a visual symbol of the company's purpose: restoring people to full life and health. At Honeywell (now merged with Allied Signal of New Jersey), the company has presented an allegorical play called *The Journey*, with group discussion that focused on the "winds of change" and their impact on "Honeydwellers," employees of a hard-working, mythical company. All around Honeydwelldom, the forces of light and dark compete. The topography of Performance Peak, Mount Innovation, and the Rock of Mutual Respect surround Lake Integrity. But not far away lurk Mediocrity Quicksands, the Valley of Status Quo, rocks of Cynicism, and a cavernous Communication Canyon. "The purpose of the play is to spark conversation about our values and the complexity of actually 'walking the talk' in today's business climate," says Kate O'Keefe, who ran the company's executive and management development program.

Candid Self-Assessment

After you have defined the core values and business practices, after policies and systems have been put in place to support the core values, after active communications, what is left? Periodic self-assessment that gauges how well your company is actually walking toward its talk. Medtronic accomplishes this in its Global Employee Survey every two years. Questions in the survey are designed to determine how well employees understand the core values of the company and how consistently they see their peers, superiors, and others put them into practice. Also included is an open-ended question that asks employees to suggest what else Medtronic might do to sustain and strengthen its culture around the world.

Just as the Twelve Steps call for continuous inner reflection, periodic assessment will help the leadership of a company assess how well its core values are understood and practiced. Without asking these questions—and being willing to hear and act on the answers—an organization can stray from its intended cultural course. A strong corporate culture does not remain so without honesty, attention, and nurturing, just as a life cannot flower without the same.

Carol Pine

Carol Pine has had a singular career as an entrepreneur and as a business consultant. Currently she is the president of Pine & Partners, a consulting firm specializing in corporate culture and corporate history working with companies including 3M, Medtronic, Hormel Foods and International Dairy Queen. She also served as Chair of the Hazelden Foundation Board of Trustees.

Carol is co-author of *Self-Made: The Stories of 12 Minnesota Entrepreneurs*, a regional bestseller published in 1982. Since then she has written extensively in business magazines and journals. In addition, she has been a business commentator on Minnesota Public Radio and co-hosted a four-part series on corporate culture that she designed, researched and wrote for MPR.

Carol has co-designed and co-facilitated a series of roundtable discussions on corporate culture, core values and performance for the Center for Ethical Business Culture based in Minnesota. She's a business columnist for *the St. Paul Pioneer Press* and her column (*On the Mind*) has been syndicated among the 27 Knight-Ridder newspapers nationwide.

CHAPTER FOUR

In this chapter Dan takes to a personal level what has hitherto been applied to the organization. He tells the stories of people he has known, from senior managers to line staff, who have faced the perils and fear of organizational change. Despite their differences in age and position, these individuals all feel lost and afraid in a world they never made. Each not only survives but also prospers, by accepting both the care and attention of others and by accepting the help of a Higher Power. "The bad news is that my life is falling apart. The good news is that my life is falling apart, which means that I now have the opportunity to put it back together again, only better this time" – a quote in this chapter from a business executive who unknowingly has delivered the key message of hope underlying the Twelve Steps. The chapter concludes with a recommended program that helps leaders reconnect with themselves and their work.

—Editor

Coping with Change and Transition

Daniel S. Hanson

A Hard Fall

Humpty Dumpty sat on a wall.
Humpty Dumpty had a great fall.
All the King's horses
And all the King's men
Couldn't put Humpty together again.

—Anonymous

Even if harsh interventions succeed brilliantly, there is no room
for celebration. There has been some injury. Someone's process
has been violated.

—The Tao of Leadership

Bill is fifty-three. By most standards he is successful. At least he was until six months ago. As president of a major division of a *Fortune* 100 food company, Bill exceeded even his own expectations. Bill's wife, Jan, is equally successful. She is a marketing executive for a financial services company. Bill, Jan, and their son, Eric, live in an upper-middle-class suburb with all the proper trimmings of a successful family.

Six months prior to the time of our interview, Bill's world fell apart. His company initiated a workforce reduction. Bill was one of the more fortunate ones. At least he was given an opportunity to take early retirement. But calling it early retirement did not ease the pain of transition. To Bill, the message was that neither his work nor his presence were valued. "It's like saying you don't count anymore," Bill told me during our interview.

Bill had mellowed by the time we spoke, but he was still bitter toward the company. "I gave them the best years of my life," he told me, "and they let me go as if all those years meant nothing." Since the loss of Bill's job, Jan had been forced to return to work full time and postpone her plan to finish her master's degree and start a new career in human resources. She tried not to be angry with Bill. After all, she knew that it was not his fault. Try as she might, however, her frustration with the situation was bound to spill over on Bill now and then. In turn, Bill found himself taking out his own frustration on Eric, who had returned home to heal from a divorce and complete his college degree. "Isn't it funny how times change," Bill said with a tinge of anger in his voice. "When I was Eric's age I was well on my way toward a successful career. Not that I had a choice. I had to work. I had two mouths to feed."

Bill talked at length about his career. He admitted that his job had never given him the kind of fulfillment he longed for, but he also reminded me that the promotions and the pay had been "damn good." Bill also admitted that he often regretted having abandoned his boyhood dream to enter the ministry. He wondered whether it was too late to resurrect the dream. Bill talked about his friends. Most of them still worked for the company. He talked to some of them now and then. It seemed to Bill that they were less happy than he was. They reported working longer hours in a stressful environment. The company expected more speed and intensity from those left behind. As bad as things were for Bill, he wondered whether he was the lucky one. At least he was out of the rat race.

A Time of Transition

Dear, dear! How queer everything is to-day! And yesterday things went on just as usual. I wonder if I've been changed in the night? Let me think: was I the same when I got up this morning? I almost think I can remember feeling a little different. But if I'm not the same, the next question is, Who in the world am I? Ah, that's the great puzzle.

–Lewis Carroll, *Alice's Adventures in Wonderland*

I, a stranger and afraid, in a world I never made.

–A. E. Housman

We live in difficult times. People feel lost, alone, and afraid. Bill, in the story that opens this chapter, is only one example. In my class at Augsburg College on self-identity at work, I am constantly amazed by the stories I hear. In spite of the progress we have made toward creating better work environments, I still hear about people losing jobs without warning. That is not the end of it. I hear stories about people being asked to run from team to team, to work with more intensity and speed and to adapt without warning to mergers and acquisitions. If there is a central theme to what I hear, it is that people feel a loss of self-worth and personal identity as a result of all the changes that have taken place over the past two decades.

In his book *The Saturated Self: Dilemmas of Identity in Contemporary Life,* Kenneth Gergen suggests that what is different about our era is that we don't know who we are anymore. Like Alice in Wonderland we feel as if we are wandering through a strange land, uncertain of what lies around the corner. We are not sure about anything anymore—including our own identity. William Bridges, author of the book *Managing Transitions,* suggests that we are in the middle of a major transition. He reminds us that it is not unusual to feel a loss of identity in the middle of a transition. He aptly names this middle time "no person's land." Listening to the experts, paying attention to people like Bill and the students in my class, or simply reflecting on my own experiences inside a large organization, I am convinced that we live in a time of acute alienation and uncertainty.

Nowhere is the alienation and uncertainty of our time felt more deeply than inside large organizations. Programs designed to make us more efficient and effective have added to the uncertainty. Introduced with good intentions, these programs often result in frequent role changes and larger work loads. At the same time, mergers and acquisitions continue at an unprecedented rate. No wonder employees begin to feel as if they are nothing more than pawns in a chess game played by executives in the boardroom. Employees are not the only people affected. Everyone feels the effects of major change. Whole communities are disrupted as businesses consolidate and plants close. Prompted by the announcement of yet another plant closing, a writer for the *New York Times* once declared that "job apprehension has intruded everywhere, diluting self-worth, splintering families, fragmenting communities, altering the chemistry of workplaces."

The irony is that many executives like Bill thought they were immune to the worst consequences of organizational change. Bill assumed that his loyalty would be rewarded and that he would continue to build his career until he chose to retire. But that was not to be. The downsizing craze eventually spread to Executive Row. Executives have learned the hard way that those at the bottom of the hierarchy are not the only expendable resources. Some of them become victims of the very programs they helped design.

I will never forget a story told to me by a middle manager of an insurance company. He was instructed to close a branch office in a small community in Pennsylvania. He told me that accepting the assignment was the most difficult decision that he ever made for the organization. He rationalized by telling himself that if he didn't do it, someone else, perhaps with less heart, would get the job done. So he caught a plane and spent a miserable month gathering records and running people through out-placement interviews. Upon his return to the home office, he was summoned into his boss's office. It seems that he had missed a name on the list of jobs to be eliminated: his own.

Many of the victims of organizational change programs are waking up to the hard reality that even programs with good intentions to improve quality and create efficiencies can have painful consequences. This is especially true if programs are implemented with only short-term results in mind coupled with an uncaring attitude toward people and toward the long-term sustainability of the enterprise and society. Waking up to the reality of our shortsightedness is only the beginning. The hard part is what to do the morning after. Like Humpty Dumpty we search for those who will help us put the pieces together again. Unfortunately, like Bill we often discover that all the King's horses and all the King's men are not able to help—nor do they want to. Can we blame them? They are most likely too busy hanging onto their own seat on the wall.

Loyal executives aren't the only victims of organizational change. Some might argue that executives are the least of the victims, indeed, that they had it coming. After all, they bought into the programs in the first place. The real victims, some people argue, are the people at the bottom of the rung who never had a choice.

A "single mom" I interviewed would agree with this line of thinking wholeheartedly. She works as a secretary for a large financial firm in order to support two children. She puts up with unreasonable demands and demeaning comments from her boss only because she is afraid to lose her job. She attends college on weekends and evenings in the hope that a degree will open new doors, but for now limits on transportation and no time to interview keep her from finding better work. Others, such as Eric, Bill's son, decided long ago that they were not ever going to get into the rat race. For Eric, success is working at several jobs that he loves and having time to balance life among work, leisure, and community involvement. Eric was blunt when I asked him about his career plans. "The last thing I want is a career. Do you think I want to end up like Dad, working for some stupid organization that doesn't give a hoot about me?"

John, a middle manager for a large health-care provider, agrees with Eric but feels powerless to do anything about it. His desire to find meaning in his work and care for others conflicts with his organization's imperative to cut costs and produce more. His department has been downsized twice. Each time he has had to tell friends of his that they no longer have a job. He feels torn between the need to support his family, please his boss, and live in harmony with his values. John's is a crisis of authenticity, or of being true to himself. He is frequently depressed. He is not alone, judging by some recent statistics.

In his book *The Hungry Spirit*, Charles Handy refers to a study by the Massachusetts Institute of Technology. The study calculated the cost of work-related depression in the United States at $47 billion a year, roughly the same as heart disease. The following headline in the October 1994 issue of *Time* magazine captured the feelings of many of the victims of organizational change: "We're Number One— And It Hurts." The article described the turnaround in the auto industry that returned America to a competitive position in world markets, including the turnaround's downside. Once again, the workers were the losers. Many were working at menial jobs part time without benefits, while others struggled to retrain themselves to adapt to a high-tech world that no longer had a need for their skills. It would seem that the short-term competitive position of the organizations of America has been realized at a cost to the individual.

Bad News or Good News?

> *Bad times have a scientific value . . . We learn geology*
> *the morning after the earthquake.*
>
> –Ralph Waldo Emerson

Trauma that organizational change causes is not always bad news. Sometimes only a crisis can bring about needed change. A friend of mine said it well: "The bad news is that my life is falling apart. The good news is that my life is falling apart, which means that I now have an opportunity to put it back together again, only better this time." The crisis might be a major illness that forces us to pay attention to what our senses have been telling us for a long time and forces us to change patterns of addictive behavior that hurt others and ourselves. In my own case, a midlife bout with cancer brought this lesson home. Strange as this might sound, I was addicted to pleasing others and being the eternal victim. I needed to let go of my need to prove that I could do everything on my own and learn to lean on others for a while in order to take charge of my life and ultimately care for those I love. This is a lesson that those who live the Twelve Step program know well. This program is uniquely focused on recovery, change, and personal transformation from despair to hope.

For those who struggle to cope with change and transition, a key lesson from the Twelve Step program is that we are not alone. When we let go, we discover that others are there for us. That discovery can make all the difference in the world. What we call "the other"—God, the Universe, or the power of caring relationships—doesn't matter. The important thing is that we let go and accept this Higher Power. To me, this is by far the most valuable lesson from the Twelve Step program. The support of others who care sends a message of hope in what appears to be a hopeless situation. It keeps us human in a world where our humanity is challenged by the imperative to value only that which can be measured on the bottom line.

In his book *The Corrosion of Character*, Richard Sennett writes about a group of IBM programmers who were victims of a workforce reduction. He describes the phases they went through as they learned to cope with the loss of job and identity. At first the group blamed the "evil organization" for abandoning them.

They moved to blaming foreign competition. Eventually, they blamed themselves for not taking the initiative to retrain themselves and find new work. It was only after they began to meet as a group that they accepted what had happened to them and found the courage to build new lives. According to Sennett, it was the group experience that made the difference. He puts it like this.

"What seems most striking in the experience of the IBM programmers is that they came to speak about failure plainly, without guilt or shame." But this result required the presence of others and drew each closer to the others. Their achievement—which is not too strong a word—is to have arrived at a state in which they were ashamed neither of their mutual need nor of their own inadequacy.

Life is about suffering now and then. The ancient Portuguese proverb had it right. "Die young or suffer much." The key is to find meaning in the suffering, a truth that Viktor Frankl, author of *Man's Search for Meaning*, brought back with him from the Holocaust. I truly believe that we cannot care deeply for others until we acknowledge and feel deeply our own suffering. A dear friend of mine who has suffered through depression and alcoholism has a wonderful way of making this point.

It is from the depths of our own suffering that we find the strength to help others. When we emerge from the darkness of despair into the light of hope we bring with us a gift to share with the world. It is the gift of recovery.

The Gift of Recovery

So why would I want anything to do with this illness? Because I honestly believe that as a result of it I have felt more things, more deeply; had more experiences, more intensely; loved more, and been more loved; laughed more often for having cried more often; appreciated more the springs, for all the winters; worn death "as close as dungarees," appreciated it—life—more; seen the finest and the most terrible in people, and slowly learned the values of caring, loyalty, and seeing things through.

–Kay Redfied Jamison, *The Unquiet Mind*

Jeanne is a recovering alcoholic. She also has bipolar disorder, an illness that causes her moods to swing from the heights of elation to the depths of depression. Her illness requires medication that produces side effects such as trembling in her hands. These facts, however, are only part of Jeanne's story.

Jeanne remembers a happy early childhood. She was especially close to her father. Her diary is full of notes about days "singing and dancing with Daddy." The happy days ended abruptly for Jeanne at the age of eight. Jeanne's father died suddenly of a heart attack. The rest of Jeanne's story reads more like a tragedy than a happy fairy tale. Unlike her biological father, her stepfather abused her frequently. What's more, he forced her to never speak of her birthfather again. What Jeanne remembers the most about her childhood after her father died is bouts of depression. Her way of coping was to turn to alcohol. By the time Jeanne was thirteen, she was already drinking heavily. Alcohol had become her best friend.

Jeanne married at a young age. She and her husband had two children. On the surface, their life together appeared normal. They lived in a nice home in a nice suburb with all the trimmings. They were both involved in the community. They were a nice couple. Underneath the facade, things were not so nice. Jeanne was struggling with her old friend, alcohol. Her moods ran up and down like a yo-yo on a string. Finally at the age of forty, Jeanne hit bottom. A suicide attempt landed her in a psychiatric ward of a major hospital. She began the slow climb out of the depths.

Jeanne's story is sad but unfortunately not unusual. What is unusual about Jeanne is the way she uses her story. Jeanne is one of those special people who emerge from the depths of suffering with the gift to share the power she found during recovery. Jeanne calls it the gift of recovery.

I felt Jeanne's power at our first meeting. I was struggling with a midlife crisis and feeling sorry for myself. Yet, there was Jeanne, a person who had every right to feel sorry for herself, talking to me about opening doors and discovering hope. Her very presence spoke of power. She reminded me that the power was not hers but rather a source of power she had learned to accept as part of her recovery. Her gift to me was the power of recovery.

Theologian and philosopher Martin Buber wrote about the gift of recovery. He called it the power of "I-thou" relationships, wherein two people meet and experience each other at a deep, caring level. The concept of the I-thou relationship goes beyond empathy. To Buber it means I feel the pain of the other as if I caused it. It is not about changing people or giving advice. It is about being present, accepting the other as different from oneself, and confirming each other. Indeed, the I-thou relationship is divine in that both parties discover that which is sacred in all of us. In the words of Buber, "It is from one [person] to another that the heavenly bread of self-being is passed."

We need not experience the suffering and pain that Jeanne went through to discover the gift of recovery. At some level we all know suffering, even if it is the loss of a job such as Bill experienced. Frankl suffered through one of the worst atrocities of our century as a prisoner during the Holocaust. If anyone earned the right to trivialize the suffering of others, he did. Yet, Frankl reminds us that suffering is like gas in a bottle. No matter how small the amount, the gas—or the suffering—fills the entire bottle. Whereas your suffering may seem trivial to me, to you it may be overwhelming.

I am reminded of the woman who hated her job so much that she would become ill every Monday morning. Her friend made fun of her and accused her of being a big baby. To her friend, there was nothing wrong that a little fortitude and a better attitude wouldn't fix. To the woman, going to a job she hated was unbearable, at times worse than death itself. Indeed, she had contemplated suicide on more than one occasion.

I often wonder why it is so hard for us to feel the pain of another person. Is it because we have become so steeped in the ethic of individualism that we have forgotten how to care? Or have we learned so well to defend ourselves from our own pain that we no longer feel the pain of others? For many people, the organization became an excuse to avoid intimacy. "I did it for the good of the organization" we would say when our conscience bothered us over a decision that might hurt someone. Not long ago I overheard an executive describe the process of closing plants: "Around here we make decisions with our heads and implement them with our hearts."

In a book titled *Descartes' Error*, Antonio Damasio contends that it is impossible to separate the rational from the emotional, the head from the heart. After studying the effects of frontal lobe brain damage in several patients, he concludes that when the part of our brain that connects the mind to the body is damaged, our reasoning powers are impaired. In other words, when we no longer feel the experience with our entire bodies, we are unable to make rational decisions. The reason this is true, according to Damasio, is because we make decisions based on somatic markers that require full body experiences. When we experience something with our entire mind, body, and spirit, our body tells us what to do and what not to do. We are also then able to experience and feel the pain of others. People who are no longer capable of experiencing with their whole body can neither reason nor empathize. I can't help but wonder what happens to us as executives when we deny our feelings for years. Do we become like the brain-damaged patients Damasio studied who lost their ability to feel? It is a question worth pondering.

You and I have the gift of recovery within our grasp. To grasp it we must get in touch with our feelings. We must dare to relive the times in our lives when we felt hurt, abandoned, overwhelmed, the times we suffered as well as the times we felt the joy of living with our total being. We must dare to relive those times with our mind, body, and spirit. It is not easy reliving the past. In truth, it often scares us to death. That is why we need the help of others who have been there. Together we might discover the gift of recovery. Having found the gift, we can share it with others. This, more than anything else, is what is needed during this time of transition and transformation.

What Leaders and Others Who Care Can Do

A Place to Shine is not a perfect place to which we travel or a utopia that we create. Rather, it is a place for caring and connecting along the way.

–Daniel S. Hanson, *A Place to Shine*

We live in the middle of transition. It is a time when people feel lost, alone, and afraid in a world they never made. During times of transition we need each other more than ever. The support we give to each other can make the difference between despair and hope. Caring for each other gives hope in an otherwise hopeless world. It is the missing piece in most change programs. Without caring relationships, the loss associated with change and transition can be frightening. It can bring out the worst in us. Caring relationships are at the heart of the Twelve Step program. It is a lesson we can bring to the workplace where change has become a way of life.

Before we can apply this lesson to work, we must relearn how to care for each other and ourselves. This will require bold steps. In my book *A Place to Shine: Emerging from the Shadows at Work,* I outlined seven bold steps that leaders might take to reconnect with themselves, their work, and each other. These steps worked for me. They helped me reconnect when I was healing from cancer. They may or may not work for you. You need to discover your own steps. My hope is that by sharing my steps you will find the courage to reconnect in your own way.

When I first shared my bold steps several years ago, I had no idea that I would be writing a chapter for a book on the Twelve Step program. I am amazed at the similarities between my steps and the Twelve Steps. It makes me wonder to what extent the Twelve Steps tap into a natural process that we all share. Perhaps that is what makes them so powerful.

Step One: Connect with Yourself

I wonder what is going to
be your next step in life:
I think of it and
even pray for it.
May you find the path
which will lead to
the highest and the truest
of yourself!
Keep the right path upwards
and hope for perpetual
discovery—
and trust life.
That's all.

–Teilhard de Chardin

We live in a world of self-help programs. To suggest that one should get in touch with oneself may seem trivial and redundant. As valuable as the exercise might prove, however, I am not recommending that you take another test to determine your personality type or preferred learning style. What I am suggesting is quite simple. Take the time to reacquaint yourself with two things that are unique and therefore the most special about you: your experiences and your feelings. Others can have your personality type or share your learning style, but no one can have your experiences or feel your feelings the way that you have felt them. They are yours alone.

When I was being treated for my cancer, I took long walks in the woods and fields near my home. One day while walking near an alfalfa patch a memory from my childhood struck me. It was so vivid it was as if I were transported back in time. I was playing "jungle animal" with my brothers and sisters in the alfalfa patch on the farm where we grew up. I laughed and played for what seemed like hours, although I know it was only a matter of minutes. It felt good to laugh and play. When I returned to reality, the sheer joy of play remained with me. I was so impressed with this memory that I included a chapter in *A Place to Shine* on the joy of play and how we might learn to play in the workplace and thus bring new energy to our work.

We learn much from our experiences and our feelings. Some of them are joyful, such as the memory of playing jungle animal in the alfalfa patch; others are more painful, such as these from my childhood: I grew up "too sensitive for my own good," as my dad put it. I was so sensitive to the feelings and opinions of others that when I was eighteen and a choir director told me that I did not have a good voice, I discounted all the awards I had received and gave up singing for several years. I let him still my song. Over the years I have joked about being overly sensitive, but it was no joking matter. In truth, my sensitive nature has made life difficult for me.

Growing up too sensitive for one's own good can be a curse. Yet, it can also be a blessing. My sensitive nature puts me in touch with my feelings and the feelings of others. Once I had learned to discount the negative opinion of others and to stand up for myself, I was free to use my gift of sensitivity to help others.

When we reconnect with ourselves, we discover that we are not so bad after all. Often what we perceive as a curse can become a blessing. What's more, we will discover that we are still in the process of becoming. Psychologist and author Carl Rogers reminds us that we are each special and that what is special about us is "comfortably lodged" in our experiences. As I wrote earlier, reliving our experiences is not easy. We are apt to discover things we do not like. This leads to the second bold step.

Step Two: "Let My People Go"

But if we are able to see our own shadow and can bear knowing about it, then a small part of the problem has already been solved.

–Carl Jung

I learned two equally valuable lessons by taking the second bold step. The first lesson applied to my role as a leader in the organization. The second lesson was more personal.

During the industrial era, or the "machine age," as historian Lewis Mumford named it, we became convinced that living the good life was about controlling things—including nature and people. Large organizations emerged to help us control the production of products and services. Growth as progress became almost sacred. Inside the organization the professional manager emerged and then was replaced with the leader, but the notion of control never went away. Leaders were expected to get things done through controlling and motivating the resources at their disposal, the most important resource being the human resource.

While I was healing my cancer, I attended a sales meeting at which a vice president of sales gave a speech about growth. "I want growth, and I don't care how we get it as long as it is profitable," he shouted. At that moment I reached for my neck and felt the cancerous tumor. "Growth isn't everything," I thought to myself, "not when it is out of harmony with the rest of the body."

Our obsession with progress, growth, and profits—or "bottom line" as we like to call it—comes at the price of the human spirit. When we control people or turn them into just another resource, we run the risk that they will become what we condition them to become. When I look up the word *resource* in my Webster's dictionary I read the words "something that can be looked to for support or aid; an accessible supply that can be withdrawn when necessary." On the other hand, when I flip a few pages forward and look up the word *source* I read, "One that causes, creates, or initiates." To me the word *source* captures the essence of the human spirit. I often comment to my audiences that a small change in the title, from "human resource department" to "human source department," might make a world of difference in how we view people and work.

As leaders we do not own people, nor do we motivate them. At best, we nurture the emergence of work environments that are like caring communities, where human sources create together around a common belief, cause, or task. I chuckle when I hear leaders in the organization say to each other, "When 'my people' get together with 'your people,' we will fix this problem." I have discovered that when I let go of my need to control and give people a reason to engage in their work—a meaningful role to perform; extrinsic rewards in the form of fair and reasonable pay, good benefits, and healthy working conditions; intrinsic rewards in the form of job satisfaction and challenges appropriate to skills; and finally, relationships that are caring and confirming— then, workers will outperform my wildest expectations. On the other hand, when I try to control people, they do what is expected of them but no more than that. "Let my people go." It is a message that God and Moses brought to the Egyptian pharaoh three thousand years ago, and it still echoes today.

The second lesson to be learned in step two is more personal. To reconnect with our work, each other, and meaning in our work, we must let go of fears that hold us back. In my own case, I had to deal with the fear that if I let go of my need to please people, conflict would emerge and things would fall apart. I was afraid to assert myself and to speak my truth. Many leaders inside the organization are afraid to appear less than perfect for fear that someone might see that they are human and therefore, fallible. We set our leaders on pedestals and expect them to act rationally and decisively; in other words to be superhuman. This places an unnecessary burden on them to be godlike. The truth is, leaders are not gods. They are human beings with feelings and the same fears that we all share. Men in our society are particularly vulnerable to this dilemma. Based on numerous studies in several organizations, Harvard professor Chris Argyris noted that fear of embarrassment in front of their peers more than any other factor kept male executives from living their values.

Another fear that I had to let go was my fear of letting people down. I am the best people pleaser who ever lived. It is both a curse and a blessing. When I let pleasing people rule my every move, it overwhelms me and keeps me from caring for others and myself. Letting go of my need to please others while learning to use my gift of sensitivity has been freeing for me. It allows me to care for others without feeling used. I find that when I am authentic and honest with others, they, in turn, are authentic and honest with me.

Unless and until we let go of our fears, we will miss out on a source of energy that is good for us and for the people around us. The fear that holds us back is different for each of us. The important thing is to face the fear and move on. When we face our fear head on, it helps to have others there who care for us. This leads me to step three and the very heart of the seven bold steps.

Step Three: Connect to Each Other

> The basis for human life is twofold, and it is one—the wish of every person to be confirmed as what he or she is, even as what he or she can become, by others; the innate capacity of humans to confirm in this way. That this capacity lies so immeasurably fallow constitutes the real weakness and questionableness of the human race: actual humanity exists only where this capacity unfolds.
>
> –Martin Buber

Step three is the heart of my seven bold steps. It is about caring for and confirming each other. It is also at the core of the Twelve Steps. I agree with Martin Buber when he asserts that our inability to care for each other is the central issue of our time.

Mihaly Csikszentmihalyi, professor of psychology at the University of Chicago and author of several books including *The Evolving Self,* suggests that we as a society have forgotten how to care for each other except from a distance. We give to charities and join in community projects, yet we are afraid to get too close to the people with whom we work or the people who live next door. Csikszentmihalyi points to our emphasis on rugged individualism as one cause of our insensitivity to the needs of others. It is the kind of individualism that encourages an if-I-can-handle-it-so-can-they attitude toward others who are more sensitive or less fortunate. Men are especially vulnerable to this kind of thinking, but it infects women as well. Csikszentmihalyi reminds us that caring is natural to the human species, but like other natural gifts our ability to care for each other can atrophy from lack of exercise. In other words, if we do not practice caring for each other, we forget how to do it. This sets in motion a vicious cycle. Because we are not good at caring for each other, we become afraid to try; because we don't try, we fail to develop the capacity to care. Eventually, our hearts atrophy.

In my book *Cultivating Common Ground: Releasing the Power of Relationships at Work,* I named six fears that keep us from connecting to each other: (1) the fear of the unknown, (2) the fear of conflict, (3) the fear of speaking out, (4) the fear of claims and responsibility, (5) the fear of being disappointed, and (6) the fear of loss of self. When we stop caring for each other, we build on these fears. After a while our fears become so large that we are unable to face them. The only way I know to overcome this is to begin to reconnect and to learn how to trust each other. Often this bold step requires a third party to get started or a group of caring others such as Alcoholics Anonymous. We need to feel safe before we are willing to open up to others and share our secrets.

It is true that living in a time of transition is not easy. The pace of change itself makes it difficult to find the time to reconnect.

Gergen makes this point in *The Saturated Self.* He also asserts that we must find ways to reconnect in new forms of community even if they are short lived. Our sense of self depends on relationships. Without work to do and others we can care for and who care for us in return, we become mere survivors, "minimal selves," according to sociologist Christopher Lasch.

One way or another we must learn how to reconnect with each other, to nurture caring communities in our neighborhoods and churches, as well as in the workplace. James Frank Mossman, a therapist who has helped countless people reconnect with themselves and others, defines *community* as a conscious commitment to holding a life and a task in common with others. I like the definition because it captures what it means to live in community. It is about holding things together through the good and the bad times. It is about learning and growing through conflict. Parker Palmer suggests that community is the place where conflict can happen because we know that others will be there to care for us. Communities have a task dimension and a relationship dimension. The two are intertwined. When things aren't right between the members of community (the relationship dimension), the task suffers. Everyone who has worked in a dysfunctional group or team has learned this the hard way. Communities are productive when people care for each other.

If we are going to survive this time of transition with our hearts intact, we must learn to reconnect with each other. It is a lesson that the Twelve Step program teaches us. Whether as individuals or as members of an organization, transition—if it is about real change—can leave us feeling alone and afraid for a while. The caring touch of someone who knows what it is like to feel alone and afraid can be a source of healing. It is the gift of recovery that I wrote about earlier. Helen Keller, who grew up without the ability to see, hear, or speak, was blessed with a heightened sense of intuition and touch. Her words from her piece *Red Letter Days* eloquently express the healing touch of someone who cares:

"The influence of their calm mellow natures is a liba-
tion poured upon our discontent, and we feel its healing touch as the ocean feels the mountain stream fresh-
ening its brine."

Step Four: Connect with a Purpose

*For the meaning of life differs from person to person, from day
to day and from hour to hour. What matters, therefore, is not
the meaning of life in general but rather the specific meaning
of a person's life at a given moment.*

–Viktor Frankl, *Man's Search for Meaning*

A plethora of books has been written already about purpose and
meaning. One of the profound yet down-to-earth books about
meaning was Viktor Frankl's aptly titled *Man's Search for
Meaning*. Of all the insights Frankl shares, three have special
meaning for me.

The first insight is that meaning is specific to the individual.
Each of us discovers meaning in the "everydayness" of our lives,
day by day, hour by hour. Furthermore, meaning differs from
person to person. I may find meaning in my work, whereas you
might discover your meaning in a special relationship.

The second insight is that we often discover meaning in our experiences, "the full granaries of the past," Frankl called it. This
insight reminds me again of the two things mentioned in my step
one that are unique and therefore, most special about you and me:
our experiences and our feelings. We often find our life theme in
our experiences. In my own case, I have discovered that helping
people shine through caring relationships is a central theme in my
life. It grows out of my experiences and feelings as a young man
"too sensitive for his own good." This theme gives my life meaning even when I feel alone and afraid in a world I never made.

The third insight is that we discover purpose and meaning
when we engage in life. This is a truth that goes contrary to

much that we have been told about meaning and purpose. It suggests that we find meaning when we quit searching for it and get involved with life. Frankl shares three ways that meaning emerges when we engage in life. One is by engaging in a special work or cause. A second way is to care for another person. A third way is by the attitude we take toward unavoidable suffering. Meaning is discovered when we see beyond the suffering. The recovering alcoholic who begins to view addiction as a way to help others who have the same illness (the last Step in the Twelve Step program) has learned the secret to this third way to find meaning.

Frankl wrote that meaning is like a butterfly. The harder we chase it, the more it flies away. When we sit still, the butterfly lands on our shoulder. So it is with meaning and purpose. The more we search for them, the more they seem to fly away from us. When we live in the present and care for ourselves, our work, and each other, meaning often lands on our shoulder.

Step Five: Become a Matchmaker

> It is man's task, his greatest task, not to learn to love, but to learn to create the conditions in which love alights upon us and remains with us.
>
> –Irene Claremont de Castillejo, *Knowing Women: A Feminine Psychology*

I wrote my step five specifically for leaders—which includes all of us, since we all emerge as leaders at one time or another at home, in the community, at church, or at work.

Several years ago Robert Greenleaf wrote a book called *Servant Leadership*. In it he argued that leadership is more of a calling than a reward, as we were led to believe in the industrial era of the professional manager. Since then others have echoed his words and called for a paradigm shift to a view of the leader as one who serves others. I would like to add to these voices the thought that leaders are really matchmakers. Together with followers, leaders create an environment where people are matched to a work that they love and others to share it with. My own way of putting it is to say that leaders build places to shine—places where people can shine in their work by doing what they are good at, being appreciated for it, and thus find meaning and purpose in it.

I have discovered that this truth is more than mere words. I was fortunate to be the leader of a group of people who cared for their work and each other. In fact, the theme of our division was "We care." People were allowed to match their skills and aspirations with the tasks that needed to be completed. We were by no means perfect, but as people began to connect to their work, we witnessed a power that is hard to describe. Csikszentmihalyi writes about this power in his book *Flow: The Psychology of Optimal Experience.* He calls *flow* an experience of getting lost in what one is doing and in which time passes without notice. Indeed, Csikszentmihalyi's studies show that people are happiest when they are working at something that is challenging to them and something that they love doing more than so-called leisure activities.

I have come to believe that the most powerful thing that we can do as leaders is to match people with a task that fits them. It brings out a power that is good for the person, good for others, and good for the organization.

Step Six: Dare to Care

> *Caring has a way of ordering activities and values around itself; it is primary and other activities and values come to be secondary.*
>
> —Milton Mayeroff, *On Caring*

This step may seem redundant. After all, in step three I already wrote about connecting to others. But it is redundant for a reason. I cannot overemphasize the need to care for our work and more importantly, for each other.

I used to think that caring was the essence of leadership. After reading the umpteenth book about leadership, I began to question my wisdom. After all, I thought to myself, it can't be that simple. I have come back full circle. I do believe that the essence of leadership is caring. It is a simple message but hard to live by because when we dare to care, we find ourselves engaged in the task and the lives of those who share the task. It is, as Greenleaf believed, truly a calling. It is a message found in the notion of the servant leader or matchmaker leader.

Other evidence supports the message of the caring leader. For example, studies of small, task-oriented groups show that leaders emerge from the group based on the approval of the followers. In other words it is the followers who decide who the leader is. They do it on the basis of who they believe cares for the task and for them. When as leaders we care for the task and the people, it shows. Leadership is a communal concept wherein a leader emerges for a time, place, and task. After everything is said and written about leaders and leadership, the one thing that all great leaders have in common is followers.

There is a warning for those who dare to care. We must care for ourselves as well. This message is especially important for those who work in the caring professions. We cannot be present for others if we are not present to ourselves. Author Charles Handy calls it a "proper selfishness." He reminds us that we are of little help to others when we are overworked, overstressed, and out of sorts physically, mentally, or spiritually. Therefore, we need to dare to care for ourselves, each other, and our work—perhaps in that order. Leaders care and it shows.

Step Seven: Simplify, Simplify

Where is the Life we have lost in living?
Where is the knowledge we have lost in information?

The cycles of Heaven in twenty centuries
Bring us farther from God and nearer to the Dust.

–T. S. Eliot

Life is complicated these days. We are saturated, as Gergen so aptly puts it, by information, images of perfection, and multiple social relationships, so saturated that we hardly know who we are anymore. Thus, one of the most important things we can do to help ourselves and each other reconnect is to simplify the task before us.

As a leader inside the organization, I have learned firsthand to honor this step. For people in my division to shine in their work and relationships, they need to understand what we do and why we do it. My challenge as a leader is to simplify things so that people can reconnect to their work, each other, and meaning and purpose to what they do together. Our work is simple yet meaningful. We put milk on people's tables. It shouldn't matter what role we play. Whether we drive a forklift in the cooler or develop a strategy in the board room, we still put milk on people's tables. When we complicate processes and keep secrets from each other, we lose sight of what we do. We also lose a source of energy that emerges when people work together on a common task that everyone understands.

People want to connect to their work and each other in meaningful ways. Indeed, we thrive on caring for work, each other, and ourselves. It is hard to connect when we can't see or understand what is going on around us. It is a simple message that is always true, but perhaps it is even more true during a time of transition when life can get more complicated than it needs to be.

Turning Transition into Transformation

What the caterpillar calls the end of life,
the master calls a butterfly.

–Richard Bach

This chapter began with a story about Bill, a middle-aged executive who lost his job and his identity for a while. I am happy to report that since my interview with Bill, he has taken on a new life. Together with friends who share Bill's experience, he has opened a center of hope for people who are struggling to find themselves while in the middle of transition. The center offers what Bill calls "a new kind of out-placement service" that provides counseling and support, as well as practical advice and employment services. Bill feels transformed by his experience. He says that he has found his ministry. Bill reminded me that he would never have been able to find new life without the support of people who care for him, people who were there for him, people who confirmed his self-worth and challenged him to grow in new ways.

For me, turning transition into transformation is what the Twelve Step program is all about. The secret ingredient is the power of caring relationships. This includes a relationship to a Higher Power as well as to other people who care. In truth, they are often one and the same: The Higher Power is revealed to us through other people. I am reminded again of the words of Martin Buber: "It is from one person to another that the heavenly bread of self-being is passed."

During a time of transition we need less of the quick-fix programs and self-help formulas and more of each other. Each of us has a gift to give to others. It is the heavenly gift of self-being, or the gift of recovery, as my friend Jeanne names it. We don't have to lose our job, as Bill did, or struggle with depression, as Jeanne did, to get in touch with our gift. At some level we know what it means to feel lost, alone, and afraid in a world we never made. What we do need to do is get in touch with our own feelings and the feelings of others even if that means taking some bold steps—not so that we can feel sorry for ourselves, but rather so that we never lose sight of our gift. God grant us the courage to reconnect and discover our gift, the heart to give that gift to others, and the wisdom to use it wisely.

Daniel S. Hanson

Daniel S. Hanson has been President of the Fluid Dairy Division of Land O' Lakes, Inc., author of three books, a full time instructor at Augsburg College, and a frequent speaker on relationships in the workplace.

A thirty-year veteran of four Fortune 500 companies, Hanson offers a unique combination of hands-on leadership experience and academic involvement that makes it possible for him to translate theory to real life situations. Through his work and speaking, Hanson is a voice for building community at work. He addresses the current need to build a new kind of loyalty to the organization based on meaningful relationships.

Hanson has written two books about building and sustaining productive work environment that—in a real world approach—bring out the best in the individual and the group. His newest book, *Cultivating Common Ground: Releasing the Power of Relationships at Work,* was released by Butterworth Heinemann in the spring of 1998. *A Place to Shine: Emerging from the Shadows at Work* was published by Butterworth Heineman in 1996.

Hanson teaches a course at Augsburg College in Minneapolis that he designed around the issue of the new social contract at work entitled "The Self and the Organization." His academic credentials include an M.A. in Organizational Communication from the University of Minnesota. He served on the advisory board for adult graduate studies at Augsburg College where he helped design a Masters of Arts in Leadership program. As part of the masters program he taught contextual leadership theory in a course on Contemporary Theories of Leadership.

C H A P T E R F I V E

Marilyn continues in this chapter the concept of transformational change on both a personal and corporate level. She tells the stories of two Chief Executive Officers who, for different reasons, face an internal crisis that threatens their selves and their companies. The path to change leads through the Twelve Steps but it is not always an easy path to accept. Marilyn also discusses the differences between change and transformation and presents a model to help explain the transformational process. As they follow this process, both CEOs are forced to surrender a part of themselves for the common good, something they had bitterly opposed through the early stages of the journey. The results of doing this, however, are startling both to the executives and to their business colleagues. As an individual's spirit can be ignited, so can a corporation's spirit be ignited, to the benefit and profit of all.

—Editor

From Personal Change to Corporate Transformation

Marilyn J. Mason

Michael's Story

Michael, a middle-aged chief executive officer (CEO) of a manu-facturing company, had just been informed that he had either to make major changes in his behavior or leave the company. Tony, the new board chair, advised Michael to seek executive coaching immediately to change what his colleagues viewed as inappro-priate and disrespectful behavior. Further, Tony told Michael the board would give him just six months in which to demonstrate changes in his behavior. Michael came to me for executive coach-ing. His first statements to me were, "What does behavior have to do with anything? And who's complaining? I thought my peers appreciated my behavior—and the profits my department brings to this company."

I was skeptical about coaching Michael at first since I had met many executives in my professional work who refused to change or even to acknowledge the need to change. Yet I also knew that a crisis such as the one Michael was confronting can often be the catalyst for true and lasting change in the individual and even throughout an organization.

Michael would have been the last person to believe that this directive for personal change would ultimately lead to corporate transformation. Some of the most growth-enhancing and rewarding changes in business start in the executive suite when corporate leaders experience an awakening crisis. Numerous events can trigger such a crisis, and we will discuss several examples in this chapter. Whatever the trigger, what becomes paramount for the executive is to find a pathway through the crisis, along with a guide or system to lead the way.

I have found in my work that the guiding principles of the Twelve Steps of Alcoholics Anonymous can provide such a pathway for individuals and for organizations. Since these principles comprise a time-tested model for personal transformation and since corporations are nothing more than groupings of people, this philosophy has universal application for people at home and at work both in theory and in practice. Whether or not we are aware of the fact, many of us who serve as business consultants use these principles on a daily basis.

It Starts with Personal Change

With gentle prodding and assurances of confidentiality, I began interviewing Michael's peers and subordinates in the company. What emerged at length was a corporate culture that exuded disrespect for its employees and stakeholders. I was told, for example, about senior management's excessive drinking at corporate functions and about blatantly sexual jokes overheard in the hallway. Senior executives provided no remedy; several, in fact, personified the problem. Michael, in particular, was called a control freak, a rogue, and other names that were far from complimentary. Many, it seemed, despised him for the way he acted toward them and for his support of the unwritten rules that all too often govern the workplace:

- Check your feelings at the door.
- Never comment on management's inappropriate behavior.

- Deny your own personal history and your involvement in problems.

- Be in control of all interaction; dominate whenever possible.

- Be physically present, but psychologically absent.

- If something goes wrong, blame others.

- Maintain secrets; don't trust anyone.

- Work long hours; give at least the appearance of perfection.

Michael's behavior was symptomatic of the disabling or dysfunctional patterns of many organizations. To start with, he had never appreciated that his first system, his childhood family, was the first organization to which he belonged and to which he must conform. Early in the coaching process, Michael began to sense the correlation between his childhood family and his corporate family: the unspoken rules, the addictive behaviors, the denials.

Michael had grown up with an alcoholic father and a fearful, hardworking mother. As Michael's memory became more vivid through conversation, he recalled that his father had often beaten Michael's brother with a belt and had threatened Michael with the same treatment. Michael had learned how to survive and even beat such a system. He brought these lessons to his job and his position as a corporate leader. With help, he began to understand that for all those years he had remained loyal to the beliefs and systems he had formed as defense mechanisms for survival. A high-stress corporate job in fact had provided a safe harbor for him to suppress and bury his feelings.

I reminded Michael of an employee assistance study conducted in the mid-1980s. This study reported that 38% of chief executive officers in the United States were raised in alcoholic families, a figure four times the national average. Michael was not alone. He took some comfort from knowing this. Nonetheless, he felt absolutely unable to confront the reality of what now had to be done.

He realized he needed to make serious changes in his behavior but did not know where to go for help. One evening he agreed to attend an all-men's Adult Children of Alcoholics (ACOA) meeting. This meeting, which other middle- and senior-level executives attended on a regular basis, proved to be a milestone for Michael. Gradually his painful childhood wounds were opened and dissected by his empathetic support group. Slowly, during a series of weekly meetings, he discovered that his story was not unique. Others had endured similar kinds of experiences and abuses and had, like Michael, shut down emotionally at too young an age. Frozen in time, these executives had developed a tough yet smooth veneer, with a heart and soul known to no one, not even themselves.

In addition to the group meetings, Michael also met with me for private consultation. The focus of these consultations was often on his boyhood. Increasingly he expressed a need to analyze himself as a youth, to understand why he was too fearful to speak up and defend himself. Out of touch with his true self, he felt out of sorts, out of control, "going crazy" as he said at one point in the process. "You're going healthy, not crazy," I stressed and urged him to continue his self-analysis. He did and made steady progress, the pain and stress notwithstanding. At long last the veneer began to crack. Michael sat one day in my office with tears running down his face, utterly defeated yet utterly victorious, no longer spiritually bankrupt, a man who for perhaps the first time in his life felt truly alive and truly grateful for his life and his family.

"See No Evil, Speak No Evil"

Denial skills learned in his childhood had served Michael well, as they have countless others. Author Ernest Becker writes, "If everybody lives roughly the same lies about the same things, there is no one to call them liars. They jointly establish their own sanity and call themselves normal." Denial allows people to become indifferent, to ignore (perhaps not even recognize) what happens right in front of them, and to create and sustain a false version of reality. Denial diminishes life and blocks from consciousness what is real.

Yet denial can be a more positive coping mechanism for those who were raised in dysfunctional family systems caused by alcoholism, drug abuse, emotional abuse, or family violence. What is experienced in one's personal life almost by definition flows into one's professional life.

Work systems function like family systems, replicating the emotional processes that those in authority impose on those with less power and authority. If one grows up in a family in which "women don't count" or "Dad must never be challenged," that individual will almost certainly struggle with the tenacious hold such internalized messages have on relationships at work. The stranglehold of rule systems—unstated, implicit patterns that senior executives dictate and employees unquestioningly follow—emanates from past family dynamics and dysfunction. Such behaviors can sabotage productivity and progress, often at significant cost to an organization. They can permanently damage the potential and success of individual employees. They can have a ripple effect, affecting the lives and emotional health of employees' spouses and family members. Michael now understood, for example, the reason his peers and subordinates had not come forward sooner to complain about his behavior. They, too, were hostages of their company's dysfunctional environment.

The Way Through

When I first talked with Michael about letting go, he replied, "Let go of what? To whom?" His support group had helped him to understand that he was not alone today and that he was powerless to control what had transpired years ago in his childhood. "But you are not powerless to face the shame your behavior has caused you and others," I reminded him. "For the benefit of yourself, your family, and your business associates, you must face the shame and accept it. Then you need to move on with your life by letting go of the shame." As Michael's frozen feelings began to thaw, he experienced new levels of spirituality and communication with his own Higher Power. He realized unequivocally that his Higher Power represented the way out of the abyss.

Michael had memorized the Serenity Prayer of AA in his group meetings and now began to recite it every morning before going to work: "God grant me the serenity to accept the things I cannot change, the courage to change the things I can, and the wisdom to know the difference."

For Michael, this prayer was to serve as a guidepost on the pathway to transformation.

Not All Change Is Growth: A Map and a Model

Change is not the same as transformation. Change can become transformation, but for that to happen there needs to be a series of steps and events that are as intense as they are purposeful. Following is a description for a model I have used in corporate seminars to help explain the transformational process.

The Overt Disabling Quadrant

Quadrant 1 (upper right corner) represents the behaviors that have led to the awakening crisis or wake-up call—whether externally or internally driven—that inevitably precede a major change or transformation. It has by now become imperative for the sake of personal sanity and career survival that the cause of a person's disabling behaviors be identified and confronted. There is a definitive call to change that is both loud and clear to the individual. Behaviors representative of Quadrant 1 lie at the far end of the continuum, where disrespect and high intensity abound. The professional life of the individual is a mess.

Characteristics of the overtly disabling quadrant: high fear, low trust, verbal abuse, sexual harassment, intimidation, compulsive behaviors, boundary invasions, highly emotional reactivity, disrespectful behaviors, and the "no-talk" rule.

Most management teams do not intentionally create dynamics that condone abuse of power, nor do they normally plot to get rid of someone by shunning and isolating them. Instead, managers merely act out what has become normalized in their work environment, often smoothed over with a veneer of tacit acceptance. Quadrant 1 is where Michael first began to admit his own dysfunctional behaviors and to understand how powerless he had felt to correct them.

As would an addict on the Step One of Alcoholics Anonymous, Michael came to realize that his life was unmanageable and that he had to face his reality. He made a commitment to change; he began to work through and identify his true value system (Step Two); and he called on his Higher Power, (in his case, God) to help him through the process (Step Three).

Covertly Disabling Quadrant

Quadrant 2 (lower right corner) contains less intense energy and less of a reactivity field, with behaviors still at the disrespectful end of the continuum. Here is where Michael could identify the covertly disabling behaviors that had contributed to what others perceived as his untrustworthiness within the organization.

Characteristics of the covertly disabling quadrant: sarcasm, cynicism, low risk, emotional abuse, silence, isolation, secrets, buried pain, gossip, "triangling"(talking to one person about another or bringing an outsider's view into discussions), emotional dishonesty, and ostracism.

As Michael moved through changes in his behaviors, he still felt reactive and at times responded in old patterns. Still, he had better control of himself. He was beginning to connect first with himself, then with others. People began to notice. He even spoke openly to his senior team about the changes he wanted desperately to make in himself and asked for honest feedback on his progress.

Gradually Michael was able to step back and look at the whole system in all its components. He began to understand how his jammed emotional processes had inhibited all of them. He read Daniel Goleman's best-seller *Emotional Intelligence* and learned that the attributes that define a person's emotional quotient (EQ)—flexibility, empathy, and adaptability in human relationships—are clear predictors of success on the job. "I.Q. takes second place to E.Q. in determining outstanding job performance," writes Goleman. Michael agreed to take an EQ test and discovered that while his overall score was low, he was already moving toward changing his self-destructive behaviors. He now realized, for the first time, that his buried emotions had blocked the competencies and skills essential to raising his EQ.

From this point on Michael became more honest about himself. He listed those behaviors that he felt were responsible for his undoing and for the sense of crisis in his professional life. Such a moral inventory is at the core of Step Four. Since Michael was by now familiar with the language of the Twelve Steps, I asked him if he wanted to work through a Fifth Step with a senior member of his ACOA group. He agreed.

Once on this path, Michael came to understand and appreciate a central principle of AA: Just as debilitating behaviors can be learned by experiencing and observing human relationships, so can other human relationships heal the wounds and foster a new beginning, both for the individual and his or her extended family.

The Transitional Quadrant

Michael was now ready to move into the third quadrant (lower left corner). Here the focus is on learning new behaviors.

Characteristics of the transitional quadrant: Growing respect, empathy, risk-taking, feelings expressed, behaviors changed, attitudes shifted, "we," not "I," and new skills learned.

Michael was by now connecting with a purpose. He could admit to his peers, "I was wrong. I'm sorry. I made a mistake." He was also learning to focus in meetings on empathy before strategy and to sit back and listen to other points of view. The effect was immediate and striking. Senior executives praised him both in public and in private. Many reported that they had never felt so comfortable in a work environment.

Michael recognized that to create an environment that supported both human development and economic growth, he would have to break many of his own unwritten rules. Although his new behavioral patterns were not yet firmly in place, as he began making amends to others for his past actions, he experienced for the first time in his professional career a higher level of commitment and respect among his peers and staff. He began to be viewed—certainly for the first time in his career as a leader—as someone who could be entrusted with the welfare of the company and its staff. It came as a revelation to Michael to be honored for the person he was rather than being feared for the person he was not.

The Vital, Spirited System

The move into the vital, spirited system involves a spiritual awareness and leap of spiritual faith. This is the stage in which a leader begins to accept a connection with a Higher Power, however the leader may define such a force. It was at this Quadrant 4 (upper left corner) that Michael realized he had to trust his Higher Power's guidance and his own heart. "I guess the old teachers were right," he confessed to me one day. "The heart has to break to open."

Characteristics of the vital, spirited quadrant: high trust, clear boundaries, safe environment, creative, expressive, committed, and high respect.

"Whoever thought I would be grateful for this crisis?" Michael exclaimed, as he worked to begin corporate training in, and implementation of, these characteristics throughout the organization. At this time Michael confided his biggest fear—that there is an inverse correlation between corporate profitability, and spirituality and humanity in the workplace. The more these principles were practiced, he feared, the less productive the company would be, and the more the workers would put their own spiritual and material needs ahead of the strategic needs of the company.

What he discovered in both the short term and the longer term was the exact opposite. With far less absenteeism and with far greater employee involvement and commitment at all levels of the organization, output, productivity, and profits rose steadily.

Michael's leadership had truly shifted from disrespect to high respect. He now complimented and supported his staff and made himself visible to his satellite offices through teleconferencing, videotapes, and personal appearances. He called for a new commitment to the company, its customers, and its shareholders and received enthusiastic applause in reply. His personal life changed in step with his professional life. Neighbors and social contacts confirmed what he felt so positively about himself. He now worked shorter hours and began taking both pleasure and pride in community volunteer work.

Michael took his senior associates out of town for another retreat. The purpose of this retreat was to provide time and occasion for inner reflection—as individuals, business leaders, and an executive team. As a group they processed their growth and discussed both their personal and corporate mission. They used silence and guided imagery in their meetings and trusted in what they could not readily see or understand. Individually and as a group they focused on their own spiritual paths within the group vision. The meeting concluded with all participants viewing themselves and their colleagues in a new and more positive light.

The dynamics of the vital, spirited system are aligned with and sustained by the principles of the Twelve Steps, especially Steps Ten through Twelve. In a more relaxed environment, staff members were able to know moments of what some call grace, or the surprise of the spirit. They knew they no longer had to fill every silent moment in their discussions. They were able to think out loud with one another and to reveal their true selves without fear of reprisal or scorn. Trust and creativity blossom in such an environment, in full acknowledgement and support of a transformational process.

It Starts at the Top

Michael's story is one of success. There are fortunately many others like his. However, there are also stories of aborted attempts to change. Michael along with many other corporate executives had to take the lead in creating a healthy, sustainable system at work. As a leader, he had a compelling moral responsibility to do so. Some cynics may say to such leaders, "Why bother?" or "Don't be naïve!" when confronted with the challenge of changing American business. Leaders must learn to ignore such admonitions and like Michael, rely on their intuition and Higher Power to guide them and their companies toward a culture of respect. It must start with them.

In his book *The Living Company,* Arie de Geus argues that when American business does assume this moral responsibility, it can become a force for societal change. De Geus analyzes the living companies that renew themselves continuously through the years, much like a healthy family might do. This book served as an inspiration to Michael in his own efforts to transform first himself, then his company. The board of directors applauded his efforts. The company's shareholders applauded his results. In the eyes of his employees and peers Michael had become a leading voice on the subject of spirited change.

Adrian Levy and RLG International

Although satisfied with both his personal income and his company's financial growth, Adrian Levy still felt something important was missing in his life. True, he had realized his college dream: At age thirty-three he owned his own successful business. In just three years he and his marketing-whiz partner had grown the company to almost three times their original projections. They now had thirty-four full-time employees on staff.

Adrian's awakening from within began with an internal monologue. He asked himself, "What is my purpose? Why am I doing what I am doing? I had realized one dream but was without another one. I'm healthy, with two wonderful children and a third on the way. I have plenty of money, a lovely home, a beautiful and loving wife, a good job that I myself created, and I'm away from my family little. Sure, there are issues and problems, but no more so than compared to other families. Why do I feel so empty? What is the next step for me?"

His pondering led him gradually away from his corporate office as he wrestled with what he should be doing with his life.

His awakening led Adrian to a personal growth workshop. There he learned that at work he had been acting out a senior executive role that he thought was appropriate for his position. In this role he had sacrificed his true self, the person he really was under the corporate veneer. This realization deeply troubled him. Amid the bustle of work during the day and in the sanctuary of his home at night, he found himself contemplating the high cost that is often extracted in pursuit of one's dreams. Henceforth, he vowed one night, he would begin stripping away the corporate veneer and just be himself, no matter the consequences.

Adrian recommenced his inward journey with renewed determination. He hired a coach to learn more about himself. He worked closely with the coach, both in person and on the telephone, in weekly and then monthly sessions. During that time Adrian studied the power of visualization and imagery and explored in depth the characteristics and personal history of his parents and grandparents. He knew that his mother had been institutionalized when he was only two years old, yet he had never felt abandoned and always felt loved and cared for. He found few clues to explain his own behaviors, but benefits were unearthed in the search nonetheless.

Moments of Insight

Adrian continued to grow and to discover more about himself. One day he had another flash of clear insight. He was away on business, and his partner called to tell him that the person they had agreed to bring into the partnership had refused to sign the employment contract as is, citing several contractual terms as being unacceptable, even though earlier the potential partner had agreed to them. In the past Adrian's reaction would have been, "Fine. If he doesn't want to sign the contract, he's not our partner." Now Adrian heard himself asking his partner, "Okay, so we're at an impasse. How would you handle this?" His partner told him how he proposed to break the deadlock, in a way that was diametrically opposed to Adrian's own solution. Nonetheless Adrian told him, "If that's what you think we should do, let's do it."

Adrian realized afterward that this was a first for him. He had broken one of his own cardinal rules of business by placing the entire responsibility for a crucial decision in someone else's hands. For perhaps the first time he was willing to let go and accept the consequences. He was beginning to trust not only his partner's decisions, but also his own willingness to trust his partner. He confessed to me, "Ever since I can remember, I have been on my own. I have always had to make my own decisions in life. It was time to let others share this responsibility—and what a relief this decision has been!" To this day, Adrian has never seen the final signed contract.

In 1993 Adrian faced another crisis. "I realized I had become a catalyst to help people with their own communications. People were searching me out. I knew I wanted to fundamentally change how business is conducted. I wanted to help people find the gifts and talents they inherently and often unconsciously carry. To do this, I had to first successfully transform my own company and then use it as an example for other companies. The first step was to give up control—this time over the entire organization, not just to my partner—and make a firm commitment to my staff and to myself to make this transformation possible."

Naturally these decisions affected Adrian's relationship with his primary business partner, who was not at all pleased with this turn of events. He offered to buy Adrian out, but Adrian refused. "Getting rid of me is not the answer," Adrian told him, "because I'm not the problem. You are. You have to change. We've gone too far in the process to turn back now."

The die was cast. The original partnership had ended, and both men knew it. Adrian approached three other senior managers in the company and asked them to join him in a new partnership. Each was to invest $100,000 in a restructured company. Adrian as senior partner would invest considerably more. All four agreed to the terms, as a consortium, but their agreement was contingent on the former partner's resignation. That resignation was scheduled to be announced at ten o'clock the next morning, along with all other components of the restructuring.

At 11 PM that night, the attorney for the consortium called Adrian. "Your new partners don't believe you've gone far enough," he told the stunned president. "What more can you offer these people to convince them this partnership's for real?"

"Nothing," Adrian replied adamantly. "I've given them all I can."

He could almost feel the heavy weight of silence. "In that case, sir, " the lawyer finally announced, "the partners have asked me to inform you that the deal is off."

The issue was control, he thought. Adrian was willing, even anxious, to cede absolute control, but not proportional control. It was his company and he would not accept a coup.

This was the nadir, the lowest two months of Adrian's life. He could not understand at first why the consortium had turned on him. "Because you don't trust us," one consortium member finally confessed to him. "Sure, you give lip service to saying you trust us, because it's easy to say. But deep down, you still believe that what you do and think is right and that what others do and think is wrong—unless they happen to agree with your position. Without confidence and trust, a partnership is meaningless." Even after all he had experienced and suffered through, Adrian still did not fully understand how great an issue is trust in one's personal and professional life. He was devastated. For days thereafter he found himself purposely avoiding his office to find comfort and guidance where he could: in his family, friends, and counselors, and in prayer.

Two months later Adrian conceded to the consortium almost everything it had sought. He still retained a majority of equity, although operational control was divided more evenly among the partners. Together they moved forward, skeptically at first but with mounting confidence. The company now had 134 employees and was represented in thirteen countries. To celebrate one spectacular year, the company invited all employees and their spouses to an all-company retreat in Hawaii. Everyone seemed pleased with both the bottom-line performance and the employees' continuing commitment to the company.

Five years passed. By this time Adrian had convinced himself that he and his partners were truly working as a team to the betterment of all. But there was yet another surprise for him the day he was again confronted by the consortium. "This isn't a real partnership," they told him. "You still have majority control—56 percent compared to the 17 percent each of us has. We're all contributing here to profits, but you still have control of the equity.

For this partnership to survive and be a real partnership, you have to share the equity equally."

Adrian thought hard. "This is it," he said to himself, "the Rubicon. How do I feel about giving up equity control of my company? What would it take for me to do this?" When the time for a decision arrived, Adrian stood before his partners and talked not about his anger or frustration or righteous indignation, but rather about his childhood. He told stories about his brothers, who he said never trusted him and never saw him as an equal. These experiences, Adrian stressed, had left lifelong scars on his psyche and had caused patterns of behavior he had grown into habits. The full extent of this behavior, he added, had only just recently come to light, and the pain of realization was agonizing. Then to the surprise of his partners, he agreed to give up equity control. "You're right," he said softly, "in this new company we must all be equal partners. It's as much your company as mine. Henceforth, we are equal partners in every sense of the word."

With these few words the mantle of total responsibility was lifted entirely from Adrian's shoulders. What had transpired in that room caused hardly a ripple in the organization as a whole, but it had a profound effect in the executive suites. Not much more was said there about this topic in the months and years that followed. There was nothing more to say.

RLG International, the company Adrian founded, is today a prosperous and purposeful company. Employee turnover rates are extremely low, while productivity rates remain among the highest in the industry. The higher corporate valuation that these results generate keep Adrian's personal net worth at high levels, despite his lower overall percentage of ownership, and he now has far more time to devote to his family, community and spiritual commitments. He describes his life as "rich beyond anything I could ever earn at RLG. Earning trust among those you love and respect is the hard part, and that's what I have achieved. With that, and God's grace, the rest comes naturally."

The Ignited Spirit

"When deep down inside the flame ignites, we light the way from inside."

–Life's Mountaineers

No matter where we find ourselves within an organization, the challenge for each of us is to ignite our own spirits, and then to ignite a broader corporate spirit. What are the signs of an ignited spirit? First, employees must work in a safe environment. They must also truly care about each other and commit themselves to making their company a touchstone for purpose and meaning. When spirits are indeed ignited at work, what we witness is an opening of hearts, true expressions of feelings, and heightened respect for one another. Certainly it is not an easy assignment. Nay-sayers, personal agendas, tunnel-visioned executives, and resistance to new systems and policies will inevitably throw up roadblocks. Nevertheless, the potential results of senior management implementing such a course are confirmed by the experiences of both Michael and Adrian.

It is happening elsewhere. At an airport recently I overheard two Southwest Airlines pilots commenting on "how great it feels to work for a company that actually cares about and trusts its employees." An executive vice president of a *Fortune* 50 company told me, "I struggled through my own crisis of consciousness. Now I spend part of each day walking the aisles and plant and counting the number of smiles I see at work. This may sound trite to some, but believe me, I've learned this much at least: If my employees are smiling, so are my customers."

As a vice president of the World Bank, Richard Barrett decided that he either had to leave the bank or make a substantial effort to change its work environment. He said he felt it was devoid of any real feeling or soul. He said there was no passion, no commitment, no feeling of belonging. There was no sense of value or purpose in his job, his high position notwithstanding. He put a note on a bulletin board inviting anyone who might be interested in discussing spirit in the workplace to join him for a brown-bag lunch. Initially, forty people showed up. As word spread, more employees expressed an interest, until there were over four hundred people at each meeting. The story was reported in *The Wall Street Journal*. Richard became a key figure in the growing movement of corporate leaders seeking to bring their whole beings to work. His subsequent book, *Liberating the Corporate Soul*, has earned international recognition and acclaim.

Not surprisingly, I have found that most large corporations are unwilling to consider a spiritual void in their workplace, at least until they are financially successful. Early stage companies may not have the energy and discipline to focus on the spirit at work. However, a crisis such as a personal emergency or an attempted corporate takeover may awaken managers to the critical importance of trust, respect, and spirit in the workplace. The role of spirit may be manifested in small, entrepreneurial companies that encourage creativity and change as necessary tools for growth and customer satisfaction.

Focusing on spirit also means examining diversity in the workplace as it relates to race, class, and gender. Two years ago I led a seminar for highly placed corporate women. I asked them to share their stories of finding their true selves. One executive stood tall when she stated that as a closet lesbian, she had felt demeaned at work by comments she continually overheard in the hallways. She decided to act. In league with other gay and lesbian employees, she marched into the president's office and announced her intention to go public with her lesbianism. Her supporters all threatened to do the same. They also stated that if the president found this unacceptable, they would quit the company and take their grievances to the press.

To their delight and surprise, the president of this *Fortune* 100 company received the message openly and without resentment. He promised to create new policies to address the situation and asked for their input and advice. A situation that in many other companies would have generated public intrigue and lurid headlines was handled quietly with dignity, sensitivity, and trust. Shortly thereafter a new CEO was announced—a woman. For this company, such an appointment was the capstone of an internal transformation. When we find the place within us that fosters commitment and purpose even in the face of what appears to be unpopular and even radical, society at large often responds positively and with respect, and the company itself is uplifted to new heights of achievement.

This is the lesson to be learned from Michael, Adrian, and countless other business leaders who are willing—however they may have come to that resolve—to test the boundaries of how an organization can and should function to the betterment of all.

Suggested Readings

Barrett, Richard. *A Guide to Liberating Your Soul*. Alexandria, VA: Fulfilling Books, 1995.

Bolman, Lee, and Deal, Terrence. *Leading with Soul*. San Francisco: Jossey Bass, 1995.

De Geus, Arie. *The Living Company: Habits for Survival in a Turbulent Business Environment*. Boston: Harvard Business School Press, 1997.

Fossum, Merle, and Marilyn Mason. *Facing Shame: Families in Recovery*. New York: Norton, 1986.

Kanter, Rosabeth. *The ChangeMasters*. New York: Simon and Schuster, 1994.

Kasl, Charlotte. *Many Roads: One Journey*. New York: Harper, 1992.

Kotter, John P. *Leading Change*. Boston: Harvard Business School Press, 1996.

Levinson, Harry, and S. Rosenthal. *CEO: Corporate Leadership in Action*. New York: Basic Books, 1984.

Mason, Marilyn. *Seven Mountains: Life Lessons from a Climber's Journal*. New York: Dutton, 1998.

Phillip Z. *A Skeptic's Guide to the Twelve Steps*. Center City: Hazelden, 1990.

Schaef, Anne Wilson, and Diane Fassel. *The Addictive Organization*. New York: Harper and Row, 1988.

Wheatley, Meg. *Leadership and the New Science*. San Francisco: Berrett-Koehler, 1994.

Wyatt, Judith, and Chauncey Hare. *Work Abuse: How to Recognize and Survive It*. Rochester, VT: Schenkman Books, 1997.

Marilyn Mason, Ph.D.

Marilyn Mason is a corporate psychologist, consultant, speaker, and author who specializes in executive leadership development. She currently serves on the Board of the Hazelden Foundation.

Marilyn has coached hundreds of senior executives and CEOs in a variety of businesses, ranging from small entrepreneurial ventures to Fortune 500 companies. The former Training Director for Creative Breakthroughs, Inc., she also consults with family foundations. She has worked with many organizations in developing spirituality in the workplace. She is the Director/Founder of Journeys Inward, leading cross-cultural outdoor wilderness "inventures."

She is currently working on *Family Ghosts in the Executive Suite: Invisible Loyalties at Work*. The co-author of *Facing Shame* (Norton, 1986), she has also written *Making Our Lives Our Own* (Harper, 1991). Her book, *Seven Mountains: The Inner Climb to Commitment* (1997) was released in paperback in 1998 with the title *Seven Mountains: Life Lessons from a Climber's Journal*.

CHAPTER SIX

At the heart of Twelve Step principles are the concepts of "values" and "spirituality." As we enter the new millenium, both concepts have assumed a new sense of meaning and urgency among many people in the corporate world. Much like alcoholics coming to grips with their addiction and powerlessness, businesspeople on all levels of the organization are struggling to find meaning in work beyond simply the accumulation of money. As Robert eloquently describes, we all must seek and discover the Divine Essence within each of us—the only true basis for authentic values—and then infuse our most sacred personal values into the values of the organization we work for. If we do not do this, our culture will remain in a continuous state of "koyaanisqatsi," a Hopi word meaning crazy life, life in turmoil, life disintegrating. Profits are essential to a business, of course; but to achieve true "profit," business must also exist to nourish both our human and spiritual nature.

—Editor

The Answer
to Our Prayers

Robert Rabbin

"*t is no use walking anywhere to preach unless our walking is our preaching.*"

–St. Francis of Assisi

Our Predicament

Every year or so, a novel spasm of possibility trembles through the business world, business being a symbol for a community of people engaged in commerce. Continuous learning, creativity, visionary leadership, social responsibility, and sustainable development are some tremors that have recently opened the body of business to heightened perception and sensation, the mind of business to greater purpose, the heart of business to greater wisdom, and the soul of business to greater meaning. With each wave of new consciousness that washes over business, we—the real and living people within the symbol—become more aware of what we do and how we do it and of the consequences to ourselves, our communities, and the entire world.

The current spasm of possibility is about values. The word has become a virtual mantra: values-based leadership, values-driven cultures, spiritual values in the workplace. We can scarcely walk through a corridor, enter a cubicle, or sit in a meeting room without seeing or hearing a reference to values. One could get the impression that before today we were a horde of heathens without values. This, of course, is not true. The simple fact is that every thought we entertain, every word we speak, every action we take, every decision we make, every goal we create is a graphic demonstration of our values. Our values indicate what is important to us and what we esteem and consider significant.

We can all agree that our values are our North Star of Significance. Values are the orienting point we use to determine our actions, our choices, our decisions, our motives, our goals—all of which generate our life experience. The entire game of our life is played on the field of our values. Our values are always on display, as colorful and loud as a band marching straight down the main street of our life. Our values are a symbol for the quality of our hearts and minds. Our values are the face by which we recognize ourselves and others, the unmistakable fragrance of who we are. The life we create and experience and the results we produce are predicated on our values, on what is important to us.

This seeming sudden and widespread interest in values implies that our past and current values have produced experiences and results we don't like or want. With even the most cursory look at the headlines, we can see that our values as a society have created a koyaanisqatsi culture. *Koyaanisqatsi* is a Hopi word which means crazy life, life in turmoil, life disintegrating, life out of balance: a state of life that calls for another way of living. In a word, koyaanisqatsi means insane, and this suggests why our interest in values has become acute.

An exploration of values is timely in the extreme, because, as Peter Russell states in his book *Waking Up in Time,* "We are living through the most exciting, challenging, and critical times in human history—possibly the most critical time in the history of life on Earth. Never before has so much been possible; never before has so much been at stake." We are hanging from a precarious ledge by the weakest of grips. What is at stake is the continued existence of our species.

As business leaders, we may not agree that safeguarding the existence of our species is our primary concern. We may feel that strengthening and expanding our business interests alone should be our main area of focus, that the success of our business and the financial satisfaction of shareholders are most important. As corporate executives and managers, we are naturally concerned with the health and vitality of our business, and we are always striving to improve our ability to deliver products and services to our customers. We are confronted with myriad daily challenges to maximizing efficiency and effectiveness, performance and productivity. We have to accomplish more with less, learn to be flexible, develop cultures in which diverse work groups treat each other with respect and dignity, attract and keep top talent, find that edge that guarantees success. To realize all of this, we need a set of values that will help us choose a course through the dangerous straits of conflicting realities: short- and long-term; self-interest and the common welfare; expediency and restraint; profit and purpose; purity and corruption; denial and truth; blame and accountability; greed and sufficiency; life-affirmation and destruction; oppression and freedom; domination and humility; reverence and disdain; rational and mystical; mind and heart; fear and love. Business leaders are often thought to be the captains whose vision and skill can navigate these straits, steering the bow of the business ship unerringly to a safe harbor of promised abundance. Most business leaders feel that profit is the true and sacred bottom line.

In today's world, however, this bottom line must be drawn with an entirely different pen from the one that dots the *i*'s and crosses the *t*'s of profit, an obsession that has driven most captains of industry insane. Business leaders now must accept responsibility for a vision of a higher order. The Dalai Lama tells us:

In our present state of affairs, the very survival of mankind depends on people developing concern for the whole of humanity, not just their own community or nation. The reality of our situation impels us to think and act properly. Narrow-mindedness and self-centered thinking may have served us well in the past, but today will only lead to disaster.

The notion that we must feed profit to sate the appetite of business before we feed humanity—indeed, the entire Earth—with loving-kindness, honesty, and decency is one of the values that has contributed to our koyaanisqatsi culture. Searching for new techniques and strategies to run our businesses more profitably is too narrow a focus. Expanding our focus to take in the world, we need instead to become more fully human. Then, with our humanity leading the way, we will know how to act properly and avoid disaster—both in the world and in our business.

We have to place our commitments as business leaders in a larger context than the old bottom line. We have to place our commitments within the context of reality itself. We have to ask and answer questions more fundamental to who we are as human beings. We have to consider the aspirations of the soul of humanity, to the longings of our true heart, and then we must place our business goals within that longing. Such unbounded commitment to new and higher principles is at the core of the Third Step of Alcoholics Anonymous.

Before we are businesspeople, we are human beings. As human beings we need to redress an array of personal and social problems that we have created. We must urgently begin to cure illness and end epidemics; feed, clothe, and house the hungry and homeless; end brutality and war; end the wholesale incarceration of people without hope and opportunity; reverse the pollution and degradation of the environment; curtail corporate and governmental corruption and greed; safely dispose of industrial and nuclear waste; educate children without crushing their free and spiritual minds. Becoming authentic human beings, responsible for the whole world, is our primary responsibility. Business can no longer exist solely to generate profit; business must also exist as a means to express our most authentic human nature. Business must become the environment in which human beings discover and demonstrate their truest and most exalted nature.

The Truth about Values

Albert Einstein is rumored to have said, "We cannot solve problems at the same level of consciousness that created them." AA defines *insanity* as doing the same thing over and over again while expecting a different result. We know we have to produce different results, and so we have to do things differently. This means we have to change our values, since values guide our actions.

Or do they?

We normally speak of our values, as I have done above, as something separate from us; over here is me, over there are my values. This is not true. Our values are not something separate from us. Our values are not something we have to align or negotiate with, as in "walk our talk." Our values are not some high-minded horizon toward which we must aspire. Our values—expressed in thought, word, and action—are who we are. Our values come into being as an image of the thoughts we give power to, the words we give passion to, the actions we commit our bodies to.

A few years ago, the owner and president of a communications company asked me to evaluate the degree to which his company expressed their corporate values in day-to-day activities and interactions.

He asked me if I wanted to review their corporate values documents. I said no. He asked if I would circulate a survey or questionnaire. I said no. He asked if I would use some form of assessment tool. I said no. He asked if I wanted to interview people one on one or in small groups. I again said no, I don't want to talk to anyone.

He asked how, in that case, I was going to proceed. I said that I was going to use my "mute button" assessment tool, that I was going to stuff cotton in my ears and then just walk around and watch people work for three days. After that, I would be able to tell him what their actual values were, based on how people conducted themselves in the course of their work. I told him that any values printed on his mission, vision, and values document were idealized. I told him I would rather watch the employees—without any explanation—to see how they interacted with themselves and each other, with customers, vendors, suppliers, the public, OSHA, the fire department. That is the true, the actual, values document: how people behave. If people don't like their behavior, they can change. But they have to see how they actually behave. Those are their values in action, the only values worth paying attention to. To superimpose a set of idealized values on our actual behavior is a sure way to institutionalize hypocrisy.

It is pure nonsense to think that what we say and what we do are two separate things that must be brought into proximity, like two ocean liners coming together, side by side, in the middle of the Atlantic. We might think that our real values are what we say they are, but that is a delusional conceit. Our real values are expressed in our actions, in what we do and how we do it. Our actions never contradict our values: Our actions *are* our values.

If we believe our values are what we say they are, then we will also believe all the reasons and excuses we give about why we do not live up to them. The simple reason we don't live up to our espoused values is that they are not our actual values. "People are our greatest asset" is an idealized value of many corporations. Though this value is declared and repeated by thousands of people every day, we can scarcely see the demonstration of it. It is not that we fall short because of this devil or that reason; we fall short because we do not value people as our greatest asset. In the daily stories about corporate mergers and downsizing and reorganization layoffs, we read about the need to optimize productivity while cutting costs to maximize profits to shareholders, but we never read about obscenely bloated executive salaries being cut. No one blinks when a hundred people are fired, or two hundred, while a single person's salary—equivalent to those hundred or two hundred casualties—remains a sacred cow.

In the corporate world, people are rarely treated as "our greatest asset."

If we want to know what we value, then we have only to watch what we do and how we do it. If we don't like what we see about ourselves as we observe this, then we can change our behavior.

We act from what we are, from what is written on the tablet of our hearts. If some values work is to be done, it is there, in our own hearts. We need to change who we are from the inside out, not because someone else says we should, but because we have looked into the mirror of our actual behavior and don't like what we see.

We lead with who we are, and our values come behind us, like approving or disapproving shadows. In sales training courses, we learn that people buy on emotion and justify with reason. In other words, people buy things because they want them. That's it. Afterward, they justify, explain, or defend their action. Their action itself, however, has to do with who they are, or who they think they are, not with any of their reasons.

So it is with values. We choose, decide, commit, go this way or that way because of who we are. Our values sit in the backseat of who we are.

We are our values, our values are us. There is no separation or distinction between one and the other. When we speak of our values, we are saying, "Look, here's who I am, dramatized in thought, word, and deed."

It is important to recognize this distinction, because we are too forgiving when we say we do not act in accordance with our values, for one reason or another. This is a delusion. For example, we may say that every life is sacred and that no one should take the life of another. Still, we sometimes do take the lives of others. For example, we may approve of state-sponsored murder in the form of capital punishment; we may shoot doctors who perform abortions, all the while screaming that all life is sacred; perhaps we invest in stocks of tobacco companies whose products kill more than a thousand people each day; maybe we spend a quarter of a trillion dollars for military weapons systems each year, the use of which has only one outcome. These actions are not in accordance with our idealized value of not taking the life of another. They are in accordance with our actual values, with what we, unfortunately, are.

It may be hard to admit, but we do not actually value human life to the extent we say we do, because we are so cavalier about ending those sacred lives whenever it suits our more valuable and pressing purposes. If we say we are nonviolent, then we must be nonviolent, and no mitigating circumstances will move us to violence, since violence does not arise within us as a possibility.

In the wake of the recent heartbreaking shootings at Columbine High School in Denver, President Clinton said, "We have to teach our children how to solve their problems without violence." Where do we have such teachers? Where do we have people in whom violence can not appear, because it no longer exists within them?

If we say we are charitable and generous, then we will not be motivated by greed of any sort. We must live simple, generous, charitable lives. We will never take or use more than we need, because it is not within us to do so. We will not be excited by wealth, status, power, or celebrity. Should any of these things come to us, we will use them for the benefit of others, not for ourselves. Meister Eckhart states bluntly, "They for whom God is not enough are greedy. The reward for all your works should be that they are known to God and that you seek God in them. Let this always be enough for you." Could we hear such conversation in corporate strategic planning sessions throughout America? Or for that matter, at home in our living rooms?

We fool ourselves when we take idealized values for actual values. Only actual values are real. Actual values are what we do and how we do it, each moment—and that is what we are. We do not need to modify, change, or transform our values. We need to transform ourselves to produce different results. We need to transform ourselves to affect the world—the world of our creation. We need to transform ourselves to create a different world, one that does not threaten itself with suicide.

Now, how do we do this?

The Higher Power

There are over eighteen million alcoholics and six million drug addicts in the United States. Tens of millions more suffer from addictions to gambling, tobacco, food, sex, Internet chat rooms, entertainment, money, and power. The cost to the quality of our individual lives and to society is astronomical. We cannot measure the personal suffering and financial repercussions of these forms of addiction, which are themselves a symptom of koyaanisqatsi.

Many people find solace, benefit, and cure through one of various Twelve Step programs, modeled originally by Alcoholics Anonymous. Embracing the themes of the Twelve Step program, addicts seek to restore balance and harmony to their lives. They seek to restore themselves to sanity, which we as a culture also must do. The Twelve Steps represent one map of how we may change. Once we are changed, our world is changed. The sage Jiddu Krishnamurti said, "The crisis is not out there, the crisis is really inward." If our life and society are out of balance, insane with excess and addiction, denial and blame, it is because we are inwardly koyaanisqatsi. What do we do? We have to change ourselves inwardly, and the first three of the Twelve Steps offer a way.

The First Step is to admit that our life has become unmanageable, that we must learn to live differently. The Second Step suggests that a Power greater than our own self can restore us to sanity. The Third Step is a decision to turn our life over to that Power.

What is this Power toward which we turn to recover our sanity, balance, and humanity? Is it something separate from us, or is it an aspect of our own self, a dimension of our forgotten or unexplored nature?

Self-Transcendence

Almost ten years ago, one of my clients, a corporate president, asked me to design a values retreat for his executive team.

Seven of us trotted off on horseback into the Santa Cruz Mountains of northern California like urban gunfighters on a mission. We made camp beneath ancient redwoods. The first day we settled in, exhaling the tension and congestion and noise and complexity of the city. I wanted the presence and silence and antiquity of the forest to enter us, individually and as a group, before we started our work.

The next day, we began. I said that any group values statement had to originate from individual values statements. If the team values were going to have any meaning, then those values ought to be the nexus of each team member's personal values. There would be no point in creating a set of idealized values that no one believed in, just to make us look good. I proposed that we take some time to reflect deeply about our life and led the team through a visualization exercise designed to get them in touch with their most heartfelt values. I thought a good place to begin to speak about what each one valued would be to access a valuable experience and mine it.

I asked the group to describe the experience that came to them in the meditation and what that experience taught them about significance. A vice president in his midfifties, and a former Marine Corps pilot, told of how, when he was fifteen, he was suddenly transported out of his body. He experienced himself as pure light and was intensely joyful. He felt that he was actually a part of all living things. He said, struggling for the words and with soft tears forming in his eyes, that this light body was the body of everything and that love was the universal spirit of life, binding every living thing together as one. He said that he experienced himself as this love and that he existed everywhere. He said it was an experience thrilling beyond words. In the midst of this recollected experience, he said that what he valued above all else was this experience of himself, this recognition that he was this light, this love, this oneness with all living creatures.

He said it was the most significant experience of his life, though he had not spoken of it for over forty years. He sat quietly for a bit, and then he said that he didn't feel anyone would understand. He himself did not understand. There was no support for that experience in his youth, and certainly no support for it in his military career and subsequent business career. He felt it was an anomaly of some kind and thought it best to forget about it. He hadn't known how to build his life from this most significant experience, and so he had gone on without it, heavier and sadder as the years went by. Instead of living from this spiritual core with its organic values, he assumed a series of roles. We explored this theme further, and we all came to admit that we, too, get lost in the roles and masks and facades of our lives. We forget that behind all of them is this universal identity, this self-transcendent beauty of being.

The fifteenth-century Indian mystic and poet Kabir speaks to us about this self-betrayal. He says:

> We sense that there is some sort of spirit that loves
> birds and the animals and the ants—perhaps the

same one who gave a radiance to you in your mother's womb. Is it logical you would be walking around entirely orphaned now? The truth is, you turned away yourself, and decided to go into the dark alone. You've forgotten what you once knew; that's why everything you do has some weird failure in it.

Our koyaanisqatsi culture is rife with the weird failures about which Kabir speaks. These failures are the breakdowns in our ethics and morality, the narrowness of our visions, our obsession with profit. We will not be successful in correcting these failures with new strategies for organizational development. And yet, we are not without the skillful means to bring sanity back into our lives. We are only forgetful of the spirit that gave us radiance in the wombs of our mothers.

There is something we have all forgotten, and that forgetfulness makes us heavy and sad. It makes us anxious and fearful and angry. The weird failures have to do with forgetting who we are and with turning away from the spirit that gives us radiance. This alienation causes us to suffer and appears in the world as koyaanisqatsi. The koyaanisqatsi of the world is ours. We own it. It persists because we tinker with idealized values and do not face ourselves directly. It persists because we try to solve problems at the same level of consciousness that created them. It persists because we let our lesser roles and identities tell us what to do and how to behave, when we should be following our human heart and letting our humanity inflate and animate the roles and identities we assume. We should never forget that these roles are subordinate to our essence. We should not become the roles we play, because we are something far greater.

The thirteenth-century Sufi mystic Jelaluddin Rumi reminds us, "You are the whole ocean. Why send out for a sip of dew? A True Human Being is the essence, the original cause. The world and the universe are secondary effects. Don't trade yourself for something worth less!"

A workshop participant asked me if who we are and v
do are not two separate things. He suggested that we c— ... act
out our business commitments in a manner that did not reflect
who we were. He said we all have to sacrifice at least a little of
who we believe we are for the sake of job requirements and corporate values. I said that was insane. If we let the rules of our
roles and masks corrupt the more significant rules of reality—of
who we are essentially—then we are sowing the seeds of our
own suffering.

If we pursue only the business of business, if we consecrate our
actions to strategic plans for profit alone, our values become corrupt and reflect an impoverished understanding of our selves.
Our business goals must reflect the more noble and worthy goal
of living: actualizing our essence, our divine nature. The affairs
of business seem complex only because we do not live in accordance with our inner knowing of who we are.

In *Forgotten Truth*, the eminent professor, author, and sage
Huston Smith writes:

> In the opening chapter of this book we argued that
> the triumphs of modern science went to man's head
> in something of the way rum does, causing him to
> grow loose in his logic. He came to think that what
> science discovers somehow casts doubt on things it
> does not discover; that the success it realized in its
> own domain throws into question the reality of
> domains its devices cannot touch. In short, he came
> to assume that science implies scientism: the belief
> that no realities save ones that conform to the matri-
> ces science works with—space, time, matter/energy,
> and in the end number—exist.

The same is true for business. We have become rum-drunk on
our plans and strategies for business success, trying to subordinate the higher truths to mere profit. The domain of business
must become subordinate to the domain of spiritual truth.

Aligning with God

Mohandas Gandhi once said, "Each of us must *be* the change we want to see in the world." This suggests that we need a transformation of self, of our consciousness, not a change of our idealized values to bring sanity into the world.

How do we do this? Again, we can turn to another step in the Twelve Step program, the Eleventh Step.

The Eleventh Step urges us to pray and meditate to improve our conscious contact with God as we understand Him, praying only for knowledge of His will for us and the power to carry that out.

The Eleventh Step does not ask us to pray to God in order to make more money, carve out more market share, increase stock value, or in any other way enhance our business life. This step asks us to implore God or whomever we view as a Higher Power to help us become fully and authentically human in mind, heart, and action. We are asked to put aside our business roles, masks, and identities to find the face of our truest glory.

What does God want for us?

I think God wants us to listen to author Tom Robbins, who wrote:

> Our purpose is to consciously, deliberately evolve toward a wiser, more liberated and luminous state of being; to return to Eden, make friends with the snake and set up our computers among the wild apple trees. Deep down, all of us are probably aware that some kind of mystical evolution is our true task. Yet we suppress the notion with considerable force because to admit it is to admit that most of our political gyrations, religious dogmas, social ambitions and financial ploys are not merely counterproductive but trivial. Our mission is to jettison those pointless preoccupations and take on once again the primordial cargo of inexhaustible ecstasy.

Epiphanies: Interventions from God

When addicts are unable to confront their own koyaanisqatsi, the people who care about them may stage an intervention, in which a circle of devoted and concerned friends and relatives shower love and compassion upon the addict in an attempt to salvage his soul. God stages interventions also when we refuse to confront the insanity of our lives. God's intervention is called grace, or epiphany. God's intervention is meant to show us the face and features of our true nature, our divine nature, our eternal essence, that we may remember and behave accordingly.

I experienced an epiphany of this last kind a few years ago at the Mt. Madonna Center in Watsonville, California. It is a retreat facility founded by Baba Hari Dass, an Indian yogi who has not spoken a word since 1952. I was facilitating a planning session for a management team of a computer chip manufacturing company. I had arranged a private meeting with our group and Baba Hari Dass, who communicates succinctly and humorously by writing on a chalkboard. We visited with him for about thirty minutes, asking a variety of questions, including several about spirituality in business. When our time was over, I went to thank him. A force emanated from his eyes that I had experienced in the eyes of my teacher many years earlier. It was a ray that could penetrate deeply into the core of one's being: it is the touch of reality, or grace, and one awakens to another world of significance.

As I walked outside with our group I suddenly felt strange, light headed, and off balance. I told my associate to continue without me, that I would catch up. I wandered into a grove of trees, found a boulder, and sat down. Something pierced my heart. I bent over and started crying. It's hard to say what occurred to me then. It is probably difficult for all of us to speak of these moments—so full of silence and beauty and awakening.

When I stopped crying, I sat still for a long time. Everything about me seemed newly alive, radiant, as though I was seeing these common things for the first time: flowers, trees, rocks, dirt. It seemed that everything was breathing! I felt light and spacious, extending beyond the familiar boundary of my body. I became aware of an orderly connection between things, much as when you finally piece a puzzle together, and you see how each piece fits into the others to form the whole. I was relieved of a burden I didn't know I was carrying. A profound peace embraced me.

When God stages an intervention, we see another dimension of life about which we were ignorant. The mask of appearances falls away, and we see something profound about life. We experience something of the timeless, the real, that which gives radiance to us in the womb. It is beyond words, and the mind hardly grasps it. In these moments, the fortifications against the soul dissolve, and a new perspective appears, a new life is born.

It is the awareness of being authentically human. Our humanity is born in this encounter with self-transcendence. Only when we go beyond the personal self can we discover the truth of the personal self. Only when we experience the subtle light and overwhelming sweetness that is the mystical nexus of all life do we know who and what we are. Only when we return from this journey to pick up and put on the masks of our roles in life can we know how we are to live. Only when we return from this journey do we find God's will and desire for us to be the same as our will and desire to know God.

Living in Reality

I am of the opinion that each of us has experienced the intervention of God in our lives. Each of us knows what it is like to be lifted to a rapture of communion with life itself, to be overwhelmed by silence and beauty, by simplicity and awe, by meaning and connection. This experience is universal. I use the word *self-transcendence* to refer to these epiphanies, in which we encounter the full measure of our humanity.

I believe that in these moments of grace, who we are becomes revealed unequivocally. It is in this intersection of time and eternity that we discover we all share the same parents, the same heart, the same longing, the same values.

Huston Smith brings needed clarity to the nature of this experience of self-transcendence. He says there are four universal characteristics imbedded in the mystical nexus of all spiritual paths and philosophies.

1. **The first is ineffability.** This means that the experience is difficult to accurately portray in words. The best we can do is to use poetry, image, metaphor, or even music, as Steven Jeddeloh does eloquently in Chapter 8. We cannot say it directly because words do not travel that far.

2. **The second is unity.** This means we feel connected to, or part of, something larger than our own body and mind. It is as though our boundaries of self slip and slide away until they embrace all that exists within creation itself.

3. **The third is immense joy.** The sudden encounter with grace lifts us to dizzying heights of bliss and ecstasy. The thrill of peace opens our inner eye to mysteries previously unseen.

4. **The fourth is certitude.** One is convinced that what one beholds is true, the way things are. This certitude is beyond reproach, beyond proof, beyond sentiment. We are standing in the oceanic rhythms of reality.

To these four characteristics, I would add a fifth: **wholeness.** Surrounded and permeated by grace, we are complete, full, and without lack of any kind. Nothing—neither experience nor knowledge nor material goods—can enhance the wholeness we feel in mind, body, and spirit. Nothing is missing.

This treasure of self-transcendence is what God wants for us. This is the answer to our prayers for sanity, harmony, balance, peace, and prosperity. This answer to our prayers is the love that saturates every atom of this universe, if only we would see, feel, touch, hear, and smell this distilled essence of life. This is why even the most downtrodden of addicts and alcoholics have hope and a way out, through God or another Higher Power.

The treasure of self-transcendence is the context in which all of our other activities and pursuits must be placed. The bottom line of life, as of business, must be drawn with the pen and ink of the Creator, who wishes that we consecrate our every action to realizing love.

We have the seeds of this kind of transcendent humanity within us, we all know such moments of surpassing beauty and unity, and we know this is real. We have only decided to live in lesser ways. Emanuel Swedenborg said, "The divine Essence itself is love and wisdom." What more do we need than to know we are that divine Essence? Productivity and profits are the twin towering idols of business, but wisdom and love are the twin formless faces of the soul.

The simple fact is that we cannot live without the soul. We cannot turn from the soul, from the Spirit that gave us radiance in the womb. We have to free our soul from servitude to lesser gods, from lesser purposes, and feast together at the banquet set and ready for us here, where we live in this truth.

We might say that we already know this, but that it is not practical enough. It does not encompass enough of our daily dilemmas and problems, nor does it embrace the complexity and pressures of our lives in business.

We may know it, but we do not yet live it. Our supreme task is to refine and clarify ourselves, until the reflection of that brightness shines outward. In this light, the dilemmas and problems, the complexity and pressures of our business life will of their own accord disappear, inasmuch as they are but images of a lesser consciousness.

In an interview with James Lipton on the Bravo television show *Inside the Actors Studio*, Sharon Stone told of sitting with her acting teacher, Roy London, during his final days. Dying of AIDS, he would lapse in and out of consciousness. One time, he opened his eyes and said, "It's so beautiful. It's so beautiful. It's all about love. I only wish I could teach one more class."

Must we wait until we are taking our last breaths to remember to live what we already know, that life is about love, not fear; selflessness, not self-interest?

Transcendence does not remove us from daily life, rather it connects us to all of life. Transcendence does not leave us incapable, but more capable. Transcendence does not destroy intelligence, but imbues it with wisdom. Mohandas Gandhi said, "I do not believe that the spiritual law works on a field of its own. On the contrary, it expresses itself only through the ordinary activities of life. It thus affects the economic, the social and the political fields."

Vaclav Havel, the president of the Czech Republic, says emphatically:

> Yes, the only real hope of people today is probably a renewal of our certainty that we are rooted in the Earth and, at the same time, in the cosmos. This awareness endows us with the capacity for self-transcendence. Politicians at international forums may reiterate a thousand times that the basis of the new world order must be universal respect for human rights, but it will mean nothing as long as this imperative does not derive from the respect of the miracle of Being, the miracle of the universe, the miracle of nature, the miracle of our own existence. Only someone who submits to the authority of the universal order and of creation, who values the right to be a part of it and a participant in it, can genuinely value himself and his neighbors, and thus honor their rights as well.

At various times in the history of human beings, cataclysms of perception have occurred to rare souls and have propelled the course of humanity in an altogether stunning new direction. We—all of us—stand at just such a moment when we can give birth to an earthquake of self-transcendent realism that will forever banish from our consciousness koyaanisqatsi, addictions, weird failures, and heartbreaking sadness.

The Final Step

Coming full circle, what do we know? We know that our values denote what we deem important and significant in any given moment. We know that our values are expressed in each thought, word, and deed, and that the external world we create—the one of relationships and situations and experiences—is a mirror of our internal values. We know there is a vast difference between idealized values and actual values. Idealized values exist on the surface of our lives as hopes and wishes, as fantasies and fancies. Idealized values are an abstract horizon of purity, a virtuous standard of conduct we never realize. We know that our actual values are demonstrated, not spoken, and that we can never be at odds with our values, because our values, our actual values, are not different from us: We are our values, acted out each moment. All of these insights show us that manipulating our idealized values does not produce any real effect. We know that if we want to affect any change in our world, we have to first create that change within ourselves: We must *be* the change we want to see in the world. Finally, seeing that we must refine our own being, we stand on the brink of the holiest and profoundest of all questions, Who am I?

In the end, as in the beginning, we must know who we are. We must know who we are in our universal essence, before we lose ourselves in lesser loyalties of roles and masks. We must remember the Spirit who gave us our radiance in the womb and recognize that we and that Spirit are one.

The divine Essence itself is love and wisdom. These are our actual values, because we are the divine Essence—every one of us. This is what we must know and be.

This is first. This Essence is the silence before the word, the Spirit before the form. If we are looking for answers and solutions, find it here. If we are looking for prescriptions and models, find it here. If we are looking for practical skills and know-how, find it here.

The divine Essence itself is love and wisdom, and we are that Essence.

Our humanity is born in this encounter with self-transcendence. Only when we go beyond the personal self can we discover the truth of the personal self. Only when we experience the subtle light and overwhelming sweetness that is the mystical nexus of all life, forces, and dimensions do we know who and what we are. Only when we return from this journey to our lives can we know how to behave.

We can do nothing until we awaken from our forgetfulness and self-betrayal and live consciously in our eternal being. The values of this awakening are demonstrated in our entire presentation of self, in thought, word, action—nothing hidden, nothing twisted.

This return—alone, by itself, and without doubt—will immediately bring balance, sanity, and clarity to koyaanisqatsi. This return will charge the Earth with a living current of wisdom and love, electrifying and enlivening us with the wishes of that Higher Power toward which we turn, from which we come, and of which we are.

Here then is my recommendation: Become the One to whom we pray and upon whom we meditate, grow your body into the soul of the universe, become the human being that exists before any lesser mask appears. We cannot wear these masks until our humanity has exploded within us, until our divine nature has become our human nature. Our divine nature is a flower of light deep within each chest, open and fragrant, more heart than heart, more soul than soul, and this flower is our humanity. Our true life is a field of these flowers, covering the plains and hills of our daily existence, piled high for the free taking on every corner of every market. Take this free flower of your essence, give it to others, throw it around freely and without care or thought.

What does this have to do with business, with management, with leadership? Just this: When we are whole and full, without wanting but to love, without desire but to serve, without motive but to heal, without sentiment but kindness, then at every moment we will know how to act from what we are.

If we are going to invoke a Higher Power, then let us go all the way. Let us become that Higher Power and act as that Higher Power acts. Do this, and you will have fewer business problems to solve.

May blessings be upon all of us, and may we return to what we have always been.

Robert Rabbin

Robert Rabbin has had a lifelong interest in the nature of consciousness, self and reality. In 1969 he began to research mystic traditions while practicing meditation and self-inquiry. During the early 1970s, while continuing his spiritual explorations abroad, he traveled to India where he met meditation master Swami Muktananda, with whom he studied for the next ten years.

Since 1985 Robert has been lecturing and leading inquiry seminars, designing executive and corporate retreats, and serving as an advisor to leaders of a broad range of companies and organizations. An iconoclastic speaker, Robert has presented his views to such groups as The State of the World Forum, The American

Management Association, Institute of Noetic Sciences, and the California Institute of Integral Studies.

Robert is the author of *Echoes of Silence: Awakening the Meditative Spirit* (2000); *Invisible Leadership: Igniting the Soul at Work* (1998); *The Sacred Hub: Living in Your Real Self* (1996); and is co-author of *The Values Workbook: Creating Personal Truth at Work* (1997) and *Leadership in a New Era* (1994). He also wrote and produced *Brilliant Business: A Road Map to the 21st Century* (1997), a video about creativity and spirit in corporate America. Over 50 of Robert's articles about mysticism and leadership have been published internationally.

His website address is www.robrabbin.com.

C H A P T E R   S E V E N

This, the last chapter in Part II, ties together the concepts of culture, values, spirituality, change and transformation found in the earlier chapters, and applies them to well-known organizations. For transformation to succeed, Douglas argues, and for a healthy work environment to be established, the Board of Directors and senior management of an organization must commit to a long term process that goes to the very heart of the organization's mission and culture. This is never an easy process, for reasons described by Pat Owen in Chapter 1 and for reasons inherent in the short-term horizons of Wall Street analysts. Further, Douglas argues, an organization does not have to be "sick" or "in crisis" for transformation to work. Change processes may function better in healthy companies seeking to become stronger. As a model for organizational change for all companies of all sizes and stages of health, Douglas presents what might be called "The Twelve Steps of Business," designed after the original Twelve Steps.

—Editor

Building a Healthy Place to Work

Douglas M. Baker

f you have experienced the joy of rebuilding your life and your relationships through Twelve Step or other change processes, you know that transformation is possible. Some of us even have faith that it can be sustained over time. This qualifies us as certified optimists, a necessary attribute as we begin to consider even larger change projects.

If we can improve major parts of our lives, why then can't we improve the place where we spend most of our waking hours? Can the same principles apply to our organizations? Can we make important progress at improving the way the place works? In the way we all get along? In how we treat our customers and clients?

The answer to each of these questions is yes—an optimistic yet qualified yes. If you think transforming individuals and their relationships is difficult, changing the ways large groups of people do things is monumental. But it can be done.

The goal is to seek the full health and potential of our organization. Some call this the overarching goal. It is a goal that is never
achieved; probably it cannot be. Still, it is the guiding principle
that will steer what we and hopefully our successors do. This
clearly falls under the category of "dreaming" big. Is optimism
helpful here? You bet.

Full health is when all corporate stakeholders have a high level
of satisfaction about the *ongoing* operations of the organization.
Shareholders and employees; suppliers and the community;
competitors and management; customers and government;
each of these stakeholders feels that the organization is meeting their needs well. It does not mean that each has achieved
an equal level of satisfaction or that corporate life has no
problems.

Not all of us will have the opportunity to lead in building a new
organization or in remaking an existing one. Perhaps we have
control of only part of the organization—a department, a section,
a division, or a program. It does not matter. The same principles
of change can be applied to all groups.

Critical Components

Unless the chief executive officer (CEO) holds enabling assumptions, this whole exercise is academic. First, the CEO needs to
believe in the value of building a healthy company that will
remain such over the long term. No quick-fix, quick turnaround
"Chainsaw Als" are needed here. Second, the CEO must assume
that all stakeholders must be well satisfied, not just the shareholders. Third, the CEO must recognize that the business proposition, values, and culture must all be equally viable. Fourth, the
CEO must hold values that will support long-term, healthy
growth. Fifth, the CEO must assume that his or her main purpose is to facilitate and support the change needed to bring
about full health of the organization.

Where to Start?

Our vision of creating or recreating superb, healthy organizations means having to deal with all three crucial elements—the business proposition (mission, strategy, and tactics); values and philosophies; and the culture. None can be avoided. For full, balanced health, all must be strong. My experience suggests that the business proposition is most vital. Without strong products and services delivered with added value to willing customers, a firm has a problematic future. Strength in the other elements cannot overcome weakness here. A firm can have strong values and a great culture, but if its business proposition is seriously lacking, the future is in jeopardy.

For example, the once-powerful computer company DEC seemingly had it all together. Then, however, upstart competitors who successfully redefined the market toward workstations superceded DEC's market niche in mainframe computers. DEC was unable to survive this weakness in its business proposition in spite of its strength in other elements.

When we begin to think seriously about our organization's future, we start with some heavy-duty questions that help us arrive at both our values and our mission. Who are we? What business are we in? Where do we want to go? What do we need to do to get there?

Three other questions provide the "culture piece" of a vision: What do we stand for? What kind of environment do we want? How do we want to work with our employees, customers, suppliers, communities, and other stakeholders? Answers to these help shape the dream of the kind of place we want to build. When we fill in the answers to the questions about the other major business elements, we will have completed the first draft of our vision. It is, after all, a dream in progress.

A firm can be strong in all the other elements, but it will not achieve its potential if it has a weak or ineffective culture.

Culture is the fabric that runs through the entire organization. Of all the crucial elements, culture contains the most uniquely human dimension. Therefore, culture is most amenable to transformation processes that work for individuals and small groups.

What Is Culture?

Culture is the sum of the human elements of our organizations: the way we do things; the way we treat each other; our norms and standards; our acted-upon values and assumptions; our positive and negative behaviors; the language we use. Culture is also the processes we use in our firms: hiring and training, research, product, service, development, manufacturing, or service processes; information technology uses; resource allocation; and so on. Culture is also the criteria by which decisions about priorities are made in the organization (one expression of the values). In essence, every organization is like a separate tribe with its own customs, language, norms, standards, rewards, and punishments.

I also like Stan Davis' definition of culture as a pattern of shared beliefs and values that gives members meaning and provides them with the rules of behavior in their organizations. Following are some words used to describe culture: being, core, ethos, ideology, philosophy, roots, spirit, style, way.

The two main elements of a culture—an organization's guiding beliefs and its daily beliefs—repeatedly give its members ideas about what is important and how things work. The guiding beliefs and assumptions give direction to daily beliefs. Guiding beliefs are the way things ought to be—part of the organization's vision—and rarely change. Usually there are only three or four of these. Daily beliefs and behaviors change as necessary

No cultures are impervious to change or are perfect and do not need revision and tweaking over time. Unless cultures are growing and changing, they will eventually decay and die.

All organizations quickly develop a pattern of behavior that is resistant to change. Their cultures acquire a unique patina that hardens over time. It is often hard to see this rigidity from the inside. To change requires substantial commitments combined with hard work over extended periods of time to break through the crust of habit and comfort. We know this to be true for ourselves. It is just as valid for organizations.

It is helpful to view cultures on a continuum from strong on one end to weak on the other. Strong is better if you are looking for support of organization effectiveness—high standards, a strong interest in achievement, positive patterns of interaction, propensity for growth in the business and the people, etc. Weak cultures tend to be those that are satisfied with mediocrity and are not working to build continuity. They tend to reward unproductive political behavior.

Pillsbury during the 1960s, for example, had a defined political culture coupled with a low-risk attitude. Top management's stated objective was to have products that were usually third or fourth in market share. Managers were not willing to support new products that had a jump on the market; they had convinced themselves that leadership was not sustainable and therefore "followership" was preferable. The decision process was further skewed to favor assumptions believed (but never confirmed) to be held by large stockholding members of the Pillsbury family.

Is Change Only for Sick Organizations?

Using any model to effect a major culture change, whether the Twelve Step process, the managerial grid, or Covey's seven habits often implies a culture in trouble. Why else would we go to such lengths and incur the difficulties unless our organization needs help?

Actually such change processes seem to work best in relatively healthy organizations that want to become even stronger. For one thing, there are not as many glaring weaknesses as in unhealthy firms. For another, the organization is building on confidence. There is a pattern of success that implies that the people are used to working smart and are committed to the future.

All organizations should consider themselves continually vulnerable. In the "white water" world (as defined by Peter Vaill in Chapter 10) in which they operate, they must be continually alert and changing constantly. They must move ahead quickly to keep up with the incredible pace of change around them. Every component of the organization must be working continually, on its own and in league with all other components, to find better ways of doing things. This includes making continual cultural improvements. Organizations that are arrogant and believe they are impervious to decline have begun to slow their growth and development. They are but a few steps ahead of an often fatal downward spiral.

For instance, in the early 1980s, General Motors (GM) was at the top of its game. It controlled the lion's share of the U.S. automotive market. GM also had impressive standings in most of the other major world markets except Japan. Although the Japanese had made major inroads into the U.S. market with cars generally superior in quality to U.S. models, GM felt confident their distribution domination would prevail. Some independent observers were predicting a dire future for GM, but inside GM there was a bravado that was breathtaking.

About this time, at a University of Michigan program for senior human resource executives, GM's senior industrial relations executive led the discussion of a case study about GM. There was not a scintilla of humbleness in this person. He would not listen to concerns that others in the room raised. He denied that the Japanese would ever have a major impact. He viewed as ill-conceived those suggestions that Ford or Chrysler might catch GM in domestic market share. It was a bravura performance. After the GM executive wound up his show and departed, those of us in the class immediately began to laugh nervously and to express shock at what we had just witnessed. To a person, we thought the GM representative was both misguided and impervious to change. Our faculty leader acknowledged that this was a similar pattern he had witnessed recently in other visiting GM executives.

We concluded that, with such an attitude, GM was unlikely to make the changes that needed to be made there. Looking at where they are almost twenty years later, clearly they have suffered much from flaunting such an attitude. Yes, they have begun the attempt to recapture the position they once held. But they were slow to start and feeble in their initial attempts. Some knowledgeable industry analysts predict that their slide will continue—and that they still do not appreciate the full extent to which they need to change.

The Drive to Achieve the Change

Culture change is the most difficult task a leader can undertake. If you have ever tried to improve a marriage or change the functioning within a family, you have a taste of the difficulties involved. Now multiply the difficulty by the size of the organization to be changed. The resulting increase is geometric rather than arithmetic.

In any organization, tremendous forces work against achieving and maintaining excellence, both from inside and out. Major change or transformation requires a commitment of several decades and usually extends through two or three senior executive tenures. Yet change is possible. A chief executive officer can fulfill a vision of developing and maintaining a strong culture and can leave a legacy of a self-renewing culture that is healthy and built to stay that way. Nonetheless, few are willing to tackle such a momentous project. Fewer still have the know-how.

In *Built to Last*, Jerry Porras and Jim Collins wrote eloquently about strong cultures that were very successful over time (at least fifty years). Interestingly, each of the firms they profiled had strong founders who worked to impose a strong culture from inception. Some firms took longer to seat the culture than others. Yet eventually the strong culture took hold and served the company well.

Why would a company want to build a strong culture? Over the years, colleagues and clients who have embarked on such a task have answered this question consistently:

> This place is where I'm going to spend most of my waking hours. I want to be proud of where I commit so much effort.

> I've worked in both fine organizations and ones that were dogs. Fine is better. Now that I'm in charge, we'll seek to be excellent, which is how we'll attract and keep the kind of people we need.

> I'm standing on the shoulders of the giants who were here before me. I owe it to their legacies to leave this place even better than how I found it.

> Before I started this firm, I spent many hours thinking about what kind of company we should be. Not just from a product and financial standpoint, but what our values should be; how we should treat each other and outsiders like customers; how we should be good citizens and help build good communities that our workers would enjoy; what our goals and standards should be. I knew we were going to have to fight like hell to survive, and I wanted it to be the best possible company in all aspects if we were going to put out such effort. We've done well the last thirty years in building on that early model. I'm confident that my successor will carry on nicely with these things since he's learned our way the past ten years.

Perhaps you are tired of working in greatly flawed organizations and want to help make a great one. Maybe you want to be of service to your colleagues and make everyone's work life more meaningful. In a nutshell, people who want strong cultures and high-performing organizations create such visions, believe they are essential, and want to leave such legacies to those that follow. Whatever your motivation, you have chosen a challenge that is both daunting and stimulating.

What Else Is Needed beyond a Vision?

Clarity about Motives

The benefits of a long-term culture creation or change will not benefit the current stakeholders much. While there can be some short-term fixes of irritating and debilitating behaviors, the major impacts are further down the line. Therefore, leaders who take on such work are interested in building a legacy that will benefit future generations. This is not something that will help next quarter's earnings. Short-term investors and most Wall Street stock analysts could not care less about such work. Rather, they will usually inveigh against efforts that seemingly work against improving the short term. The people must believe that a strong culture will perform immeasurably better over time and that starting such a process will bring greater long-term value to the shareholders, employees, and customers. Numerous studies have verified this. But many leaders do not have the long term in mind. Others do not have the fortitude to stick with such a plan once stormy seas arise. It takes an immense amount of courage for a leader to start such work, not to mention sticking with it when many are criticizing him or her.

Leaders Who Change Cultures

Cultures are almost impossible to change from the bottom, poetry and mythology notwithstanding. While others may develop the vision, values, or standards, change requires the support and commitment of the very top to pull it off. Guiding beliefs are changed at the top. Culture and the business proposition are from the top down. Care for the culture cannot be delegated.

A Serious Commitment to the Time and Effort

Building and changing cultures takes tremendous commitment. Such a change process will not survive in an organization that is used to new programs or "fads of the month." Think in terms of decades. Even smaller organizations need to think in terms of many years. No quick fixes work in culture change.

For example, at American Express Financial Advisors, a major culture change effort began in 1984. Much of the change seemed cemented at the headquarters by the early 1990s, but the field organization took more than another seven years to come closer to the original vision.

Commitment to change is as major a stumbling block to many leaders as it is to many addicts. In many organizations, leaders do not stay long enough to see the results of a long-term change process. Either they are promoted quickly, or they move on to other firms. Such movement keeps many leaders from developing a long-term outlook. What usually becomes the focus for such leaders is a series of quick fixes that can help make short-term numbers look good.

Committed Colleagues

Even the best leaders need friends and followers in high places. No one can pull off a major culture change independently. A team of senior people is needed who support the basic objectives if not each of the specific tactics.

It will take time to build this group commitment. Since the current senior team is probably the one that reinforced if not built the present culture, they may need some heavy-duty convincing.

The late Richard E. Byrd taught the value of engaging a strong team of lieutenants, who could in turn educate their senior bosses. In effect, the bosses are sandwiched by a committed CEO on the top and their most able colleagues on the bottom. Perhaps Machiavelli would approve.

For example, in a diversified financial services client of mine, this technique worked smoothly twice in a five-year process. The CEO had asked a team of several of his direct subordinates and a few other key leaders to present options for a new corporate mission. This group was assembled not only for its competence but also for its ability to influence others. With the CEO they narrowed the options and then individually reviewed their work with the rest of the senior management team. When the senior group met shortly thereafter, the choices were three viable options, all of which could be strongly supported. Interestingly, the group ultimately forged and settled on a fourth option that was a combination of two others. It called for a dramatically changed definition of the primary client group for the firm; this new target client group had been only suggested in the other options.

Next, a second team of talented officers was created to recommend the culture factors and values that were needed to achieve the new mission. This group made it a practice continually to brief their senior managers individually. By the time they made their final recommendations to the total senior management group, they had built a workable consensus so that alterations at that point were polishing rather than reconstructing.

A Succession of Committed Leaders

This is why strong cultures look to develop their own leaders rather than consistently going outside. There is a much greater chance of having a culture change continued if the new leader is a part of the change process and is committed to its aims. One new leader with a different vision or set of values can undermine the great beginnings of a predecessor.

In *Reluctant Dissenter,* James Shannon describes an amazing cultural review that a large international organization—the Roman Catholic Church—undertook. The book captures many of the difficulties that such a project can encounter. Some of the potential roadblocks to major long-term success of such a change effort included its enormous scope; a lack of agreement among many participants that such change was needed; loss of the change leader early in the process; and the new leader removing a key item on the agenda just prior to the conclusion of the advisory group's work.

In January 1959, Pope John XXIII announced the Second Vatican Council to be held each year for four years from 1962 to 1965. This was a gathering of all bishops of the Catholic Church; an average of nearly 2,500 of the 2,900 eligible attended each of the yearly sessions. Shannon attended the fourth of these gatherings as a newly consecrated bishop.

Pope John set the tone "to seek a wide-open dialogue . . . to review the role and refine the methods for preaching the gospel of Jesus Christ in the modern world." Pope John also sought to "adjust the norms of ecclesiastical law to the needs and thoughts of our times—to update or bring into step with the times." He wanted to "open the windows in the church to let the fresh air come in."

During more than three years' planning for the council, a large number of scholars, philosophers, and historians from around the world were invited to provide enlightenment on major questions before the council. Great numbers of the media were nearby but were excluded from the discussions, as were all outsiders except some of the experts who helped frame the papers to be discussed. However, some of the participants provided daily briefings in all the major languages of the world.

After Pope John died suddenly in June 1963, his successor, Pope Paul VI, had the "difficult task of guiding the dialogue which John had invited but which many Catholic traditionalists considered dangerously innovative and entirely too responsive to the secular winds of change."

Nevertheless the council passed sixteen major papers that covered "such cosmic themes as the dignity of the modern person, the universal community of humankind, the nexus between religion and human culture, marital morality, war and peace, economic development, political relations, and the community of nations."

Shannon describes in great detail an intention of a majority of bishops to endorse a new view of human sexuality that enlarged "the limits within which [loving spouses] could share their conjugal love and keep faith within the formal doctrine of the Catholic Church." Such was included in the final papers that the Pope approved to become the official teachings of the church. The bishops were disseminating this idea, along with the other revisions emanating from the council, to all the church's communicants. It was a monumental task that continues to this day.

Yet less than three years later, the new Pope reversed one new direction and reinstated the church's traditional position against contraception as the official teaching of the church. Suddenly the bishops had to reverse course and revert to pre-Vatican Council teachings on this topic.

A Solid Plan Coupled with a Solid Strategy

Here's a blinding glimpse of the obvious. It is easier to build and maintain a strong culture from scratch. As Emerson pointed out, every spirit makes its own house; every house then tries to control this spirit. All gatherings of people try to develop conformity. Changing spirit and conformity is a task of even a higher order of difficulty than creating one initially.

Creating a new culture requires substantial thought. What are the elements of the culture you need to fulfill your new vision?

What values will you need? How do these blend with the values and culture that exist? It is rare in changing an existing culture that you will have to change everything. Some elements are bound to be worth preserving. Others may be irritating but are insignificant in the total picture.

These and other questions need a proven structure to frame the examination needed. I have worked with several over the years—the managerial grid and the Covey model—that can work. I have also successfully used a process that mirrors the Twelve Step model. The same psychological and spiritual brilliance encapsulated in the Twelve Step process can work as well for groups of people as it does for individuals.

The crucial matter is one of substance, not form. Many possible processes can be used successfully if the crucial seeking of the truth is employed. All culture changes are messy and difficult. There will be natural tendencies to seek a less difficult path. Forces will rise up to argue strongly against painful reflection and apologies (such as, the reaction to apologizing for the U.S. history of slaveholding). You must be sure that regardless of the process chosen, the heavy lifting necessary to discover the truth about the past is not avoided.

For instance, in 1984 when American Express bought its financial planning arm, American Express Financial Advisors (AEFA, formerly IDS), its new CEO concluded that shifts both in firm's direction and standards were required if the company's potential were to be achieved. Not only was a shift to a client-focused financial planning process prescribed as a new business mission, but a revised set of company values were formulated to achieve the mission.

The process to construct the new mission and values took about six months. Changing a national organization that was sales driven, with all systems designed to reinforce this emphasis, continues today. Not only did the sales force and its leaders have to change, but also the rest of the company and the clients had to accept the new direction.

The strategies to inculcate the new mission and values were reviewed and tweaked frequently during the first five years. Once they seemed safely launched, the culture was reexamined. A statement of the kind of company desired in the future was drafted. Then a detailed examination of how the place measured up to the new vision was carried out. Where changes were needed, attempts to change were put into place. Over the ensuing years other cultural fixes have been implemented especially in hiring, retention and pay.

It sounds neater here than how it happened. Such a process can be messy and stop-and-start. Yet the results for AEFA have been amazing. Not only has its financial success been remarkable, but also it has developed into a workplace of note.

A Model for Organization Change

It is unusual for an organization to be changing both its business proposition and its culture simultaneously. It feels unwieldy to try to deal with changing both in the same series of discussions, but that may be more due to matters of scale than anything else. Smaller firms may not have the size to support separate efforts. Nevertheless the following model can be run as a dual-track process—one for culture change and the other for revitalizing the business purpose.

If the purpose of the change process is to seek the full health and potential of the organization, the senior management group has to be committed to a set of difficult behaviors. These ethical concepts are vital to bring forth honest interchange. These include employing brutal honesty, being committed to truth, having no sacred cows, being open and committed to changing everything, having willingness to admit mistakes, being willing to accept help from all quarters, taking responsibility for past and present actions, and maintaining the fortitude to continue with the change over time. These happen to be the same factors needed for successful individual transformation at the core of the Twelve Step principles and philosophy.

Here is a model designed after the Twelve Step principles:

- **Step One.** *Acknowledge that the current situation is in crisis and needs to change dramatically.* We admit that we are powerless to control all the forces at work in the world. At best, we can influence our world, but there is no way we can predict the future. The organization does not have to be in crisis but does have to acknowledge that its performance falls far short of its potential.

- **Step Two.** *Realize that your current values and standards are insufficient.* Have faith that there is a better way. One definition of *hitting bottom* is that we are not achieving our best. Perhaps an outsider is needed to come in to give a new definition of *bottom.* As a colleague recently said, organizations either endure the pain or set a new vision.

- **Step Three.** *Abandon the false god of shareholder primacy.* Set your own assumptions about how stakeholders should be ranked. Since clients are important to every concern, perhaps serving them well should be your top priority. Here is where your mission should be reexamined to see if it is still valid. Same with your values—are they what is needed to carry out your new vision, mission, and priorities?

- **Step Four.** *Make a brutally honest inventory of how your organization is behaving against your revised set of values.* Identify the behaviors you need to change. There is no easy way to do this. It is holding up a mirror and looking at what the organization needs and how it is currently behaving. If it can be done without finger pointing and blaming, then it has a better chance of succeeding. It helps if someone who has been around and is respected leads this exercise with a team that includes some newcomers who aren't blinded by history.

- **Step Five.** *Share this inventory widely with a large cross section of the organization, to seek input and collaboration in the changes needed.* Continue to commit yourself to the truth, not to anyone's particular view of the situation. The organization will be able to tell in a heartbeat if you are trying to white-wash how things are working. A few strong souls with good b.s. detectors should always be part of this effort.

- **Step Six.** *Make a commitment to see the changes through, painful though they will be.* It is always easier to set resolutions than to carry them out. So usually it is at this point that individual and group change efforts break down. Renewal of the purpose of this whole exercise is helpful. Remember too that seeking perfection in this task is not helpful. Stick with the major changes that can have the most important effect.

- **Step Seven.** *Seek help from all stakeholders in making the changes.* An argument can be made that this should be part of Step Five. At any rate, in this change process it is useful to engage other external stakeholders in addition to the internal associates in the organization. Suppliers, customers, community leaders, board members, and shareholders can provide useful advice and help in carrying out the changes desired.

- **Step Eight.** *Acknowledge and be willing to make amends for harm to stakeholders in the past.* This step almost seems un-American. Yet the psychology is sound. If you want your associates to believe you are sincere about new values, then this step will help begin to lay that foundation.

- **Step Nine.** *Make the amends in Step Eight where appropriate.* *Appropriate* is the key word here. There are many instances where the harm occurred so long ago that to reopen the wounds might not be useful. In both Step Eight and Step Nine there will be significant resistance from legal advisors who will warn against acknowledging past actions that can open you to legal action. Creative leadership can accomplish these steps while preserving the organization's assets.

- **Step Ten.** *Continue your moral reevaluation of the system and progress against the objectives.* It is necessary to frequently

measure how the organization is doing against its plan.
Build this into your process.

- **Step Eleven.** *Continue the cycle of honest assessment and
courageous change.* To establish such healthy examinations
as an ongoing practice means that honest assessment will
have to be repeated as needed over time. This is needed
because the organization is going to try to recapture its old
habits. My guideline is to conduct the process again in two
years and at longer intervals thereafter. Smaller organizations may want to do it annually.

- **Step Twelve.** *Become an example to other stakeholders to adopt
the same principles and practices.* You can offer other stakeholders assistance from your organization in establishing
such change processes for them. Another legacy you can
leave is to spread such healthy practices to other organizations you become a part of through community work or
through board membership.

Douglas M. Baker

Douglas M. Baker of Minneapolis is an author, executive coach,
business consultant and speaker. He is a founder of The Chief
Executive Academy and is an Executive Fellow at the Graduate
School of Business, University of St. Thomas. Baker has held senior management positions for American Express and Litton
Industries. His extensive community service includes building
houses, preparing meals, and serving on boards of spiritual,
educational, charitable and arts organizations. In his words, he
is most proud of "my wife, Carole, our grown children and their
spouses, and a marvelous brood of grandkids."

PART III

CHAPTER EIGHT

In Part III of this book we consider the future of business, in light of what has been presented in Parts I and II. Whatever the future may in fact bring, it is being met today largely with fear and anxiety. The traditional bond between employer and employee has disappeared. Acquisitions, divestitures, downsizing, e-commerce, start-ups, bankruptcies amid unprecedented growth have combined to drive business at light speed. With this as a backdrop, Steven contemplates the role and functions of a leader in the future—how the concept of leadership is even now evolving in the workplace. He considers both the internal and external world of the future leader and cogently compares these worlds to those of a jazz musician. Again using the metaphor of a jazz musician, he also discusses the critical role of followers in an organization, since an effective leader in the future must learn to collaborate with followers and channel discord and dissension towards a creative output. Included in this chapter are numerous exercises recommended for leaders of the future, as well as specific references and ties to steps within the Twelve Steps.

—Editor

The Future of Leadership: Continuous Transformation

Steven Jeddeloh

was sitting in with a group of jazz musicians assembled in orderly rows, greatly anticipating the leap from a classical context to a jazz improvisation. The odds of getting to where we wished to go were against us. We assembled as a music class, not as a group of experienced improvisers. The leader was a classically trained trumpet player. He obviously knew his way around a musical score and definitely had the will, desire, and excitement for delving into a jazz experience—but he had no experience playing jazz, let alone leading a jazz group.

Out of twenty musicians, perhaps three had improvisation experience. I certainly wasn't one of the three, but I was there with desire, curiosity, and lots of trepidation.

We read the chart, made music and began the journey to learn and experience the art of playing jazz, of improvisation and, hopefully, of making a little magic. As part of that first session we were each to take a solo, a stab at improvisation in a simple, predictable system of chord modulations.

As my solo approached, I vacillated between sheer terror and a sort of blissful connection to the musical flow. When I began my solo, I had a sense of letting go of the score and the way the music was written, and I surrendered to the flow of the music. In a way, I lost consciousness except of the rhythm and tones of the musical world in which I was floating. I lost track of the written music, the instrument, my "self," time, and my surroundings.

I soloed long past my prescribed section and played until my sense of what I was playing seemed naturally to finish its course. The rest of the musicians had already stopped playing. My terror returned. My first sense was that I had just committed a heinous crime, a musical murder in the first degree. On the contrary, the expressions I first took as anger or disgust were looks of awe and wonder. There were cheers such one would hear upon scoring the winning point in a championship game.

In his book *Flow: The Psychology of Optimal Experience,* Mihaly Csikszentmihalyi describes this blissful connection as a flow state, where the technical proficiencies and optimal emotional state align. The group I was in had not played together before even as beginners, much less as experienced improvising musicians. Our musical system wasn't technically proficient. Yet for me it happened.

Though this event occurred more than twenty years ago, it is still vivid in my mind. This experience created a turning point in my life resulting in four extremely wonderful years playing and improvising music on a small-scale professional level.

It wasn't until twenty years later that I realized the value of the experience, how much I had learned from that process, and how much it affects both my own leadership and the business advice I give to my clients.

We live in a time of monumental change and turbulence—in our businesses, our organizations, and our lives. In Chapter 10 of this book, Peter Vaill terms this state of constant turbulence and change *permanent white water.* This permanent white water will continue. We need leaders more than ever, yet we also value and demand our individualism, our independence more than ever. We often feel resentment when someone tries to tell us what to do, to manage us, especially if we perceive that we know as much as or more than the manager. On the other hand, there has always been a need for strong leadership—to be a keeper of the place where the buck stops and to make decisions in times of crisis.

Acquisitions, rightsizing, mergers, e-commerce, start-ups, overwhelming growth, decline, and bankruptcies have all contributed to our insecurity and anxiety about the future. At the same time that we lament a lack of strong and positive leadership, we also have an enormously difficult time defining what leadership means and what we want from our leaders. Each of us has a socially constructed worldview that includes our meaning of *leader.* This view is based on experience and memories not only from our own lifetime but also from the lives of our ancestors, contributing to our cultural view. We have socially constructed a mental model of how we are, and this influences how we act.

Since our world is evolving at a tremendous rate, and every one of us has an idea of what leadership is and is not, there naturally is a lack of consensus regarding characteristics of the leader of the future and how to develop these characteristics. A productive way to look at continuous learning and improvement of leadership skills is by focusing on a set of underlying guiding principles that if taken to heart can have a significantly positive effect on leadership.

I am using the term *leader* as A. Bryman does in *Handbook of Organizational Studies.* A leader is anyone who influences others to move toward a common goal. It relates to being ahead of the change curve, to serving those being led. It is the person who, through words and deeds, personifies the importance of simple governing principles such as guiding visions, strong values, and organizational beliefs. This could be a political leader, a chief executive officer (CEO), a congregational leader, a temporary group leader, a parent, or anyone who pulls others together for a common purpose.

I use a familiar metaphor of an improvising jazz ensemble to explore what I perceive is a positive means for developing future leadership characteristics. The application of this metaphor is not universal or a one-size-fits-all strategy. The best organizational strategy is the one that fits the business and gains the support of the people involved. I will also interpret the language of the principles and Traditions of Alcoholics Anonymous to apply to leaders in a way to guide their growth and development.

Driving the Business at Light Speed

As well as in a time of constant change, we live in a time of great exploration. The new worlds we seek to explore, however, are not uncharted waters and vast continents. Rather, we explore worlds of information. The paths we take are virtual and ever-expanding networks. Our communication and transportation systems have made proximity almost instantaneous. We are able to drive, fly, or virtually connect with people at a moment's notice. Yet, as R. Kegan describes, with all this opportunity to connect, we purposely strive to stay less connected in our families and communities. We start our days early and get home late—exhausted. The last thing we want to do is go out and connect with our neighbors next door or down the hall. It is common in many communities never to meet the people next door. Yet we still look for meaningful connection where we spend most of our waking hours—at work.

One of the things that fascinates me in my consulting work is how unaware business leaders are about the needs and wants of their customers. True market research is too infrequently used to develop new products and services. When asked, leaders will say they understand the markets they are in and what their customers want. Yet my experience is that when asked to describe the information they gather and the methods used to collect it, leaders often describe anecdotal information collected from their sales reps, industry reports, and journals. Often there is a reluctance to put systems in place to gather customer data on a regular basis. Leaders of the future will need to become more externally focused, spending less time dealing with data about internal functions and more time on customers, collaboration, and global networks.

Our business world has become relationally elongated. By this I mean decisions are often made in isolation, far from the place where the work is done and the impact felt. For example, an executive may make a decision from a New York office that affects a group of workers in a plant in Singapore. It would take a special effort to consider the potential impact on the people, community, and environment at such an impersonal distance. This effort is especially difficult to maintain when quarterly financial reports and shareholder value drive decisions.

Step One of the Twelve Steps underscores the powerlessness we sometimes feel. We become aware that we are much less powerful than we once thought—that we really cannot succeed as leaders on our own. We need the help and guidance of our followers and our Higher Power.

Today, we have a much harder time identifying the best and the brightest leaders, that sort of "take-charge-hit-the-ground-running" figure. This is the person who came into the room and, to everyone's relief, had all the answers. The supreme, all-knowing, charismatic leader has become obsolete. Though these take-charge qualities are still needed in times of crisis, this sort of leader is the exception rather than the rule. What has caused this change is easy access to information. Each person in the room is now an expert and leader in his or her own right. The culture focus of the workplace has shifted. Followers now believe that their first loyalty is to themselves and their immediate family or work group.

Why worker loyalty to the company has waned is moot. The truth is that even in secure work environments, the majority of workers believe they have less security than they did in years past. Even the most secure worker is fully aware of the layoffs, acquisitions, and quick changes affecting multitudes of workers—enough to wonder about his or her own situation, enough to plant and nourish a seed of doubt. This in turn has caused a shift in how we view our work, not as a necessary and vital part of our existence (many jobs are available in the current economy) but as a competing player for our interest. In this climate, worker attention will go to the companies and the leaders who are willing to offer the things that these new workers want: to be recognized, to be treated in a respectful, caring way, to grow and develop, and to be paid fairly and equitably.

Yet modern society seems to be more fascinated with the technology than with the consequences of the information we receive. It is easy to become fascinated with the medium and neglect the critical eye necessary to filter and turn the data delivered into meaningful information. Yet this information carries the meaning that needs to be developed in our organizations, the stuff that leaders need to carry forward so that subordinates and colleagues will find compelling reasons to participate and to follow. The leader of the future will need to not only be aware of information systems and the data these systems contain, but, more importantly, the meaning of the data.

All this confirms that our professional and personal worlds have changed and will continue to evolve. It makes perfect sense that the leader's role must evolve to accommodate these transformations. What will it mean to be a leader in the future? What new roles lie ahead for effective leaders?

A Quick Look at History

Our mental models of what leadership means come from a long line of figures, both benevolent and ruthless: Attila the Hun, Machiavelli, Martin Luther, Alexander the Great, Hitler, Churchill, Cleopatra, kings, queens, popes, scholars, murderers. It is thus easy to understand how we equate leadership with ultimate power and almost mystical capabilities. Leadership of the past was based on hierarchy, on a ladder of power and influence.

Leadership in our business world did not truly emerge until the industrial revolution and has been in existence for less than 150 years. The models we used to define our Western notion of leadership when the industrial revolution started continued to be based on the class system, with nobility at the top of the hierarchy. The wealthy industry owner started a business and usually anointed his sons to be the heirs and managers of the business. Choice of leaders at that time was not so much based on knowledge as it was based on fate and family. Unfortunately that style of leadership was based on accepted levels of coercion and brutality. Such practices today would spawn a spate of lawsuits.

As businesses grew and the need for more managers increased, the wealthy were able to afford higher education and influence the academic community to design coursework about management and leadership. The early academics and practitioners were working with models where the leader was the omnipotent figure at the top. Since the leaders controlled the money, the consultants—beginning with Frederick Taylor, who developed the idea of scientific management—catered to the needs and whims of this group. The breakthrough Taylor offered was material on creating efficiency in jobs. What his theory lacked was the human factor—a factor he could not break down into its smallest parts, streamline, and reassemble into a more efficient whole. Taylor's methods fit with the science of the time since Descartes and Newton. Still, this so-called modern method is operating today in many businesses and in the minds of their leaders.

As history advanced, leadership training and education evolved, building on the earlier educational curricula and gradually pushing a more inclusive, humane, respectful set of practices. Our mental models have gradually changed as we learn that getting cooperation from followers is easier and more effective through methods of attraction and alignment rather than coercion. Yet our basic mental model about leadership is still reminiscent of the nobility model: leaders firmly in power, creating the vision and challenge for the organization to move boldly into the future.

Leading at the Speed of Transformation

Leaders contend with masses of data from a variety of sources. It is possible to differentiate two worlds that every leader must confront: the external world or outside of self; and the internal world, or inside of self. Keep in mind that in a systems view of the leader's role and life there is a separation here only of convenience. The two worlds I describe are, in reality, inseparable and interdependent. Leadership cannot exist in isolation without situations and followers with which to interact. Successful leadership is not based on heroic individual endeavor but is contingent on the efforts and input of followers. This creates an interdependent system, a partnership for success based on a shared vision or purpose. Mark Haskins writes about an ethic of collaboration as the fuel or energy that gives an organization its power.

The Leader's External World

The mass of data mentioned previously comprise a sea of relationships, problems, and risks and opportunities. This is where collaboration takes place, where networks are developed. Here is also where the leaders need to stay out in front of the mission and meaning of the organization. Traditional managerial skills include financial skills, control of costs and processes, organization, marketing, product development, technology, and a host of other, equally necessary skills. It is easy to see how managing and leading can be enormously challenging tasks. Add to this list the requirement that a leader needs a good understanding of psychology to successfully navigate the human side of the enterprise, and we have a role that is, at times, seemingly impossible to perform.

As a company expands, one of the inevitabilities inside the organization is the creation of bureaucracy. Bureaucracy ideally is a system actively creating efficiencies—that is, instituting policies and procedures so that incidents and processes can be standardized and made efficient. This frees up the workers to do their jobs without their being concerned with such matters. The downside of bureaucracy is that it can create roadblocks to innovation and even to everyday work. The leader of the future will need to create organizations that avoid the negative aspects of bureaucracy and allow just enough to operate efficiently. Larger and older companies will need to rethink structure, to create efficient, streamlined, smaller, and versatile subunits. Smaller companies need to be focused on what they do and quickly respond to changes. All companies will need to operate like smaller, more flexible business units. Future leaders will need to shift their focus from simply designing a structure and expecting workers to function in it. Rather, they must allow a structure to emerge and define itself after focusing on worker and process needs— and especially customer needs.

The Musician's External World

One of the things that music gave me without presenting itself as a theory or a lesson is my ability to "hear" things, the sounds of the world as musical melodies and rhythms. Just as my consciousness fills with the sounds of my current business consulting work, the sounds around me present themselves as harmony and dissonance, begging to be developed. In fact, once a sound gets into my head from the outside world, it becomes an internal matter, at times to the

*point of distraction. My consciousness plays with the poten-
tial music. A birdsong could be included, the rhythms and
beat of a train on the tracks, but even a child crying down
the street, a siren, the wind blowing, the rain on the roof. All
these sounds seem to move into my consciousness and ask to
be developed as musical themes or improvisations of other
melodies already lodged in my memory. Some end up as simple rhythms, others as full songs with verse and refrain.*

*The jazz musician is constantly scanning the outside world
and interpreting the sounds, sights, and other stimuli coming in through the senses. The combination of outside stimuli and the inside world taking the stimuli and working
with them is the jazz musician's supply chain.*

One of the difficult undertakings of organization leadership in
growing a business is knowing when to let go of a product, service or practice that has served the organization well for a long
time and when to reach for the next innovation, the next level.
My experience with leaders is that many, understandably, wish to
hold on to the old, the tried and true, to keep a sense of security
while the next wave is developed. The new skill is a sharpened
sense of the optimal time to let go and move into reinventing the
organization.

*Jazz music is the practice of continuously looking back at
what was done, the melody, the last improvisation, the last
rhythm change, and, at the same time, looking ahead to
improvise something new based on what came before. This is
an effective way to describe personal and organization
reflection and learning.*

The Leader's Internal World

The leader's internal world is a world of consciousness, process-
ing data, evaluating, mentally scanning and sorting data, feelings, ideas.

We begin to develop mental scanning—the skill of sensing what is going on around us—even before birth. We develop the skill as a survival mechanism and we become more sophisticated with the process as we get older. Political as well as physical survival depends on our mental scanning abilities. Mental scanning is a circular process and relies on a leader's intellectual capabilities, emotional sensitivity, and willingness or attitude. Reflecting back and making changes in building our reality and theory is an example of double-loop learning, where we are not only reacting to the situation, but we are also mentally reviewing the process and learning new ways to operate.

Ego acts as one of the main mental scanning filters we have and seems to surface as a major issue in the leaders I meet who are having trouble. Leadership ego, on the one hand, is necessary to maintain a confident and healthy sense of self. It becomes a liability, however, when the leader becomes self-centered and seeks an unreasonable amount of ego reinforcement.

In his book *Managing Strategic Change,* N. Tichy states that the success of action resulting from mental scanning hinges on what is acceptable to the immediate organization's technical, cultural, and political norms and values. If a proposed action by a leader is not acceptable to the culture, then the action, even if seen as socially responsible, will be resisted. Difficulties occur when we attempt to forcefully implement action based on faulty data or not engaging the collective energy in the effort. Failed leadership occurs even with a highly skilled leader when he or she is unable to understand and work with the technical, cultural, and political power of an organization.

If the leader, or anyone, is attempting to behave in ways contrary to the organization's cultural norms and values (that is, trying to institute change), even if the changes are in the best interest of the culture, resistance is inevitable (ironically even from the people who will benefit).

A healthy ego and confidence level speak also of faith, the cornerstone of Step Two of the Twelve Steps. This faith is the leader's sense of belief in self, followers, and a Higher Power to provide what is needed to do the right things for customers, the organization, and the world.

Steps Two, Three, and Five have to do with a willingness not only to accept one's powerlessness but also to accept the help and support of others—to develop a willingness to listen and take others seriously while at the same time not taking oneself too seriously. These others are not only the close circle of confidants but also others inside and outside the organization who have the knowledge and expertise to help.

In leadership language, Step Five is the ego management step. The key is to maintain a healthy ego without becoming self-absorbed. The trappings of leadership are tempting and create comfort but often also create distance between the leader and followers. Leaders must have the ability and the desire to draw constantly on followers for feedback and input to fuel the mental scanning.

The Musician's Internal World

Most musicians I know view music as their art form. As artists they play primarily for themselves and oh, by the way, if someone listening happens to enjoy it, all the better.

When I developed musical thoughts inspired by the outside world, the melodies tended to drift in and out of my consciousness. When my internal, emotional, passionate self was ready, these musical thoughts came to the fore and inspired some sort of melody or riff. The riff could lie dormant a long time and influence me when I was either practicing or playing with the group.

It is emotional to be in a musical group that is playing a standard melody or creating a new melody and to feel the musical riff emerge as I play, massaging it as an improvised melody to see what happens. This is the work of the musician. It creates the satisfaction one feels with oneself and the sort of collective satisfaction the group feels when Something Big happens. This is also the process of developing trust within the group, creating awareness of each others' sameness and differences, creating a certain amount of predictability coupled with a certain amount of unpredictability to keep the group always at the edge.

One of the welcome trends in leadership, which will become even more important in the future, is that the individual leader does not dictate a course or direction but engages the organization in developing meaning. The future leader will be vigilant about including all constituencies and sensitive to exclusion. By engaging co-workers in developing meaning, resistance either is nonexistent or fades away as trust and faith in the engagement process increase. The leader of the future will be less concerned with the "how" of solving a problem and more concerned with the "way" or process to use.

There are good leaders who engage, and there are good leaders who do not. There are leaders who do not share their true intent. Even if we do not appreciate the intent, we do appreciate honesty and clarity. This has to do with leader authenticity. More and more, knowledge workers—perfectly capable of doing their own mental scanning—review a leader's authenticity and intent and base their decisions to trust the leader on the outcomes of their mental scan. Authentic leaders running an honest program with good intentions for the organization and its workers will project an energy that attracts knowledge workers.

In my consulting practice I coach leaders to be honest and clear about intent, even if it is selfish intent. I think the honesty and clarity has to come before the personal and organizational plans for change. This is in essence what is behind Step Four, in which leaders are asked to take a "fearless inventory" of their behavior and the input of their organization.

An honest inventory provides a healthy avenue of reflection for leaders and followers alike. This indeed is an opportunity to note which behaviors and emotions cause trouble or negative impacts to self and those around us, and to the world.

Networked Collaboration

A critical factor in this network leadership is communication. Leaders need to model and reinforce communication as a means not only to share data but also to share and develop knowledge. This in turn becomes a critical factor in an organization's ability to innovate and learn. Thus future leadership will be lodged in less hierarchy and more in a shared process of leading between small, versatile collaborators, some free agents, some internal staff, and some larger companies. Critical to this sort of networked business is a climate of trust that can be fostered only through example of the leadership. The need to trust the process is paramount, as an overabundance of control will put off collaborators who view their role in the project as a voluntary endeavor.

Leadership, rather than visualized as an individual exhibiting an enormous amount of charisma, may be viewed in the future as both a realization of how powerless we are and how much we rely on the collective energy and knowledge of followers to succeed, best nurtured by group processes. A climate of trust based on competence, a certain amount of tenacity to stay the course, the creation of meaning, and the ability to learn from mistakes will all be imperative characteristics.

Musical Language and Communication

Jazz music has its own language. There is the language based on music theory: the staff, the key, the time, the notes. There is also a secondary, unwritten language in jazz music. This has to do with subtle nuances, interpretation of what is written (how much to bend a note, how long past the note' s value to hold it, etc.), and how much liberty the players take with the music.

Another part of the musical language has to do with the interaction among the players. This language is based on experience and familiarity in the group. It is a language of subtle cues offered among players. It can be as obvious as a key change, or as subtle as a slight quickening of the tempo. In the groups I played in, there was a point where we were in the groove, when communication among players was no longer overt. The signals seemed so subtle as to be psychic, effortless. We all knew each other well and had enough skill and trust to anticipate what was coming even in a constantly changing musical piece.

In addition to the art of listening and inclusion as leadership skills, leaders also need to be vigilant about processes. There is a tension between doing things the traditional way and questioning why things are done, a willingness to break the old lines of thinking and inviting followers to try new processes. In the end it is not so much that a new process is designed and implemented, but rather that it becomes a process owned by the group with a commitment to making it work the best way possible. This sort of paradigm-busting attitude is a cultural norm that leaders need to sanction and model. Peter Drucker talks about the old management paradigms as a set of faulty assumptions on which leadership and management theory rested for years. The old assumptions will not work in a future environment with no one best company design, no standard set of rules for working with people and systems. Even MacGregor's theory of working with people as collaborators rather than as subjects to be ordered about is not a universal truth. Each worker has a preferred way of being led. In fact, as businesses become more global in their reach, diversity in the workforce will multiply, creating more diverse leadership models. It will be the leaders' responsibility to determine the best method for leading an organization.

Because networks and information are so widespread, our old notions of command and control are not just outdated but can become negative forces for many workers, stifling learning, collaboration, and innovation. The organization of the future will be even more diverse and widespread, connecting more disparate, smaller units into the whole. The workforce, after years of rightsizing and insecurity, will become less loyal to the company and more focused on self. The trend for freelancing is booming, creating networks of independent contractors able to plug in to different organizations at will, yet working as non-employees. As F. Herzberg describes in the *Harvard Business Review*, this creates a critical need for leaders to handle an evolving workforce differently, where the leverage with the postmodern follower includes meaningful, interesting work, recognition, opportunities to learn, and fair monetary reward.

Collaboration

Jazz music is a great metaphor for describing independence as well as interdependence within a collaborative framework. During an improvised piece, there are opportunities for soloists to step forward. At this time the rest of the musicians are supporting the soloist as well as the whole piece. Jazz musicians call this support "comping." The collaborative network that is developed and fine-tuned with familiarity is a good example of interdependent teaming.

The soloist could conceivably play alone. Personally I have found it much more compelling to improvise with other musicians than alone. The end result of collaborative music has always been much more energetic and satisfying.

The requirements for making good, satisfying music include: the musicians need to come with a set of baseline skills, abilities to read charts, and play at a level that is not too different from the other musicians' skills; and the musicians' need to have a comfort with the general direction, style, and vision of the musical group. Just as the musicians need to have sameness, they need to bring differences also that beget dissonance and just enough healthy conflict to promote innovation. The musicians need to bring themselves, their muse, their energy, and passion to fuel the music and make it come alive.

To play with musicians who are unfamiliar with each other is much harder and takes some getting used to. It takes more energy in the listening, communicating more overtly rather than subtly, accepting, trusting, and willing to go down new, strange, musical paths with others.

Once during my consulting work I worked with a group of consultants, trainers, and writers. Each of them was a knowledge worker creating products and services for customers from the raw materials of their knowledge. We also employed a number of volunteers who helped assemble products. Volunteers as well as knowledge workers, I learned quickly, needed to be led differently through stimulating work, relationships with coworkers, and recognition of the good work they did. I agree with Drucker that more leaders will have to lead their workforce with the idea that they do not own the workers but are graced with volunteers who are assets to be cherished and protected. These volunteers will soon find other places to volunteer if they are not treated well.

Leader as Other-Focused

A constant leadership characteristic is influence on others. After all, one cannot be a leader without followers. Followers create the human dynamics that leaders contend with. I recall one leader saying to me somewhat in jest, "This would be a great place to work, except for the people who work here." For us to discern what leaders need to do, we need to first examine the needs of their followers.

Followers want essentially three things: to be recognized; to be treated in a respectful, caring way; and to grow. To fulfill these employee needs, the leaders of the future must above all learn the art of leadership communication.

Leadership Communication

We interpret what we sense. The leader as speaker or writer is secondary when it comes to the notion of *meaning*. Meaning is more developed by the receiver. Even after explanation and dialogue, we can never be certain that the interpretation is as we wish it to be. We can only hope to close the gap between what we have communicated and the meaning that was perceived. That is why a key competency of the leaders of tomorrow will be the skills required to gain understanding and consensus not only about the organization's mission but also its plan and the actions that result. Followers will have the requisite knowledge for success. Leaders will need the means to facilitate a collective consciousness and energy. Both are needed, and dialogue is the way to put the two together.

Leadership communication of the future will be based on the concept of dialogue, a process of communicating with deep listening as D. Bohm describes in *On Dialog*. Dialogue is developed as a set of interpretations of the group. In this regard, the interpretation of what a leader says and wants is only a portion of the group consciousness. The leader who relies on dialogue both to learn and to facilitate change must believe in two things: (1) future success resides in the knowledge of the followers, and (2) engaging the workers in dialogue about the future is critical to organization success.

In an *Atlantic Monthly* article titled "Who Owns Intelligence?" Howard Gardner describes a set of human intelligences and suggests that one that effective leaders need is emotional sensitivity. This is not a skill of taking care of others but an ability and desire to understand, empathize, and create opportunities for others in their best interest. Relating to others is also how a leader deals with conflict. Holding a long-range view of difference and conflict as a healthy characteristic of a developing organization and embracing these characteristics are abilities that do not come naturally to most people. We are not comfortable with the deep listening required to be sensitive to what others are saying. This is a skill that takes practice and resolve.

Consider an example. The senior leadership team conducts a monthlong planning process. When completed, the plan is shared throughout the ranks of management. Each manager reads the plan, interprets the meaning, and applies his or her own perception of the strategies and tactics necessary. Now, suppose just for a moment that the organization developed the plan via dialogue sessions with employees, managers, senior executives, customers, suppliers, and other stakeholders. Consider how much more aligned their perceptions would be about what the plan means and how the strategies will be implemented.

Connection

Almost everything in our world is connected and has a vital role to play. We cannot act as separate, disparate entities without a thought as to how we affect each other and the world. The leaders of the future will need to recognize this for a number of reasons:

- *Leaders cannot be effective on their own.* They must recognize that they are part of an interdependent network of people and resources. It is an empowering act of strength to seek help and support from followers. The new perception will be that leaders show strength when they seek support and assistance from others.

- *Competition, a socially constructed phenomenon in our business world, will be here in the future but with a different meaning.* As businesses rise and fall in an interdependent world, it is vital that bridges within the network are not burned. If one business successfully kills another, this may start a chain of events that actually results in harm to the stronger businesses. Leaders will need to figure out how to work with competitors to "win."

- *Leaders must take the discord, dissention, and disagreement and channel it into creative output.* Leaders of the future will see value in differences and diversity and welcome them as contributing to learning and growth.

- *Leaders need to operate not as ship captain or shipbuilder, but as ship designer.* They bring disparate talents together to make the ship and its course a reality.

Businesses of tomorrow will be so complex that one person cannot possibly know and understand everything. Leaders of the future will give this notion more than lip service. They will need the humility to admit that they don't have all the answers, that they are powerless over many things, and that they will have to rely on others to succeed. The notion of seeking collective wisdom and energy from followers is a different, legitimate way to feel pride and confidence in our role as leader.

Self-Transformation

Leaders of tomorrow will be dedicated to transforming their vision and creating learning through modeling transformation of organization and self. Leaders of tomorrow need to take responsibility for their own development and transformation just as they need to offer this benefit to their followers.

In the language of Step Six, the "removal of defects of character" has a transformational quality to it. Broadly put, defects can mean any known or unknown shortcoming or liability that prevent us from good work. If we are truly committed to becoming the best we can be, then self and organizational transformation become a constant imperative.

Step Seven presents a humble request to remove these shortcomings or liabilities. It also speaks of having the right mind. We rely on ourselves, others, and our Higher Power to help us with these shortcomings—we understand we cannot learn and grow completely when living in isolation.

Making the list referred to in Step Eight has to do with being public about mistakes and errors that have a negative effect on others and becoming willing to make things right again. This flies in the face of the spin-doctor approach or the damage control that goes on in many organizations trying to cover up negative acts.

Reflection

One of the things sorely lacking in the primary, secondary, and even postgraduate curricula is the skill and practice of self-reflection. The frenetic pace of the work environment leaves precious little time to accomplish what needs to be done. Our tendency is to get caught up in the pace (and even enjoy it as long as we feel in control) and neglect to sit quietly and reflect both on the past and the future. My own experience in the corporate environment is filled with examples of too much to do in too little time. In fact, at one point I took a look at how much time I spent on each task I had to perform. The average length of time spent on each focus was less than three minutes per subject. Though I made a to-do list each day, it was the other, unanticipated events, requests, and focuses that drained the time from the day. When I started reflecting each day and working to stay consciously in the areas that I needed to, I found that less of these unanticipated events came to my attention. Staff who gradually felt capable and empowered to manage them took care of many of them.

Facilitating reflection will become an important characteristic of future leaders. Learning is based on reflection, sorting out the behaviors or practices we can change, cleaning up any debris we left, and testing new behaviors. Deep learning and change do not occur without reflection. We need to look back (reflect) on our behaviors and impact while looking ahead to anticipate (improvise) the changes we will make. Modeling this reflective behavior on an individual basis will legitimize it and encourage followers to do the same.

Step Ten makes the previous three Steps a way of being and acting rather than an isolated event. This then becomes a transformational or learning loop: being open and willing to improve, reflecting on what happened, righting our wrongs, and moving on.

Transformational Jazz

> There is a well-known quote from Charles Mingus, "You can't improvise on nothing, man, you gotta improvise on somethin'." What he means is that jazz musicians are constantly looking back, improvising on the melodies previously played, while simultaneously looking forward, constantly pushing new ground, twisting, turning, altering a melody almost until unrecognizable, changing the key, changing the rhythm, changing the style. There is the theme here of reflecting while looking ahead and moving forward.
>
> Personally I learn the most, I feel the most alive, and I get the most energy from reflecting on what I have done and using that reflection as a way to spring forward and improvise a new and energizing present and future.

One of the exercises I advocate is for the leader to keep a transformation journal. The journal itself is not to be shared but kept as a private way to inventory self, practice, and the transformation journey. I recommend that the journal writer jot down answers to these or similar questions:

1. *What did I learn today? How did I solo? How did I comp? How did events of today align with my personal values and the organization's? How did my behaviors model the values of the organization?* These first questions are really a fearless and personal moral inventory of one's behavior. This question seeks self-awareness of how comfortable the leader is with

letting go and trusting others to make good decisions and take positive action.

2. *What did I do today that resulted in building trust? Are there amends to be made?* These questions evoke an inventory of behaviors that empower others, that give followers the courage to take risks and promote an atmosphere of communicating vital information, both positive and negative. This embodies the information leaders need to improvise their organization's and their own plans for the future, to make adjustments to current plans, to obtain the right information needed to seek new opportunities in the external environment.

3. *What did I do today that gave me energy—made me feel alive? Where was I at my best? How did this affect those around me?* These questions are actually the most important. They are meant to evoke mindfulness, which implies both being aware and acting in an appropriate way, congruent with personal and organizational values. If we can identify the practices that give us passion and energy, then we can take that reflection and improvise it into the future. The fact that we inventory it each day raises it from our subconscious to our conscious and causes us to be aware of it and practice it more readily. The bonus is that followers are attracted to the positive energy exhibited by people who are energized. We all have had the experience of meeting people and immediately wanting to get to know them better. We perceive a positive energy about them, they are on the right path, they seem genuinely happy and sure of themselves. Confidence can breed success.

4. *What did I do today to eliminate innovation barriers for my followers? What opportunities did I provide so others could thrive?* These last questions are a key practice for leaders in the future. Eliminating barriers in the form of bureaucracy, providing adequate resources and other leadership tasks are critical to allowing collaboration across boundaries to happen. This is also a "development of others" practice. By

eliminating barriers that followers perceive are stopping them from innovating, leaders create opportunities for followers to risk, to experiment, and to learn.

The above questions are intent on eliciting self-awareness about the following leadership attributes:

- *How aware am I of self?* This is knowing your strengths as well as your weaknesses. You can learn this somewhat from reflections but you will also need bold and honest feedback from those around you.

- *How do I become energized and passionate?* This implies that there are many places a person's style and skills may fit and also many places where they may not. Business literature is deep with accounts of leaders who are successful and have made a great impact on their organizations. Usually context and environment are minimized as factors in this success. There are fewer accounts of leaders who succeed in one organization and fail miserably in another.

- *How do I learn?* In *Sources of Executive Learning,* D. T. Hall examines a study in Boston that suggests that 75 percent of executive learning is accomplished through experience. Little, after attainment of baseline knowledge, is accomplished through readings, seminars, or college courses. Many leaders learn by speaking. That is, they test out ideas and possibilities through speaking, to see the reaction of others, and more importantly, to hear themselves say what they are thinking. This clarifies the thoughts and makes them real.

- *What values drive me? What values do I live by?* In *Leadership from the Inside Out: Becoming a Leader for Life,* Kevin Cashman describes authentic leaders as those whose behavior aligns with their personal values and what they believe is meaningful. Have you taken an honest inventory of your values?

- *How do I relate to others?* Do I collaborate naturally or did I get where I am through my own individual strength and means? Where am I on my list of priorities? Do I take care of myself and my career first, second, or third? What is important to me: other people, the work, the accomplishment, creating a legacy?

- *What do I or can I contribute?* What can I do to see that plans are implemented? How do I affect tactics once plans are in place?

Continuous Learning and All That Jazz

The jazz musician's development, like the development of leaders, is honed through a number of venues: natural potential, education, and experience. A nature vs. nurture debate goes on still. My sense is that both come into play. A jazz musician, much like a leader, needs the potential to become a good performer. This natural ability is contained within the cellular memories, the DNA handed down from past generations. This natural ability includes intellect, emotional intelligence, physical and mental coordination, and stability. Who would want to argue that Mozart became a great musician solely because of his training? His greatness was based primarily on inherited potential.

Just as musicians and leaders need talent, they also need nurturing. The encouragement and establishment of values at an early age builds a foundation from which to guide the inherited potential. The education we receive gives us the basics for shaping that potential further: language, math, reading, whether reading musical charts or business spreadsheets.

So now that we have the talent, the potential, and the education, will we be a wonderful Jazz musician or leader? No, there is a key component missing.

Experience!

Some of the most deeply affecting experiences that have influenced my music had nothing to do with music. They

included events that contributed to the fullness and richness
of my experience. These experiences provided the grist and
emotion to fuel my muse.

Experience in life—the handling of setbacks, mistakes, successes, relationships—adds to the breadth of a person's skills and attributes and the richness of life at home and at work. For musicians, experience provides not only the comfort and confidence in abilities to improvise but also the passion, the emotion, the energy to express in music that which causes us to feel. Likewise, leaders without this life experience are limited in dimensions, uncomfortable or unseasoned in how to deal with the things leaders of the future must handle: global economics and politics, networks and collaboration, and a knowledge-based workforce. It seems that the more examples of trauma and angst we successfully handle, the more our eyes open up to the world.

To me, Steps Eleven and Twelve are the most spiritual and perhaps the most meaningful Steps. They call for a regular practice of prayer, meditation, and reflection to quiet oneself and become open to transformation and change. Often leaders become evangelists with a new idea or practice. This is not what these Steps are about. The most effective way we as leaders can touch others is by quietly modeling behaviors that are aligned with our vision and values, and are perceived to be in the best interest of our followers and the world.

Impermanence

At some point, suffering or loss affects us. Loss of a loved one, loss of one's possessions, loss of family, near-death experience, loss of freedom all open our eyes to the impermanence and frailty of life. Traumas such as these bring us closer to our mortality. Our consciousness suddenly becomes open to transformation. Many people report a renewed appreciation of nature, sights, smells, fresh air. The ego is rocked and torn asunder. Often we are moved to ponder the meaning of life more deeply.

No one can possibly live a long and full life without major set-backs. Setbacks are normal and necessary for us to stop, retreat, and work through changes we need to make. Often, strong leaders cite an event that caused them to transform how they view life and the world. The transformation resulting from a significant loss does not, however, result in a loss of power. Actually, just the opposite result is more likely. W. E. Rowe reports in *Human and Organization Development* that those who have gone through transformation have reported it has made them stronger, more peaceful, more focused, and patient. The leadership drive is still there; the ego is probably more developed. The energy that once drove the competitive self is redirected toward a collaborative self.

Leaders of the Future

Leaders of the future will be role models. The opportunity for self-leadership and leadership of those around us will increase exponentially as the pace of change increases. Leaders of the future will be dedicated to setting an example of values, ethics, and a broad notion of spirituality in the business environment.

Transformation allows the leader to convey meaning through a collaboratively developed vision, a new confidence, purpose, authenticity, caring, and an insatiable appetite for knowledge.

This leader authenticity includes:

- Knowing who you are and who you are not, understanding your strengths as well as your shortcomings
- Not being in denial about strengths and weaknesses, but being realistic
- Leveraging strengths and shoring up deficits through interdependent networks with others

The role of the leader is to reflect not only on self but also on the organization. This includes facilitating a reflective process throughout the ranks of followers. Such reflection and inventory needs to focus on reality: truth about environment, competition, capabilities, and how well the culture aligns with the espoused set of organizational values. The leader's job is to ask and hear the tough questions and allow the organization to struggle to find truth and alignment. It is the struggle—knowing when to promote it, engage in it, direct it, and facilitate positive decisions and action from it—that provides the opportunity for creativity and innovation. The organization, however, can be perfectly aligned, and inspiration and passion may run high, but unless a leader can help turn this aligned energy into action, the organization will fail. This suggests a balanced focus between obtaining results and the manner in which those results are obtained.

Jazz Dissonance and Revolution

Jazz music has a discordant quality to it. Not in a dissonant sort of way, although dissonance creates interesting music, but in a relational way. This is the relation between musician and the musical chart and also among the musicians as they play. Sonny Rollins said, "You can't have jazz without protest." If there were no dissonance, no protest, no diversity, there would be no improvisation. All the music would be the same.

One quality of jazz improvising is that of always pushing outside the mainstream, the mundane, the tried and true; in actuality, creating difference. If jazz musicians repeat something, playing the same exact riff more than once, they are not really improvising.

The environment surrounding jazz musicians pushes conformity. The audience has an idea of what they want based on what they have heard before and liked. This is a tremendous pressure on the musicians to present the music that others want to hear. For example, our group played in all sorts of clubs and venues. Often, someone in the audience would request that we play Proud Mary. First, we would play enough of the melody for the audience to recognize it, then improvise enough to satisfy our own artistic intent. I am not sure if you would call this playfulness, resistance, or passive-aggressive behavior on our part. But it did allow us to stick close to our values and still satisfy the audience.

The point of this is that multiple forces were always pushing, pulling, and trying to get their own wishes met. At any one time there are as many agendas floating around a jazz group as there are musicians, customers, and supporters. Inevitably jazz musicians choose from a multitude of options, what to play, where to play, how to play it, who solos, who comps.

Imposition of Will

As our workplace and what we do become more complex, managing others becomes more challenging. The literature suggests that knowledge workers need to become self-managed, sort of free agents, with an expectation to be self-initiating, self-correcting, and self-evaluating. With this shift in expectations about workers, what is expected of leaders?

The leaders with the most difficulty want too much control in an environment or culture that expects self-management. Leaders who impose their own will rather than seek consensus from self-managed workers first meet resistance, then lose trust, then experience rebellion and turnover.

What is the alternative? The new role of leaders is to pull the ideas and meaning that self-managed workers bring to the table into a collaborative vision that fits with the overall organization mission and vision. This also implies assisting self-managed workers to find the right fit with the meaning they bring.

One leader I worked with had the overwhelming need to set the course for the group he was leading. All he got from them was

chaotic disagreement and dissent. When he was finally convinced to trust the process and allow the group to develop the
direction with his parameters and encouragement, they came to
essentially the same conclusions he had wanted to impose. The
difference in this case was the group agreement and ownership
of meaning and vision embodied in the new plan.

Musical Imposition of Will

*Leadership in a jazz musical group illustrates the phenome-
non of shared leadership. Jazz musicians as a rule are an
independent lot. This is a group of individuals who come
together not to exert control or to be controlled, but to develop music together. My experience of contending with this as
a potential group leader was my own discomfort with the
tendency of my musical cohorts to be thoroughly content
simply practicing together. Though there was desire and certainly a monetary need to go out and play for an audience,
the primary motivation was development of the music within the group. My own anxiety about needing money for food
got the better of me, and I ended up taking more of a leadership role, marketing and selling the group to places willing
to pay and suggesting to the group that we build playlists
that we could mix and match for various audiences. I
learned early that my imposition of will on the group was
acceptable as long as it was outside the realm of the music.
It was unacceptable to impose will on the music and how
each of the musicians interpreted and played. In fact, my
own sense is that the act of improvising needs to be done in
a space void of as much control as possible, as it is the feeling of disequilibrium and tension that pushes the musician
to new heights.*

*If we see the soloist as the leader within the musical frame-
work, we can see that leadership rotates among the players —
it is the shared leadership network. Outside of the music
there are obviously tasks that need to be accomplished. Jobs
have to be obtained, support services have to be contracted,*

space has to be let, schedules have to be set up and confirmed, problems need to be solved. And someone has to start the music. Once the music is started, assuming the players are skilled, the roles of leader and follower rotate, with no one imposing their will. So what happens if the group gets stuck, hits a musical crisis, or gets into an uncomfortable place? If the players are skilled, the discomfort is what drives the next breakthrough. If the insecurities or crisis is too great to over-come, then either the group stops (a performing disaster) or one group member steps forward and leads the musicians through the crisis. There is an enormous sense of pride for professional musicians to get through a musical crisis while the audience perceives no crisis at all.

Once I was sitting in the lobby of a hotel awaiting the arrival of three people I knew through professional connections. I knew that the gentleman sitting next to me—I later learned he was a Buddhist—was waiting for the same group. We started talking, and I reminisced about my experiences playing jazz. I was think-ing about that magical space when a musician becomes self-less or "one with the universe," where the music no longer exists as a separate entity but seems to flow through the body. I lamented that as soon as one tried to re-create that state, it is lost. It seemed addictive, so pleasurable that I was always trying to get it back. He smiled and said that he attained similar states during medi-tation. He asked me to hold out my hand, which I did a bit reluc-tantly. (Which introverted Midwesterner wouldn't be reluctant?) He told me to squeeze my hand as if I was clutching something. When I did this, he told me to open my hand slowly. When my hand was flat out in front of me he said, "See, you still have it in your hand." Amazing! I was struck by such a powerful lesson about control delivered in such a simple, straightforward way. In the context of leadership, it is the control and imposition of will that causes us to lose or never attain that magic moment.

Trust among organizations emerges only when they have suc-cessfully completed transactions and perceive one another as trustworthy. We mentally scan and evaluate all the time, attempting to gain comfort in our predictions as well as postengagement assessments. Who will start the process of collaboration? This becomes a leadership characteristic and responsibility. Leaders of the future will need to model trust (a form of risk taking) and expect trust among collaborators within the organization and outside. Leaders need to create signals of trust both to model expectations and positively reinforce trust behaviors.

This will be an essential skill of future leaders: the ability to bring workers together in a collaborative process, facilitate the group's development of meaning and vision by setting parameters and trusting in the capabilities of the group. This authentic letting go is an essential first step that is scary for leaders who are used to imposing their will. Implied here is the appropriate use of will. It results in an ego that is in harmony with the environment.

Summary

Leader as a Facilitator of Meaning

The leader of tomorrow is a "keeper of the meaning." The new leadership role is to "let go" of the old control aspects of management and facilitate the collective energy and talent of a knowledge worker talent pool.

Leader as Transformer of Organization and Self

The leader of tomorrow will be an improviser, constantly looking back at the past as a source of energy and ideas with which to improvise a future. This includes the use of reflective loops not only to develop self but also to collectively develop the organization. This also includes developing a set of organization and personal values that are aligned.

Leader as Networking Collaborator

The leader of the future will be concerned less with the traditional view of competition and be much more concerned with collaboration across boundaries, both imagined and real, local and global. Communication will not be primarily directive but will be based on dialogue.

Leaders who will be successful at collaborating across boundaries will also be comfortable with diversity, reveling in differences, differences of ideas, people and methods.

Recommendations

For our world to develop strong leadership capability, I have two specific recommendations.

First, step up our efforts to research leadership not as an individualistic entity but in the context of the systems in which leaders operate. We can no longer afford to be myopic in our views—that our 'western' culture is the best method, the best economy, the best way.

Second, examine leadership development—be mindful of how we develop our leaders. Develop networked educational opportunities between business, universities, government and nonprofits to provide open space to dialogue and reflect on self, organization and what it means to lead.

References

Barrett, F. J. "Creativity and Improvisation in Jazz and Organizations: Implications for Organizational Learning." *Organization Science* 9 (no. 5), 1998: 605–622.

Weick, K. E. "Improvisation as a Mindset for Organization Analysis." *Organization Science* 9(no. 5), 1998: 543–555.

Alcoholic Anonymous. New York: A.A. World Services, 1976.

Argyris, C. *Organizational Learning: A Theory of Action Perspective.* Reading, MA: Addison-Wesley, 1976.

———. *Overcoming Organizational Defenses.* Englewood Cliffs, NJ: Prentice Hall, 1990.

Bateson, G. *Mind and Nature.* New York: Dutton, 1979.

Bennis, W. B., and Patricia Ward *Organizing Genius: The Secrets to Creative Collaboration.* Reading, MA: Addison-Wesley, 1996.

Bohm, D. *On Dialogue.* New York: Routledge, 1996.

Bryman, A. *Handbook of Organization Studies.* Thousand Oaks, CA: Sage, 1996.

Capra, F. *The Web of Life.* New York: Anchor, 1996.

Cashman, K. *Leadership from the Inside Out: Becoming A Leader for Life.* Provo, UT: Publishers Press., 1998.

Clegg, S. R., and Cynthia Hardy. *Handbook of Organization Studies.* Thousand Oaks, CA: Sage, 1996.

Csikszentmihalyi, M. Flow: *The Psychology of Optimal Experience.* New York: HarperCollins, 1990.

Deming, W. E. *The New Economics: for Industry, Government, Education.* Cambridge, MA: Institute of Technology Center for Advanced Engineering Study, 1993.

Drucker, P. F. "Management's New Paradigms." *Forbes* (October 5, 1998): 152–177.

–––. *Management Challenges for the Twenty-First Century.* New York: Harper Business, 1999.

Gadamer, H. *Truth and Method.* New York: Seabury Press, 1975.

Gardner, H. "Who Owns Intelligence?" *Atlantic Monthly* 283 (2), 1999: 67–76.

Goodman, G. W. "Sonny Rollins at Sixty-Eight: Reformed, Redeemed, and Ready for Reincarnation." *Atlantic Monthly* 284 (no. 1), 1999: 82–88.

Greenleaf, R. *Servant Leadership: A Journey into the Nature of Legitimate Power and Greatness.* New York: Paulist Press, 1977.

Hall, D. T. *Sources of Executive Learning. Leadership Development.* University of Minnesota, Boston University, 1996.

Haskins, M. E., Jeanne Liedke, and John Rosenblum. "Beyond Teams: Toward an Ethic of Collaboration." *Organizational Dynamics* (spring 1998): 34–50.

Heifetz, R. A. *Leadership without Easy Answers.* Cambridge, MA: The Belknap Press of Harvard University Press, 1994.

Herzberg, F. "One More Time: How Do You Motivate Employees?" *Harvard Business Review* 65(5), 1987: 109–120.

Holland, J. H. (1998). *Emergence: From Chaos to Order.* Reading, MA: Helix, 1998.

Jaworski, J. *Synchronicity: The Inner Path of Leadership.* San Francisco: Berrett-Koehler, 1996.

Kegan, R. *In Over Our Heads: The Mental Demands of Modern Life.* Cambridge, MA: Harvard University Press, 1994.

Morgan, G. *Images of Organization.* Thousand Oaks, CA: Sage, 1998.

Quinn, R. E., Spreitzer, Gretchen M. "The Road to Empowerment: Seven Questions Every Leader Should Consider." *Organizational Dynamics* (fall 1997): 37–49.

Rowe, W. E. "Domains of Transformation: Development of a Model and Measures for Assessing 'Transformative Change' Resulting from the Experiences of Significant Interpersonal Conflict." *In Human and Organization Development.* Santa Barbara, CA: Fielding Institute, 1999.

Senge, P. (1990). *The Fifth Discipline.* New York: Doubleday, 1990.

Tep, B. *Spirituality Retreat.* North Branch, MN, Spirituality Retreat, 1999.

Tichy, N. M. *Managing Strategic Change: Technical, Political, and Cultural Dynamics.* New York: Wiley, 1983.

Vaill, P. B. *Learning As a Way of Being.* San Francisco: Jossey-Bass, 1996.

Varela, F. J., E. Thompson, and E. Rosch. *The Embodied Mind: Cognitive Science and Human Experience.* Cambridge, MA: MIT Press, 1997.

Weisbord, M. R. *Productive Workplaces: Organizing and Managing for Dignity, Meaning, and Community.* San Francisco: Jossey-Bass, 1987.

Wheatley, M. *Leadership and the New Science.* San Francisco: Barrett-Koehler, 1992.

Zuboff, S. *In the Age of the Smart Machine.* New York: Basic Books, 1988.

Steven Jeddeloh

Steven Jeddeloh has over 20 years experience in helping individuals and organizations improve performance. He has been a business leader, a small business owner as well as a Human Resources Manager and Consultant, providing Strategic Planning and Implementation of Large Scale Change Initiatives, Business Transformation, Total Quality Initiatives, and Building Effective Teams.

Mr. Jeddeloh contributed to two training modules published by Hazelden Publishing: *Chemical Health on the College Campus*, a strategy for system change, and *Roots and Wings*, methods for effective parenting. Other modules include *Building High Performance Teams, Conflict Resolution, Engaging the Total Organization in Strategic Planning*, and *Dealing with Continuous Change*.

Mr. Jeddeloh received two Master's Degrees from the University of Minnesota in both Education and Organization Development. He has continued his studies in Organization Development, Total Quality and Change Strategies, and is currently completing a Doctorate in Human and Organization Development.

CHAPTER NINE

Craig and Wallys agrees with the premise put forth by Dan Hanson in Chapter 4, that today, despite conspicuous wealth and a healthy Nasdaq, the vast majority of Americans are unhappy and unfulfilled at work. Many of us are addicted to work, but are enjoying it less. Creating and distributing material wealth seems to be all that matters. Not surprisingly, this emphasis on materialism has resulted in unprecedented levels of ethical, moral and spiritual decadence, as well as a feeling of emptiness and powerlessness so familiar to addicts of all descriptions. But there is hope. A transformational revolution in consciousness has already begun. Fueled by a spiritual renaissance in America and by a powerful movement for corporate social responsibility, "conscious businesses" are emerging that understand the "humanness" of their enterprises and the critical need to foster an economy based not on exploitation and extraction, but on the principles of sustainable living. Among those leading this revolution will be the millions of people in recovery who have already exhibited the courage to accept change and to allow personal transformation to happen.

—Editor

The Essential Path: Linking Personal and Workplace Transformation

Craig Neal

A Few Perspectives at the Outset

Business in America appears to be booming. For some time now the Dow Jones has had the 12,000-point mark in its crosshairs. Unemployment and inflation are at historic lows. Opportunities abound for entrepreneurs. Confidence in business and economic growth is high. Yet, an honest inventory of the workplace reveals disturbing, unhealthy trends—most notably, widespread dissatisfaction with the work environment and the gap between workplace and personal values. There is thus a shadowy side, a soft underbelly, an uneasiness at the foundation of our economic good fortune that few people want to face. Unless there is a shift toward sustainability and away from our current focus on material wealth as the sole aim of our economic system, the widening disconnect between personal visions and workplace values will intercept our progress and undermine our organizations. Prosperity will then become more illusive.

An Activist Agenda

This chapter calls for participation in the revolution of consciousness already underway among individuals and organizations. This revolution is moving our workplaces and our society toward a higher plane. As a political, social, and educational activist guiding and nurturing grassroots and professional organizations, I have witnessed the influence individuals and organizations have in creating the kind of world in which they want to live. My twenty-five years of leadership inside socially responsible companies such as The Garden Way Companies, Rodale Press, and the *Utne Reader* magazine have convinced me that companies can indeed "do well by doing good." The opportunities business provides are a significant new form of leadership in our society. As a founding member of the now fourteen-hundred-member-strong Business for Social Responsibility, founder of the Conscious Business Alliance, and active member of the Social Venture Network, I understand how broad and deep is the reservoir of sensitivity and goodwill within the business sector. Today we are ready to tackle even the most daunting challenges and capable of sensing the unrest beneath our smooth veneer of success.

As a society, and as individuals and organizations, we can reverse the negatives and enhance the positives, thereby helping to create a world that works for more people on a more regular basis. A positive shift is occurring because of a largely untapped source of energy: the awakening of personal and spiritual consciousness. This growing movement has the potential to stimulate broad institutional self-examination, create environments of truth and wisdom within our organizations, and move people and institutions to reach their highest purpose.

Transformation Is Fundamental Change

The revolution that is underway is a massive cultural, social, and economic transformation. It is important to distinguish *transformation* from *change*. These terms are not interchangeable. As

Marilyn Mason articulates in Chapter 5, *transformation* means going from one state to another. It assumes the need for a fundamental shift to another level of action. *Change* is a variation of a situation, while transformation is an alteration of its essence. The transformation of essence is a change of consciousness. It is preceded by an insight—the insight that creates the change that is needed. Transforming thoughts are lasting and serve as fundamental insights—an actual rebirthing.

A Transformational Tool: Essential Meetings

Because of its dominance in our world today, business or organizational life has a singular role to play as the delivery system in effecting a new era in which people can find the meaning they seek from life and work. Meetings at any level are the most common means through which business is conducted and through which change ultimately occurs within an organization. The ways we conduct our meetings communicate our organizations' values. By simply shifting the focus and intent of how we meet from merely tactical, action-oriented sessions to deeper, more essential articulations of our visions, we can create essential gatherings, large and small, within organizations that can, in fact, transform the nature of our relationships and ultimately our organizations. These "essential meetings" (EMs) are a new synthesis of both ancient forms and modern organizational techniques reflecting many traditions. Organizations can begin to leverage the transformational work in which individuals have been engaging, free innate sources of human intelligence, model the values they wish to practice, and support individuals by providing an environment of caring, truth and courage as they endeavor to tackle the difficult issues in this time of great change.

The Workplace in the Throes of Change

Moving successfully toward a desirable future requires a firm grasp on current realities and emerging developments. It is important to recognize that in modern society, we have been condoning a legitimized schizophrenia within ourselves and our organizations. Everyone in business has felt it—that uneasy sensation of putting on a mask, of playing the game, of donning the suit to do what one seems to have to do to be successful. We have tended to accept this artificial separation between work and life. As Barbara Bailey Reinhold has pointed out in her book, *Toxic Work*, burnout and stress are among the results. Stress is linked to chronic illnesses and pain such as hypertension, heart disease, headaches, and arthritis. The American Institute of Stress (AIS) has documented that 75 to 90 percent of employee visits to hospitals are for ailments related to stress.

It is no surprise that for most Americans work is not a happy place. A recent Roper Starch Worldwide Survey reports that barely one-quarter of the working adult population is satisfied with their work. The most satisfied individuals, according to a 1997 Gallup survey, are those who work for smaller firms or own their own companies. Many come face to face with troubling issues at the workplace. A 1996 Gallup poll showed that one of every four employees is angry at work. Another 1996 survey found that only one-third of workers perceived management as trustworthy and fair minded. Research consistently reveals a gap between the high value managers claim to hold for people as assets and the low importance actually given to efforts to develop their employees. Employee concerns routinely receive low rankings in action plans.

Yet, Americans are working more. In her definitive book *The Overworked American*, Harvard economist Juliet Schor cites research indicating that from 1969 to 1987, the average worker added the equivalent of one full month of extra work—163 hours annually. In addition, it is more difficult to separate one's so-called work life from one's personal life. For many Americans, "workaholism" is as serious and growing a problem as alcoholism or drug abuse. Hard work and long hours are unhealthy when people confuse their inner essence with the position and rewards they seek. Defining one's life and one's value as one's work, especially if the work is defined as a maniacal seeking for growth and material goods, leads to a flatness, a feeling of deadness in the pursuit. We as a society live to work; we don't work to live.

Despite outward signs of success, businesses and institutions are experiencing considerable internal turmoil. Many companies have made a practice of instituting constant change in an effort to keep up with the turbulence in their industries. Even in 1994, before the pace of change had accelerated to today's levels, four out of five companies reported being in the midst of major change. Yet, in that same year, a Gallup/Proudfoot study found more than half of the executives they polled had doubts about their firms' ability to address changes.

In our new "first-to-market," service-oriented economy, in which an institution's major assets are human knowledge, information, and creativity, corporations are being held to a higher level of accountability. Companies that are aware of the dichotomy between personal values and professional life fear getting eaten from the inside out. They fear an implosion. As individuals seek change and some opt out of the rat race, companies and organizations, for their own part, are struggling with two critical and interrelated management issues: retention of the best people and improvement of productivity.

Clearly, the schizophrenia that we condone and the unhealthy, unsustainable environment in which it operates have a destructive impact on both individuals and the institutions in which they work. As a society, we are at, or close to, our tolerance level of these conditions.

Reflecting on the Legacy of Materialism

Organizations as we know them now are relatively new, a hallmark of the industrial age. Those who created them did so out of innocence, not malice, to make sense of conditions confronting society. Our organizations are structured in most part around the principles of creating and distributing material wealth. Currently, the prevailing theory is that if enough material wealth is created for enough people it will, through its own momentum, trickle down, positively affecting the population and culture. In reality, we have created ever-increasing material abundance for most people in this country. It has not, however, resulted in a collective inner well-being.

Most organizations and businesses operate in a material, intellectually based paradigm, isolating the spiritual, soulful, heartful aspects of life and work. Business's traditional *modus operandi* depends on an extremely high level of unconsciousness to core human values and morality to maintain acceptance of the status quo—the rules, the regulations, the immediate linear solutions. To the degree that people remain oblivious to the missed opportunities and the real damage that our ways of doing business create, society is condemned to be locked into historical repetition of the missteps of the past.

Outside-in Perspective

Most of our organizations operate from a competitive notion of self preservation, as if life and death were in the balance at all times if their goals are not achieved. Individuals' self worth, the worth of the organization, and success all seem to hinge upon our complying to outwardly oriented values.

World cultures are linked through an intricate and interdependent web of commercial and economic imperatives. Today's cultural heroes are business tycoons and entrepreneurs, along with entertainers and athletes. We seem to be operating in a perpetual global cycle of "doingness." People have become addicted to thinking that the point of life is to achieve external goals and possessions. Many believe that the outer world will ultimately nourish the inner world. We expect someone or something to supply the answers for which we yearn. Quite often the seeking and the acts of daily life cover up that yearning. Rather, we might look inside for the answers.

Common perception is from the outside-in when we should be considering the inside-out.

Fear

Currently, the dominant reality in the workplace is fear; not just fear of one's inability to keep up with the rapidly changing business and technological environment, and fear of possible reorganizations or downsizing, but also fear at the personal level, of revealing one's vulnerabilities, of seeming out of line, of getting too close to others, of standing up for what seems right. Management commonly uses fear as the ultimate motivator; however, fear can be abused and all consuming, driving people into a perpetual state of stress and anxiety.

Fear contributes mightily to the stasis in business regarding the values gap. To overcome the overriding fear and achieve greater balance, our organizations must create and nurture cultures of courage, safe environments in which people know themselves, have a sense of what must be done and possess the courage to act on their convictions, and are supported in doing so.

Powerlessness

Lacking a sense of genuine personal power, people feel less and less like individuals in this cookie-cutter culture. Yet, ironically, we are emerging through technology and more decentralized organizations into the age of the individual, of the company of one, of diversity and entitlement. The material security we experience in our society at the moment goes hand in hand with unprecedented levels of moral, spiritual, and ethical decadence. This is a human tragedy. Many people feel lost, unconnected, and not whole as human beings.

Our traditional organizational structure is quickly becoming outdated, in large part due to an inaccurate sense of the essential nature of the human being. Command and control management techniques are increasingly less effective. In the new global business environment, organizations must tap into every aspect of their human and creative resources. Organizations are the manifest reflection of their individuals. Leaders who are clear that their organizations are, in fact, living organisms will profit in the coming millennium.

Accelerators of Transformation

Nothing short of a revolution in consciousness will get us out of the deep rut we have created for ourselves. This revolution is a radical change in thinking and perceiving, an awakening to better ways of carrying out our human purpose and the positive roles our organizations can play in fostering a sustainable society. This revolution is, in fact, transformational because it requires a complete shift in consciousness. The self-examination many individuals have undertaken is an essential building block in the evolution of our culture.

At the personal level, individuals are seeking self-actualization, transformational experiences, and health and balance, and are examining every aspect of their lives. Our workplaces, where so much of our time and energy are expended, can be powerful venues through which individuals can carry out their purpose. Organizations through their workers can likewise move to higher ground via collective awakenings.

Forces are already moving in the direction of organizational transformation. Each individual can play a significant role in this effort regardless of his or her position in society or its organizations. One of the key accelerators of transformation is the convergence of two major social movements—one operating in the culture at large and one affecting organizational life.

America's Spiritual Renaissance

The first powerful movement now influencing the workplace is America's spiritual renaissance. Interest in religion is on the rise virtually everywhere. The Princeton Religious Research Center documents that almost two-thirds of Americans say that religion has a growing influence in their lives. A large segment of the population has participated in the recovery movement, a process involving considerable self-examination and values clarification in which trust in a Higher Power plays a significant role. In 1992, there were some fifty thousand chapters of AA alone, and over 500,000 support, self-help, and recovery groups of all kinds in operation. A *Christian Science Monitor* article the same year documented 140 different kinds of support groups in the United States with approximately forty-five million members. The millions in this great social movement of self-realization and empowerment are a potentially powerful force for change in organizations.

Furthermore, there has been a thirty-year trend toward the exploration of personal spirituality, with individuals turning inward for guidance; listening for intuitive wisdom; embracing a wide array of personal practices such as prayer, body awareness, and meditation; and accepting individual responsibility for serving the collective good. In fact, this large social movement—which public opinion researcher Paul H. Ray for the Institute of Noetic Sciences and the Fetzer Institute identified as led by the "cultural creatives" in studies done on the emergence of transformational values in America—encompasses nearly one-fourth of American adults, or forty-four million persons.

Corporate Social Responsibility

The second important development influencing the workplace is the movement for corporate social responsibility. For over two decades, this movement has encouraged businesses to play a role in improving their communities. It calls upon companies to use their power, contribution dollars, and employees to take stands on important social issues in an attempt to effect change in the organization, community, workplace, marketplace, and environment. Well-established organizations such as Business for Social Responsibility and The Social Venture Network provide opportunities for such companies to learn from one another and create programs for change.

Conscious Business Movement

These two powerful forces—America's spiritual renaissance and corporate social responsibility—have been running on parallel but separate tracks until recently. Their fusion is spawning a third movement, known as "conscious business." This revolutionary awakening supports the actions of corporate social responsibility, encompassing the convergence of values-centered, spirit-infused ideas to improve the business environment. It also supports efforts to have our workplaces take on more responsibility for nurturing the human spirit and soul. The conscious business movement connects personal and organizational transformation. It aligns the best interests of companies with the needs of employees. It also is focused internally, on making the work-place one in which the highest personal values of employees are upheld.

Committed companies and organizations are finding ways to integrate conscious business practices into their day-to-day operations companywide. Aveda Corporation, Quad/Graphics, Dreyer's Ice Cream, and Tires Plus are examples of the organizations that are committed to workplace and organizational transformation. Other companies have pockets of enlighten-ment—approachable managers, empathetic department heads, networks of managers who are implementing conscious business practices. Recently, several hundred CEOs and global business leaders called for members of the world business community to sign a resolution entitled *The Twenty-First-Century Agenda for Business: A Global Referendum for New Corporate Values and Priorities.* This resolution envisions socially responsible policies and holistic management approaches based on principles of servant leadership, learning organizations, evolutionary corporations, and conscious organizations.

Integration of Management Theory with New Science

There have been considerable evolutionary leaps in the science of management, which now embraces such new concepts as chaos theory and self-organizing systems, as elucidated by Margaret Wheatley and Myron Kellner-Rogers.

Chaos theory comes directly out of physics, and the new science and self-organizing systems originate with biology and the study of the natural world. Both concepts are now finding their way into business and organizational theory, helping us understand that organizations are organisms capable of living and dying. These concepts also teach us that information and relationships are critical to organizations. This unlikely marriage of science, natural forces and management is another instance in which business and our other cultural expressions are becoming more integrated.

People and organizations are so poised for change that only a slight but crucial shift in confidence and courage is needed to transform the workplace and to bring about a new reality. This shift can occur when, on the one hand, people realize they no longer have to live in fear in the workplace and when, on the other, business decides it can be successful and operate on sustainable principles without human or natural exploitation. Essential meetings (EMs), discussed later in this chapter, are a means of leveraging these trends within the framework of current organizational structures.

Economic and Organizational Change: A Call for Sustainability

The exploitation of human and natural resources has been fueling a good deal of our economic growth over the last hundred years, resulting in increased limitations in natural resources. We can no longer afford to perpetuate an economy based on the principles of exploitation and extraction. As we navigate into the new millennium, the key question is not how to disassociate ourselves from the negative forces in our work organizations so that we can survive and thrive outside the organization. Rather, it is how we can live our purpose in and through the organization, since it is and will continue to be a central aspect of modern life. The awakening of organizations will be a realization that to be truly successful in this millennium, nearly everything we hold true will need to be reexamined, including how we measure the bottom line. Will our society have the insight organizationally and collectively, and then the courage, to act on that insight?

A sustainable economic system is one that reverses current exploitive, extractive practices based on obsolescence and reaches a system of renewal and regeneration, based on whole systems and natural laws that can bring us into balance. Business economics have been operating on short-term payback horizons for over a hundred years, glorifying financial return on investment (ROI) as the key indicator of health. Using the natural laws of regeneration, or self-renewing systems, it is time now to look instead at the big picture. Already emerging is a healthy new way of looking at organizations as being more organic, decentralized, and synergistic in nature, creating partnerships or relationships based on mutual trust, not fear. The only companies that can thrive in the long run are sustainable organizations that nourish individuals and are as concerned with the long-term impact on society and culture of their actions as with their financial returns. We need to begin slowly to embrace the overarching principles of a sustainable environment and adapt practices such as those espoused by the Natural Step, an environmentally based process for managing successful and sustainable entities.

Business and society collectively have done phenomenally well mastering much of the material plane. Now is the time to master the internal frontier. Much has been said about how to extract and exploit, create more product, sell more product, and turn a profit. What is not in place is how to tap latent aspects in our organizations and individuals, aspects that take into account the spiritual, physical, and environmental well-being of the organization and, therefore, its impact on the individual and the planet.

I propose we literally transform the consciousness of our organizations beyond overlying short-term, feel-good programs or "best practices." We can do this by questioning and revitalizing the fundamental vision, mission, goals, and objectives of the organization. It is imperative that our organizations begin to function out of wisdom, compassion, and basic respect for the human condition. They must exist to serve the highest values of humanity and our collective best interests.

Linking Personal and Workplace Transformation

It is abundantly clear that individuals and organizations are already in a transformational process and that these searches are inextricably linked.

The evolution of personal transformation is an awakening of consciousness to what I call the prior condition: who we really are when in the fully conscious state. There is an innate desire for the self to make sense of and to know itself. This is the nature of consciousness at both the individual and the collective level. This seems to be our inner job. It is our birthright as human beings to realize our full human potential. In our organizations, self-realization and fulfillment are about understanding the nature of the self and how we fit into the larger whole.

On the new frontier, our priorities shift away from fulfilling external, material needs and gratifications and toward discovering our inner self. People tend to think they need to change themselves, when actually all that is needed is to bring to the surface what is already inside. We each possess the collective wisdom of the centuries; we just need to awaken to that fact. The main obstacle is fear—of finding out that we are eternal, connected to all things in the interdependent web of life, and that we might discover untapped power ready to be ignited. Opening to this awareness is often the first insight, which may be followed by the recognition that we don't live this way, that our lives, in fact, don't work well. This recognition parallels the important First Step in the transformational Twelve Step process.

Many people are coming to realize that we can have surprising control over ourselves and our future. As human beings, we may already know what to do and how to do it. However, we may lack the courage, the support, and the environment needed to do it. The bottom line is taking personal responsibility. By being true to ourselves and demonstrating what we believe in, we can influence others by example and thus change the environment around us. That is the essence of personal power. The shift that is needed among individuals is one of awareness—seeing things in a different light, as individuals and in our affiliation with organizations. The insight is the leverage point, the moment of realization that our new perception of reality seems to be working.

Elements common to personal growth and transformation are directly reflected in organizational transformation. Organizations, like individuals, are living organisms in constant change. Nowadays, in the era of the "fast company," organizations must change constantly to survive in the marketplace, yet most inherently avoid chaos. Organizational transformation can take many forms. One way is to elevate and make visible the basic humanity of all those in the workplace. If we do not value people in organizations enough, it is a reflection of the extent to which we undervalue ourselves and our potential for carrying out our higher purpose.

Organizations need environments of honesty and clarity where ideas can be shared on short-term goals and long-term objectives. Individuals who are clear on their own purpose and higher selves are in the best position to contribute to these discussions. What is needed right now is for our organizations to reflect the elevated consciousness that the individual is working with and through.

Toward a Congruence of Values

Business can no longer just take care of business, nor can society just take care of society. We live in a global environment in which we are increasingly interconnected and interdependent. The idea that there should be linkage between the values of organizations and the values of their people is not new. However, with the advent of the self-managed "knowledge worker" as the linchpin in the new economy, there is an economic as well as personal benefit to congruency. Peter Drucker, the dean of organizational management, argues this point in his 1999 book *Management Challenges for the Twenty-First Century.*

To link individuals to organizations and to society at large, we must have a vision of ourselves as an important piece in a larger whole and a vision of the changes we would like to see in our environment that will, in turn, support us in our individual journeys. We are social creatures who come together in organizations and workplaces to share our highest manifestation, our highest yearning in our life to create something that is bigger than any one of us. That is the ultimate purpose of all organizations.

The journey can be difficult. Organizations do a poor job in adapting to or utilizing self-actualized people, primarily because the personal priorities of these people may not be aligned with the priorities of the organization. Often, leaders are the most self-actualized through their wider, strategic perspectives and, therefore, the most torn within their organizations. They have achieved their positions after enduring the rigors of being tested as a warrior in the prevailing culture—often finding themselves in the limelight, microphone thrust into their faces, having to defend a paradigm they do not fully accept. Decisions—not about what is right or wrong, but what is best for the organization—have to be taken within an environment of fear, which most people do not recognize for what it really is.

Our organizations are fast realizing that to become cultures of caring and courage as described by Carol Pine in Chapter 4, wisdom must be honored, because in wisdom comes an inherent sense of self-sustainability. When organizations nurture this cultural expression, they are able to utilize the full potential of their healthy employees and maximize the impact of individual transformation.

Organizational Cultures of Courage

Organizations can create conditions that are congruent with institutional and personal goals, supporting individual transformation and allowing individual fulfillment to play a part in the collective wisdom. These are organizations where people:

- Can deal with even the hard issues'

- Are encouraged to know themselves and be themselves

- Feel safe in their diversity

- Understand the work they do in its relationship to the mission of the organization and its global impact

- Are nurtured to be fully healthy human beings

- Recognize the interdependent relationship with their co-workers

- Can realize shared understandings and shared goals

- Feel their contributions are valued

- Are aware of the past and have a stake in the future of the organization

- Understand the nature of fear and its debilitating effects

If you are a leader in a position to influence the direction of your organization, you can make considerable progress toward realizing this vision by:

- Becoming fully aware of all the realities in your organization

- Communicating your own personal values and letting people know you as a whole human being

- Encouraging open discussion about values and principles that people would like to see underlying organizational action

- Creating an impenetrable container of safety and respect for the people in the organization, where fear is acknowledged and people are free to be vulnerable and allow their true self to emerge

This kind of environment will foster a richer, more diverse organization, one in which people will know themselves individually and collectively and in which both individual and institution will be working to realize shared understanding and shared goals.

Bringing Wisdom into Our Organizations

Meetings are still the dominant means of communication in our society and a most telling indicator of organizational culture. In our work with individuals and organizations, we have created a new form, called Essential Meetings (EMs), that by design brings to the surface and uses the collective wisdom that is inherent when groups of people meet. These meetings are a means through which people in every organization can integrate that enlightenment with the flourishing of the organization—materially, socially, and culturally. This new form synthesizes traditional methods for business meetings with indigenous council ceremony and modern organizational development practices influenced by Peter Senge's work with learning organizations, David Bohm's work with dialogue, and open space technology as espoused by Harrison Owen, among others. EMs create the environment and groundedness for an organization's work while retaining the highest level of individual inspiration. They have been an important breakthrough model that works in the Age of Information but leads us into cultures of caring and wisdom.

EMs provide a forum for exploring the common experience. The impetus is that people are starving for real dialogue about how to deal with the rapidity and unrelenting nature of constant change in their life and work. Sometimes new leadership, downsizing, an industry challenge, or a corporate reorganization is the catalyst for creating these safe places where people can explore their values in relation to their work.

Storytelling is a key element of EMs. Many great cultures, if not all, have been passed on through the oral tradition. The strength of storytelling is the direct communication of ideas and concepts from one person to another, through repetition and embellishment, from generation to generation. Everyone is a teacher, a learner, and a leader.

The format is simple. Cohorts are invited to engage through discourse on issues of compelling interest to them. A brief conversation starter sets the stage by addressing the theme of the EM from three perspectives:

- What is a compelling issue facing our organization today?
- How is the organization addressing this issue—its successes and failures?
- How am I dealing with this issue? What are my successes and failures?

Dialoging through a series of large and small circles, participants gradually open to share experiences, observations, and responses with other members and attendees. Participants share thoughts and insights as individuals and in groups. A portion of each session is designed to respond to attendees' most immediate concerns. Continuous feedback tools allow participants to provide insights, make suggestions for future meetings, and exchange concerns anonymously.

In EMs, the setting of a safe container nurtures the wisdom of the group to manifest itself. These meetings are a method for mirroring healthy behavior to one another, a safe container that provides the opportunity to bring to the surface the innate creativity, knowledge, and intelligence lying dormant and ready to emerge. Individuals working in a setting of mutual trust and respect are far more likely to integrate the richness of their personal values with the value system at work.

Those who have participated in these gatherings have found a safe haven because EMs provide a respite from the conflict most people feel in the workplace. Some participants come to the meetings having already undergone a deep process of personal transformation on their own; yet they are reluctant to share their inner contemplation for fear of being seen as soft or unprofessional.

EMs are a new communications pipeline into, around, and out of organizations—a new element in the massive message delivery system that already exists through organizations in our society. They allow individuals to express their technical know-how while linking inner values and gathering strength from other individuals. This can reverse the "garbage-in-garbage-out" (GIGO) syndrome from which our communications pipelines have long suffered. The capability for human beings to adapt, grow, and prosper is dependent on the level to which they can communicate their humanity in all its forms.

At a deeper level, EMs bring our personal transformational light to the surface, helping to create cultures of courage within our organizations. An inevitable outcome of EMs is the speaking of truth. In what may have seemed a highly personal process, our vulnerability now becomes a shared asset. In the presence of support and safety, what only minutes ago may have seemed painfully personal becomes common knowledge and experience. In the absence of fear, connection to and a recognition of our interdependent condition emerges. Self-revelation in the midst of others is the outcome. We already have the answers within us. We must simply reveal them to ourselves.

There is no technique; rather, a letting go, a suspension of belief, and an opening to the essence of our common condition. Empathy and compassion come into play. It is our experience that a shift in consciousness occurs spontaneously in the group when people speak the truth about their personal condition. Individual insights emerge in a collective way to heighten the dialogue. Truth becomes manifest. A collective sense of wisdom develops of the right thing to do. The outcome is a shared, elevated sense of well-being.

Organizations do have the capability to release the wisdom of the well intentioned. Processes like EMs will work in a wide variety of settings—static smokestack industries desperate for a new lease on life, high-growth "fast companies" that must create a vision from scratch for how they want to operate, and even start-up shops that capitalize on their unique qualities and human-scale relationships.

EMs are a way for people to find one another and then to move ahead with confidence and courage.

The Essential Meeting (EM) Model

The more static we are in our everyday environment, the less we are able to focus on the fundamentals and the less aware or conscious we become of our own condition. Essential Meetings are a valuable means for removing ourselves from the fray to achieve clarity of purpose.

Creating the Container of Safety

Creating the container of safety is a deliberate and conscious acknowledgment that we must design places in which leadership and freedom can emerge. Inside is a realm where participants have permission to tell their truth. We create containers of safety for ourselves through personal practice—a religious faith, for example, or meditation that allows us to discover our essence or spirit. Organizations need tools to do the same. Traditional gathering techniques do not explore deeply enough or take into account the inner life within the organization.

The nature of the invitation to EMs is important, as is the expression of the principles by which these group experiences will operate. Getting those willing to step inside the container for the first time requires leaders who engender faith and confidence and who possess both a track record of trustworthiness and an expanded vision of the organization beyond short-term interests.

Giving Permission through Leadership

Active leadership becomes more important once the container is created—a leadership of vision, values, compassion, and clarity. A successful EM is characterized by attendees who can come from where they are in their history and are able to be exactly who they are in that moment, free to explore what is really alive and essential inside each of them. Leadership provides by example the permission to speak freely and be honest. Part of leadership's role is to be aware of the underlying fear. Most organizations negate fear and so are condemned to live with its many manifestations. The entrainment process—the integration of body, mind, and spirit—naturally occurs in the absence of fear.

The leader who understands the need for affiliation and group support either is aware or intuits a law of human development—the yearning to bear collective witness. As a society, we do not awaken alone. We do it together, and the same is true of organizations. It is important that members model for one another our highest selves, our highest being, which is present but may not have been allowed to surface, and to support that behavior in one another. It is this new concept in group purpose that makes these meetings so unique and potentially powerful.

Shift in Consciousness

As discussion continues in this contained environment of acceptance, forgiveness, trust, and freedom, people begin to discover their deepest bond—their humanity. This is where a profound shift of consciousness begins to occur. People open up to one another, sharing their challenges, hopes, and aspirations, and begin to understand that they all share a common experience. There is an awakening to the possibility of an entire new culture. When hearts and minds are open, empathy and compassion emerge.

The Expression of Truth

Being in the presence and articulation of wisdom is the most challenging place to be for both an individual or an organization. We come to a place of awareness and awakening, but are we prepared to take responsibility for that? This is where courage is essential. Courage is born out of knowing one's essential self, usually in an atmosphere of support. The spontaneous expression of truth provides wisdom and, therefore, support. Without that foundation, nothing of lasting consequence can happen within any organization.

Thus, action—or transformation in organizations—comes after people have arrived at wisdom, courage and support. Without the nurturing environment, it is hard to initiate or sustain individual or organizational change.

Realization of Common Experience

The awakening of insight into one's true nature in the presence of others is a powerful and profound experience. It is as if lights turn on around the meeting room, sparking the realization of the common experience. When we allow ourselves the possibility of sharing our higher self and all that it brings, the collective experience paves the way for the possibility of true organizational transformation.

Awakening to the Possibility of Transformation

The bottom line is that EMs open the door for personal insight, the awakening to shared experience, and the common realization that transformation is, in fact, possible. Personal awakening, insight, and personal growth are linked to the awakening of other people. This is not a top-down effort to effect change, but rather a transformation of the systemic makeup of the human community within the organization as it comes to a collective awakening and begins to make appropriate changes from that perspective. This collective awakening, which many may doubt is possible, can take place in the absence of fear and the presence of our higher selves. Each person leaves with something new—a spark of hope, the courage to act, the will to make a difference.

Heightening Awareness through Self-Examination

Individuals, leaders, and organizations can facilitate the transformational process and heighten their levels of awareness through intense self-examination, either within the context of the EM process or through individual practice.

For individuals who have awakened to a personal clarity of purpose, a logical issue to confront when working inside an organization is one of congruence of values. As challenges arise in the workplace, we ask ourselves, Are we in sync with the organization's values and do they fit with our own? How do I feel intellectually and emotionally? What is the response of my heart and gut? Am I energized by it, or does it shut me down?

Leaders can do a great deal inside the organization to foster an awakening. Having an honest conversation with oneself about what is working, what is not, and what are the contradictions can lead to the beginning of insight. Leaders can ask, What is my vision for my life? What is the vision of the organization and the practice to which I am aligning myself? How do those visions relate? Where are the issues still unresolved?

Organizations benefit, too, from this heightened level of self-awareness. New kinds of measurements emerge from a conscious inquiry and awakening. Organizations might ask, Are we strategically in place to thrive in twenty, fifty, or a hundred years? Are we contributing to our employees' health and well-being? Are we contributing to our community, our society? What is the impact of our products on the individual and collectively on the environment? Are we practicing sound and sustainable business and social practices? Are we taking care of the corporate body, mind, spirit, heart, and soul? Are they healthy?

What is so important about the personal growth and recovery movements are the potential outcomes. Recovering individuals, who are present in great numbers in our organizations, may be poised to become leaders in the organizational transformation process. They have already demonstrated the personal courage and strength to make change. They will be all the more sensitive when workplace values are in conflict with their own.

People who open up personally and begin to see how life works will begin to ask: Am I willing to make the changes that are needed in my life to start to affect the organization I am working with? The leader's responsibility to that question is to have the wherewithal, the information, and the personal integrity to take the next step, and then the courage to enter into dialogue with others. This juncture is one place where the exploratory, self-revelatory EM model applies so well.

At the Edge of Revolution

Is it worth taking all the individual and organizational risks to endeavor to achieve cultural change and transformation? Some would say there is no alternative—one either leads change or accepts the personal consequences of an unacceptable status quo. Some find fulfillment in living out their values, being true to themselves, and supporting others who do likewise. Some believe their actions will contribute toward productivity and competitive position in the marketplace. All of these motives and rationales for linking personal and workplace transformation are valid. However, the most powerful reason to reinforce one's personal practice through the workplace—or to begin to discover such practices in the company of others in the workplace—is the ultimate impact of more of us and our organizations operating sustainably, out of wisdom, in tune with universal principles, for the betterment of life on this planet.

I began by painting a dark picture of how miserable many people perceive the workplace to be today and how few people feel fulfilled. I believe staying the current course is leading to mutual destruction. But my message is a hopeful one. The modern workplace is poised to change for the better, first, because we have reached the limits of tolerance of the current situation, and second, because human beings are yearning to find and express their true spirit-infused selves. Transformation in the workplace is inextricably linked to personal transformation, and vice versa. Together, we can find ways—simple ways—to release the godliness in ourselves and others. Together, we can replace the culture of fear with cultures of courage. Together, we can unleash the wisdom to restore our organizations, ourselves, and our planet to health and balance.

Notes and References

The Garden Way Companies of Norwalk, Connecticut; Rodale Press of Emmaus, Pennsylvania: www.rodale.com; *Utne Reader* magazine of Minneapolis, Minnesota: www.utne.com.

Based in San Francisco, Business for Social Responsibility is a membership organization of companies seeking to sustain their commercial success in ways that demonstrate respect for ethical values, people, communities, and the environment. 415-537-0888 or: www.bsr.org. The Conscious Business Alliance, based in Edina, Minnesota, is a network of individuals and companies that gather in major business hubs to envision new models for linking business and spirit and to support one another in the pursuit of these goals. 612-925-5995. The Social Venture Network, also based in San Francisco, supports its members' efforts to seek ecological sustainability and workplace fulfillment, personal and spiritual growth, and social justice and to find a balance among the three, and helps members create new ventures that further these goals. 415-561-6501 or www.svn.org.

Cited in Barbara Bailey Reinhold, *Toxic Work: How To Overcome Stress, Overload and Burnout and Revitalize Your Career*, New York: Dutton, 1996.

Richard S. DeFrank and John M. Ivancevich, "Stress on the Job: An Executive Update," *Academy of Management*, August 1998, p. 55.

Amy Aronson, "A Shaky Economy, Or Just Frazzled Nerves?" *Working Woman*, April 1995, vol. 20, no. 4, p.16.

Michael Hopkins and Jeffrey L. Seglin, "Americans @ Work", *Inc., Annual Report1997*, vol. 19, no. 7, p. 77. Special Issue: The State of Small Business.

Elaine McShulskis, "Workplace Anger: A Growing Problem," *HRMagazine*, December 1996,, vol. 41, no. 7, p. 16.

John Draper, "The Cynical Work Force," *Communication World*, September 1996, vol. 13, no. 7, p. 26.

Juliet Schor. *The Overworked American: The Unexpected Decline of Leisure*, New York: Basic Books, 1992.

A 1994 survey found that more than four out of five U.S. firms were in the midst of major change, yet a Gallup/Proudfoot study in the same year found that more than half of the executives they surveyed had doubts about their firms' ability to address changes. Cited in Catherine Romano, "Managing Change, Divesity and Emotions," *Management Review*, July 1995, vol. 84, no. 7, p. 6. Also see Catherine Romano, "Change for Change's Sake?" *Management Review*, September 1994, vol. 83, no. 9, p. 9, reporting a Kepner Tregoe study of senior executives. Kenneth Marbler, "Change Management: Still a Scary Prospect," CMA: *The Management Accounting Magazine*, February 1994, vol. 68, no. 1, p. 27.

A 1997 analysis by the Princeton Religious Research Center of surveys conducted over a year by the Gallup Poll, cited in Bill Broadway, "Poll Finds America as Churched as Ever; Beliefs in God, Afterlife Have Changed Little Since 1947, but Faithful Sample More Forms of Spirituality," *The Washington Post*, May 31, 1997, Section B, p. 7, col. 1.

Documentation of the size of the recovery movement may be found in the following resources: Alice Dowd, "Making Room for Recovery," *Library Journal*, May 1, 1992, p. 49; Marilyn Gardner, "The Marketing of Recovery," *The Christian Science Monitor*, May 19, 1992, p 12; and, Ron Rhodes, "Recovering from the Recovery Movement," Reading from the *Scriptures Ministries* (posted on the Internet, no date).

Paul H. Ray. *The Integral Culture Survey: A Study of the Emergence of Transformational Values in America. Research Report* 96-A, Institute of

Noetic Sciences, Sausalito, California, in partnership with Fetzer Institute, Kalamazoo, Michigan, 1996.

For more information on conscious business events and regional networking opportunities, contact the Conscious Business Alliance, 612-925-5995.

Aveda Corporation of Minneapolis,: www.aveda.com; Quad/Graphics of Pewaukee, Wisconsin,: www.qg.com; Dreyer's Ice Cream of Oakland: www.dreyers.com; Tires Plus of Burnsville, Minnesota,: www.tiresplus.com.

Posted on the Internet on July 16, 1999, and signed initially by 225 international business leaders, the Agenda is available for reading and signing at: www.renesch.com/THE-AGENDA.

Margaret J. Wheatley, *Leadership and the New Science: Learning about Organization from an Orderly Universe*, San Francisco: Berrett-Koehler, 1992; Margaret J. Wheatley and Myron Kellner-Rogers. *A Simpler Way*, San Francisco: Berrett-Koehler, 1996. Wheatley and Kellner-Rogers are founders of The Berkana Institute (www.berkana.org), an educational and research foundation that supports collaborative research, new thinking, and practice about the organizing of human endeavor.

Brian Nattrass, Mary Altomare, and Brian Naijrass, *The Natural Step for Business: Wealth, Ecology and the Evolutionary Corporation*, Gabriola Island, BC: New Society Publishers, 1999. For more information on the natural step process and educational conferences, contact The Natural Step (TNS), a nonprofit organization headquartered in San Francisco. 415-561-3344, or www.naturalstep.org.

Trends and case studies covered in *Fast Company*, a monthly magazine published in partnership with *U.S. News and World Report*. 617-973-0300, or: www.fastcompany.com.

Peter Ferdinand Drucker, *Management Challenges for the Twenty-First Century*, New York: HarperCollins, 1999, pp. 158-159 and pp. 175-178.

Peter Senge, *The Fifth Discipline: The Art and Practice of the Learning Organization*, New York: Doubleday Books, 1994. David Bohm and Lee Nichol (editors), *On Dialogue*, London and New York: Routledge, 1996; Harrison Owen, *Expanding Our Now: The Story of Open Space Technology*, Berkeley, CA: North Atlantic Books, 1997.

Company References

Aveda Corporation of Minneapolis, Minnesota, www.aveda.com

Dreyer's Ice Cream of Oakland, California, www.dreyers.com

The Garden Way Companies of Norwalk, Connecticut

Quad/Graphics of Pewaukee, Wisconsin, www.qg.com

Rodale Press of Emmaus, Pennsylvania, www.rodale.com

Tires Plus of Burnsville, Minnesota, www.tiresplus.com

Utne Reader Magazine of Minneapolis, Minnesota, www.utne.com

Organizational References

The Berkana Institute (http://berkana.org), an educational and research foundation that supports collaborative research, new thinking and practice about the organizing of human endeavor founded by Margaret J. Wheatley and Myron Kellner-Rogers

Business for Social Responsibility, headquartered in San Francisco, California, is a membership organization of companies seeking to sustain their commercial success in ways that demonstrate respect for ethical values, people, communities and the environment. 415-561-3344, or www.bsr.org

The Conscious Business Alliance, based in Edina, Minnesota, is a network of individuals and companies that gather in major business hubs to envision new models for linking business and spirit, and to support one another in the pursuit of these goals. 612-925-5995.

The Natural Step (TNS), a nonprofit organization headquartered in San Francisco. 415-561-3344, or www.naturalstep.org.

The Social Venture Network, also based in San Francisco, supports its members' efforts to seek ecological sustainability and workplace fulfillment, personal and spiritual growth, and social justice and to find a balance among the three, and helps members create new ventures that further these goals. 415-561-6501 or www.svn.org.

Bibliographic References

Bibliographic references are provided in full on the Web site of The Heartland Institute, www.hearlandinstitute.com.

Craig Neal

Craig Neal is co-founder of the Heartland Institute in Minneapolis, with his wife and partner of 20 years, Patricia, to promote the reality that business and organizational life is the conduit and delivery system to a global renaissance as we enter the 21st century. Heartland produces the Thought Leader Gatherings™, a learning community of change agents and visionary Bay Area and Minnesota organizations. Members include Levi-Strauss, Medtronic, Sony Electronics, Honeywell, Seagate Technology, and Northern States Power among others. He also founded the Conscious Business Alliance, the Minnesota Magazine Publishers Association, and served as a board member of Business for Social Responsibility. He is a member of Social Venture Network and Business for Social Responsibility. Most recently he was Publisher of *Utne Reader* magazine.

Craig has written extensively in various books and journals, including an article entitled "A Conscious Change in the Workplace" published in the *Association of Quality and Participation Journal*, and a chapter entitled "Toward a Healthcare Revolution: Linking Personal Meaning with Workplace Transformation" in a book *(Managing Change in Healthcare)* published by McGraw-Hill.

In writing this chapter, Craig worked closely with his colleague, Wallys W. Conhaim, a strategic planner and futurist. In her 35-year career, Wallys, a co-owner of Conhaim Associates, Inc., has focused on assessing trends affecting businesses and institutions, helping organizations develop realistic views of the future, bringing leading-edge concepts into practice, and building capacity by using innovative participatory techniques that tap into a full range of human and information resources.

CHAPTER TEN

This chapter is concerned with change that is truly growth. A major dimension of growth must be a reduction in the sense of worry and fear so prevalent in the workplace today, a principle expounded in the two previous chapters and in the Twelve Steps. Another dimension is the need to integrate one's personal values and goals with the goals of the organization, and vice versa. Indeed it is management's responsibility to help employees integrate their goals with those of the organization. This is not a "natural law" to many executives today, but for change and growth to occur, existing power structures and cultures of control must be abolished. Change will occur in any event. Peter coins the term "white water" to define the world of continuous, swirling change we see all around us every day at work. The way through this white water, he argues, is found in the processes and language of the Twelve Steps, in a program of sustained recovery and growth based on one's personal and spiritual values.

—Editor

Change as Growth

Peter Vaill

*T*he *Human Side of Enterprise,* published in 1960 by Douglas McGregor, an MIT professor and management consultant, should be on anyone's short list of the most influential management books of the century. As announced in its title, McGregor's book persuasively attached top priority to a dimension of organizational life that, while not entirely ignored, had nonetheless played second fiddle to the idea that economic success was an organization's main purpose and that it could be achieved only through top-down direction and control.

McGregor proposed an alternative principle of integration and control where management was not seen as extracting effort from presumed sullen and recalcitrant employees. Rather, management was seen as responsible for helping employees to integrate their interests with those of the organization: Management's job is "the creation of conditions such that the members of the organization can achieve their own goals *best* by directing their efforts toward the success of the enterprise."

McGregor's principle is one of the first to claim that the so-called world of work can and should be a satisfying and fulfilling place, that there need be no fundamental opposition between the needs of a person and the needs of the organization. Moreover, though McGregor did not stress the point, other interpreters quickly saw that his argument did not apply just to lower-level workers. The principle of integration also could be applied to the exploding white-collar population that we have come to call "knowledge workers."

This principle of integration has been a guiding philosophy of enlightened management ever since. It is a cornerstone of the consulting profession known as organization development, which was just beginning to crystallize as a body of professional practice as McGregor's book was published. It is not an exaggeration to suggest that organizational change essentially has been viewed McGregor's way ever since: Change meant healing what he viewed as an artificial and unnecessary split between members of the organization and the organization itself.

This chapter is concerned with change that is truly growth. Certainly the many thousands of devotees of McGregor's principle would see it as promoting growthful change. In fact, as far as I know, the validity of McGregor's principle has never been challenged. Yet for several reasons, subsequent trends and events call his principle into question. In 1960, it was a radical idea for American management, but as we will see it may not have been radical enough. Indeed, if McGregor's principle has the weaknesses discussed below, it may be that our whole way of thinking about change as growth in the organizational world needs to change. This chapter, in other words, raises the question of whether humanistic management and all the thousands of dedicated people who have believed in it have been on the wrong track for the past forty years.

Are contemporary beliefs about organizational life and about change a path of growth? If they are not, what needs to change in our thinking? I do not have an elaborate technical definition of *growth* in mind. I am, however, talking about change that is more than tinkering with symptoms, more than re-solving problems that one thought had been put to rest. Certainly growth has to be change on one's own preferred terms rather than change just to please someone else or to stay out of trouble. Growthful change brings a person into fuller, richer modes of thinking and feeling. It seems to involve greater balance among a person's various priorities and needs. A major dimension of growth must be a reduction in worry and fear, something both the Twelve Step movement and many management writers have emphasized. In fact, Elton Mayo, father of the Harvard Business School's path-breaking human relations curriculum, believed fearful obsession was the number one problem of industrial civilization. Worry, fear, and obsession usually are in relation to other people. Growth must mean fuller, richer, more satisfying relationships with others—better communication, more trust and empathy, a clearer feeling of being valued by others. Finally, increased openness and thus greater learning and creativity are characteristic of growth, with a corresponding reduction in the kind of denial that recovery writers have shown to characterize drug and alcohol addiction.

Before we can address change as growth in more detail, we need to reflect further on McGregor's principle because it has had such a profound effect on what we think change in an organization needs to be. McGregor's principle can be critiqued from three points of view: first, its coherence on its own terms; second, its appropriateness to the contemporary organizational world of rapid and continual change; and third, its relevance to what we have learned about change that is really growth and not just desperate coping to survive. This third point of view will draw heavily on what we have learned about recovery from various unhealthy addictions and dependencies. This third topic will lead naturally into a final section about what is involved in change that is really growth in organizational life.

The Principle of Integration: A Category Error?

McGregor's principle may contain an intrinsic error. Logicians use the phrase *category error* when two or more things are compared as if they belonged to the same general category when in fact they do not. In everyday life, we have the familiar experience of finding someone comparing apples and oranges—putting things in relation and comparison to each other that do not go together. The two things that McGregor's principle compares are "[employees'] own goals" and "the success [the goals] of the enterprise." McGregor would have management integrate these two goals.

Do they in fact integrate? Is a manager possibly setting himself or herself up for failure by the very possibility that employees' goals and the organization's goals are apples and oranges? Employee goals belong to a category that might be called "the psychology of the employee." Employees are concrete persons; they have identifiable existence in the world, and their nature can be studied in both theory and research. Organizational goals, on the other hand, belong to a category that is usually called organization theory and behavior. An organization (or enterprise) is more abstract than a person: you can't point to anything in particular and say, "That is an organization." The goals and successes that organizations have are themselves abstractions and as such are matters of continuing debate. Organization success, in fact, is such a vague notion as perhaps not to be a category at all. (Some may think profit is quite real as a form of success, but in fact profit itself is an accountant's abstraction and does not refer to any concrete pot of money. An organization can be profitable while having no liquid assets at the end of the period in which the profit is calculated; and it can have a large pot of money without being profitable.)

So what exactly is being integrated between the concrete goals of specific persons and the abstract goals of abstract entities?

This question might be merely academic if it were not for the thousands of managers and consultants in the past forty years who have taken McGregor's proposition seriously and spent millions of dollars in pursuit of this integration. McGregor's principle exhorts a manager to create conditions whereby the integration can be achieved or at least approximated. If, however, the two kinds of goals have fundamentally different properties, the integration cannot be achieved. It doesn't mean a manager can't do things that will create benefit in each category, but it raises doubt that any given managerial action—say a new performance appraisal policy—can reconcile and integrate the two categories or that this integration can be achieved consistently across a broad range of managerial actions.

There are only two ways to understand McGregor's principle without committing the category error. One way is to say that the organization's goals are merely the sum of the separate goals of employees, which any organization theorist would say is nonsense. The second way is to drop the idea that there is something separate and independent called the enterprise that has goals of its own apart from member goals. Instead, we need to think of the variety of concrete persons grouped within the enterprise, sometimes called stakeholders. A stakeholder can be anyone with a stake in the organization's performance, but the key stakeholders seem to be employees, customers, suppliers, competitors, investors and owners, and communities. We would then ask of all of them: Are there ways to conduct an organization so that stakeholders can feel they are making positive progress toward the goals that are meaningful to them?

This way of phrasing the challenge resolves the apples and oranges problem and helps us to see more clearly what is the real issue in organizations: identifying and resolving conflicts among various players in the organizational arena, of which a major group are the managers. Managerial leaders are thus in a paradoxical position of necessarily being involved parties to the very conflicts they should be taking the lead to resolve. McGregor did not highlight this paradox nor in fact did any of the early writers on the human side of enterprise.

This identifying and resolving conflicts among stakeholder priorities is what the change process is all about in an organization. McGregor's principle of integration misframes the issue. Without realizing the inherent paradox identified above, thousands of managers and consultants set about the organizational change process, hoping to create conditions wherein employees would energetically and enthusiastically pursue organizational goals.

There were many examples of apparent progress on this question in various corporations, government agencies, health systems, and other organizations. But over time, the changes did not last because the underlying power discrepancies between various stakeholders usually were not addressed. Attempts to seek greater employee commitment, it is now apparent, rested on various assumptions about organizational mission and purpose, about products and customers, about the rewards that were available, about the actions of competitors, about the economic climate, and most importantly, about the continuity of leadership an organization was going to receive. When changes occurred that invalidated these assumptions, as of course constantly happens, there tended to be a reversion to more unilateral, top-down modes of management in which employee needs and goals once again were subordinated to the goals of more powerful stakeholders, such as top managers and stockholders.

Thus, the misunderstanding of McGregor's principle promoted a misunderstanding about what one is doing when introducing change. One is *not* integrating employee goals with organizational goals. What one is doing is dealing with power discrepancies and power conflicts among stakeholders. Change will therefore involve these various parties coming to think and act differently about power. In organizational life, power is essentially the ability to control the allocation of resources and the distribution of rewards. Power is about control. Change will *not* occur while an existing power structure and culture of control are essentially unchanged. Change will occur by growing beyond the strictures of the existing power structure and culture of control. The question is, what does this "growing" entail for everyone involved?

Leading and Managing Change Is All There Is

The reality in organizational life for several decades has been continual change. The organizational world of the 1960s that McGregor saw was one in which leading change was only one among several kinds of managerial behavior. In those days it was assumed that the need for change could be clearly determined; the goals of change could be clearly stated; the pace could be controlled; progress could be measured; there was time for those affected to be consulted; other factors impeding change could be removed or sequestered. Change, in short, was viewed as a fairly straightforward process whose principal ingredients involved being as clear as possible about objectives and gaining the understanding and loyalty of those who were needed to make the change happen (hence the importance attached to the subject of motivation). This was the kind of mental image that McGregor and his colleagues of the 1950s and early 1960s apparently had. *Planned change* was felt to be a genuinely meaningful phrase!

Even though we constantly speak of change today, we have not yet really come to terms with the meaning of continual change. To say that change is continual is a cliché, yet when we speak of continual change, do we realize that we must mean some or all of the following?

- Change in what is already changing
- Change interacting with, crosscutting, canceling out, and amplifying other change originating at other points
- Change where the knowledge base involved is also continually changing or is unknown entirely
- Change that is interrupted, evaluated, and redirected in midstream

- Intended change that is unpredictably affected by unintended change

- Change that is not initiated to seize opportunity, but rather change that is initiated to avoid extinction (what I call the "dinosaur problem")

- Unanticipated and dramatic social changes emanating from what seemed to be reasonable and needed technological changes

- Changes in the infrastructure—transportation, banks, water, electricity, mail, for example—that we would like to take for granted as predictable and reliable resources in our environments

- Changes in the very employee needs and organizational goals that McGregor said were to be integrated

- Changes that for all these reasons create acute confusions and anxieties and self-protective behaviors in the people—managers and employees alike—who are responsible for making these changes effective

When we speak casually of continual change, we clearly are making a more sweeping statement about the nature of our world than we may realize. We are talking about a veritable swirl. In short, change itself is continually changing. Drawing on the image of rafting down a wild river, I like to use the metaphor of "permanent white water" for such a world of continually surprising, novel, multifaceted change. A real rafting trip, of course, comes to an end.

The managerial and leadership mentalities and abilities that McGregor was contemplating are perhaps not adequate to this new kind of environment of continual change—an environment that is becoming even more affected by continual change every year.

The kind of mentality existing at the time McGregor wrote was what might be called an engineering approach to change. At its simplest, the classical idea of managing something involves knowing where you are, knowing where you want to go, and having the authority to organize and direct needed resources to close the gap. For a variety of reasons, many of which are suggested above, this simple model of management is inadequate to the present situation. In this classical model of management, the change process was conceived in linear terms as a series of steps, phases, or milestones. The presumed linear nature of change is still echoed in such familiar phrases as *course of action, getting on the right path, getting things straightened out, getting the kinks out, moving straight ahead, getting squared away, smoothing out the wrinkles, getting our ducks in a row,* or *finding the groove.* Despite all the contrary evidence, it is as if we still want to think change is an arrow to be shot neatly into the future.

In addition to this linear mentality, it was assumed that the planning of change was done mainly at the beginning and then implemented according to plan. ("Plan your work and work your plan" was one of the most popular management slogans of the 1950s and 1960s.) The change was presumed to be aimed at a specific objective. Anything that stood between the present situation and the objective was regarded as a potential resistance to change, and this resistance was to be overcome. The imagery was of pushing change through a resistant medium. Moreover, change was thought of as a one-time affair and not itself a learning process about initiating change in complex systems. The persons presumed to be competent to introduce the change were those who were specialists in its content. Accountants were regarded as the experts in changing financial systems; computer specialists were the experts in changing information systems; engineers were the experts in changing manufacturing processes and the design of jobs. That these content experts were for the most part not schooled in change processes for their own sake was not regarded as important.

This then is a sketch of the way we thought about implementing change all through the postwar years. This mentality can still be found in organizational life today. However, just as the nature of change is changing, this mental model of leading and managing change is itself changing. It no longer makes sense to think of creating conditions in a stable environment wherein McGregor's fixed entities of employee and organizational goals will be integrated. Leading and managing change in permanent white water is something else—something that we are just beginning to understand. Leading and managing and living with change are all there is.

Controlling the Uncontrollable

Between the lines of the management ideas we have been reviewing was an assumption about control; namely, that the person initiating change had control. The only question was whether that control was going to be used wisely on behalf of McGregor's principle of integration. Control was to be directed toward creating conditions that the principle of integration called for. McGregor apparently believed that if management did create the conditions in which employees could achieve their own goals best by pursuing the goals of the enterprise, then the main problem of controlling people's behavior would disappear. People would exercise self-control because they would be acting on behalf of their own goals as well as the organization's.

As we have seen, though, the principle of integration may be flawed in its formulation, and even if not, subsequent trends and events have rendered it inapplicable to the actual conditions of permanent white water that exist in organizations. As the principle of integration becomes more difficult to implement, the question of control becomes more problematic. Yet just because effective control is more difficult to exercise in an unstable, changing environment, it does not mean that managers reduce their control needs and shift easily to some other form of action. For many managers who feel the heavy responsibility of producing results in a fast-paced, competitive environment, control is not just an option; it is the main thing they think they need to do and the main thing they *think* they know how to do.

This is a rather stark way to put the matter, and it has been softened somewhat by shifting to the word *leadership*, but it comes to basically the same thing. When we say leadership is needed, we are often really saying that someone has to get control of the situation—to get it straightened out, so to speak. To the extent that leadership is primarily about control, do we possibly misunderstand leadership in permanent white water, and to that extent do we possibly misunderstand change as growth?

Those who would exercise leadership and control in an unstable and rapidly changing environment may find themselves increasingly relying on one or a combination of three strategies. One is simply to work harder, more hours per day, days per week, and weeks per year, and to push other people to work harder as well. A person acts on the assumption that with enough time and effort, everything will get done. This may be called a workaholic approach and represents a form of addiction. One of the most noteworthy symptoms of the workaholic approach is to become acutely time conscious. It is understandable that this should occur because the workaholic is forced to be superefficient in the use of time. Indeed, another name for workaholism is "the hurry sickness," because no matter how hard he or she tries, the workaholic is constantly running behind.

It should also be said that many workaholics say they love their work, and indeed from an objective point of view many of these jobs are interesting: stimulating problems, interesting people, travel, comfortable work surroundings, and so forth. But for someone with workaholic tendencies, a fascinating job is not necessarily a blessing, any more than being a bartender would be for someone trying to recover from the disease of alcoholism. Unfortunately and ironically, as with an addict struggling against temptations, many workaholics can't find work that does *not* have the dangerous characteristics. The knowledge and skills they have, plus their financial requirements, commit them to hyperstimulating environments. This is a problem of the postindustrial age that begs for more study.

A second response to the swirling white water is to assume there must be a simple solution somewhere and to search actively for new technologies and approaches that will solve the problems the organization is experiencing and thereby regain control. The hope is that despite all the turbulence, there is a "turnkey" solution or a system of some kind available that will not be too difficult to install. (Obviously, a huge consulting market has arisen to feed this hope.) This may be called a technoholic approach. The essence of the technoholic's frame of mind is that the problem is outside oneself and so is the solution. The technoholic is preoccupied with how to do it, where the "it" (the problem or objective) is given. Technoholism is a subtle form of closed system thinking: the system or technique that will solve the problem is presumed to be efficient provided uncontrolled variables don't intrude to impede the system's operation. Of course, such uncontrolled variables always do intrude, which only makes the true technoholic all the more control-conscious and all the more determined to fix it once and for all.

The technoholic style typically does not include philosophizing too much about the situation, especially in terms of its ethical and moral aspects or about the varieties of human feeling and perception at play. Competing values and human subjectivity bring the possibility that no technical system exists to solve the problem, that instead what is needed is a change in the interpersonal and cultural climate—the soft, touchy-feely stuff. To the true technoholic that is an upsetting thought. (It is worth noting in passing that in the past decade, attempts have been made to create technical systems that address the soft, qualitative aspects of human organizations. The lesson has been painfully relearned: Problems of interpersonal relationships and corporate culture cannot be engineered out of existence.)

Technoholism is a common malady in our technological society. (In 1999, over seven thousand books were in print with titles that begin *How to…*) In an organization full of energetic technoholics, the organization becomes a Christmas tree of uncoordinated and even competing procedures, systems, and gimmicks. They all, of course, are put in place to achieve greater control over some aspect of operations but often are not coordinated with other devices and systems that are attempting to do the same thing.

A third mode of response to the swirl is a more political approach where one seeks safety in being on the inside, knowing the right people, having advance warning of changes that are coming by working the system. This third style we may call a powerholic strategy because it is obsessively conscious of who is in power and is so eager to stay in step with them.

The powerholic strategy has at least two different forms. There is the relatively cynical and manipulative form, in which a person is quite consciously out to advance his or her own interests over everyone else's—a style Charles Kelly memorably characterized recently as the "destructive achiever." Organizational life for this person is a selfish, self-centered power game lived by such mottoes as, "Don't get mad, get even," "Look out for number one," and "Do unto others before they do unto you!"

There is another way to be a powerholic and that is to be a compulsive volunteer and caretaker, being on the inside of things and gaining power by accepting the responsibilities that no one else wants. One resolves the feeling of chaos and things being out of control by taking it into oneself. Even though compulsive caretaking may seem benign, its essence is power and control and is exacerbated in an environment of chaos and confusion. To be sure, there are healthy ways to be responsible and helpful; I am talking about a compulsive way that is not in control of itself any more than the workaholic and technoholic approaches are. The addiction recovery movement probably deserves the credit for identifying this pattern of compulsive caretaking in the syndrome of codependence.

These three broad modes of response to permanent white water comprise much of the organizational behavior we see. To the extent this is true, it makes change a different proposition from how McGregor and his colleagues encouraged us to think about it. The suffix *-holic* is meant quite literally: Managers are normally accustomed to achieving and maintaining control of things by working hard, using effective technical methods, and learning and practicing effective social skills in the organization. These methods have become unconsciously habitual. When these routine methods of control are not working effectively, a person may be drawn into more extreme and intense forms of the same behavior; and as turbulence increases, the temptation is to further increase the intensity of effort—with no upper limit that they can see. Like the addict, they find that as time goes on, increasingly large doses of the addictive substance or behavior are needed to get the same effect.

The three forms of compulsive control behavior described in this chapter are probably not the only methods; and within each of the three are many more specific forms. Perhaps we need a more general word to refer to someone who is unable to control his or her impulse to control! Cybernetics (from the Greek, *kybernetes*, meaning "helmsman") is the science of control. Perhaps we can speak of a cyberholic as one who, because of the compulsive inner need, has trouble seeing what kind of control in what amounts for what reasons and over what periods of time are in fact appropriate to the kind of situation one is in. The cyberholic overdoes it and micromanages situations or possibly goes to the other extreme after a while and withdraws abruptly. The cyberholic is quite likely to personalize situations and see himself or herself in a struggle against others for control. This would be particularly true of one who favored the powerholic modes described previously.

Many thousands of managers and employees are asking themselves today how much longer they can go on like this. Questioning how much more stress and confusion one can stand is getting close to the kind of attitude known in addiction recovery circles as hitting bottom. However, in the go-get-'em, can-do atmosphere of modern organizations, it is difficult to take seriously the possibility that fundamental change is needed to relieve the conditions that are causing so much stress. It is easier to fall back on a rhetoric of achievement and organizational challenge. This rhetoric functions to keep managers in denial.

Denial of Loss of Control

Understanding the phenomenon of denial is one of the great contributions of the Twelve Steps and the recovery movement to our understanding of change processes. In cyberholic forms of coping with continual change, we can see the mechanism of denial powerfully at work. Denial appears in the setting of more ambitious objectives; in the tighter scheduling we do of ourselves; in the longer hours; the reliance on "labor-saving" technologies like cell phones and laptop computers; in the endless quest for more job-related education; in the preoccupation with increasing our social and political skills at work; in the use of black humor, like the *Dilbert* comic strip, to distance ourselves from the stress of work environments. Denial is seen most poignantly in the maintenance of what we call a "professional" attitude no matter how great the pressure, stress, and anxiety.

Two well-known management thinkers, William G. Scott and David K. Hart in their 1989 book *Organizational Values in America*, powerfully sketch one form of managerial denial. Scott and Hart believe that something they call the organizational imperative has arisen in our society. It is as follows: "Whatever is good for the individual can only come from the modern organization." To fulfill this imperative, managers of organizations have adopted something Scott and Hart call the managerial credo. This formulation I consider one of the most penetrating insights of the postwar era. Though Scott and Hart do not put it this way, the managerial credo keeps a person in denial.

Scott and Hart's managerial credo is composed of six propositions that, taken together, provide a person with a belief system for doing everything he or she can to enhance the organization's interests. If anyone objects to what a manager is doing, the credo provides the explanation. The credo functions as a mechanism of denial. The credo consists of six statements, which I will quote and then elaborate on briefly:

1. *We believe in the decency of managerial intention.* It is important to be able to believe that one is acting for the good of the organization and not for oneself or with the intention of hurting anyone.

2. *We believe in the humaneness of managerial escalation.* Given the organizational imperative and the decency of managerial intention, it is proper that managerial control be extended as widely throughout the organization as possible.

3. *We believe in the job over all else.* Following directly from the importance of the organization, nothing in a manager's life can be more important.

4. *We believe in the homogeneity of management.* The same values, standards, and principles are applicable in every organization. In terms of managing organizational affairs, there are no unique or exceptional situations.

5. *We believe in the vocationalization of education.* Job relevancy becomes the standard for whether a manager ought to seek a particular degree or otherwise undertake learning and self-development. This principle follows directly from the organizational imperative and from Principle 3.

6. *We believe in the sovereignty of management.* The values associated with managing the organization should always win out over values associated with any specialized function. The systems of the organization must be followed, whether they fit an individual case or not. In a grading dispute for example, the registrar's system wins over any individual professor's habits, preferences, or beliefs.

This is a powerful and bitter critique of the managerial credo. "The most destructive ethical problem in America today is not insider trading, or influence peddling—it is the corrosive influence of managerial power upon all those who work in organizations, whether in the private or public sectors." Some might say the managerial credo is a caricature: A modern manager can't possibly believe without qualification such simplistic ideas about the role of management. One would hope it is a caricature, but after many years of working with executives and with management students, I think it is an accurate description of the dominant belief system of American management, operating as a set of assumptions that are rarely questioned. It is a belief system that supplies words and phrases to support the compulsive cyberholic behaviors so many managers use to deal with permanent white water. As such, it is a belief system of denial.

There are endless permutations of cyberholic denial. The problem, of course, with all denial-based coping mechanisms is that the underlying condition that is being denied continues to grow in strength and in its negative effects. In the case of permanent white water, the problem is that the kind of changes we are facing in organizations require changes on our part that many of us are not prepared to accept.

Change as Growth in Permanent White Water

Among the many important lessons from the experiences of addiction recovery is the idea that we have to be careful about giving others advice about what they need to do to recover. The most important things they need to hear are the "experience, strength, and hope" of others who are also trying to recover from addictive attitudes and behaviors as put forth in the Twelfth Step. In keeping with that learning, I want to speak more personally about my own learnings about growth and change in the white water.

The nature of white water itself demands that I talk personally, because turbulence, confusion, and disorder are very much in the eye of the beholder. What feels like a chaotic situation to me may not feel like a chaotic situation to you. Millions of us are experiencing breakdowns and transformations of values and behaviors and intensified feelings of turbulence and chaos. We are all in some kind of white water, but the specifics vary widely from person to person, profession to profession, industry to industry, and across cultures, age groups, and genders.

In various ways throughout this chapter, I have been saying that growth has to mean something more than general improvement in various skills and the kinds of knowledge one possesses. Permanent white water has changed the meaning of organization- al life, so change as growth is going to be more of a transformation for many of us than simply adding to our existing repertoire.

The three most important modes of growth for me are proving to be, first, what the addiction recovery community calls the process of "letting go"; second, the spiritual development that becomes possible as one lets go of old defenses; and third, what I have come to call "Ms. Murphy's Law." I see myself in a recov- ery process from my own forms of cyberholism. This recovery process is the growth process.

Letting Go

I have painfully come to see that I have a case of Scott and Hart's managerial credo, especially of its first and third principles. I have paid all of the prices that compulsive adherence to nonstop "do-gooding" brings with it. My form of technoholism is not so much a fascination with physical equipment as with technology as analytical method—the belief that there must be a way to think and act that will get us past all the crazy absurdities of per- manent white water.

So I am constantly thinking about what the issues are and the best ways to approach them. It is easy for me, as the therapeutic community might put it, to "get up in my head"—in other words to analyze the white water, look for some solution to it in con- cepts and strategies and then come up with compelling verbal interpretations of the issues. It is only recently that I have seen that mode of coping as possibly unconscious technoholism. "Those who know do not speak; those who speak do not know," says the *Tao Te Ching*. When I am really gripped by technoholic analysis, it is almost impossible for me to see the wisdom in this statement.

These two forms of cyberholic coping lead me to try to push the river, rather than to transcend it. I have come to see that trying to out-work and out-analyze the white water often only expresses my assumption that I must understand what is going on at all times.

Another form of cyberholic control I can see in myself is the fantasy that the white water is going to subside if I can just hang on a little longer. Things will settle down, I find myself hoping, "after we get into the new building," "once the new software is up and running," "when the new Dean arrives," "once we get through the budget cycle," "once we roll out the new degree program," "once I get my book written," "after payday," "once manager X leaves," or any other future event that seems to promise an increase in comprehension, control, and order, and a reduction in pressure. My growth, if it can be called that, has been finally to understand that I will be functioning in these unstable, unpredictable, uncontrollable environments for the indefinite future, environments where the unpredictability and instability is likely to *increase!* It is this world of continual change in which I am going to have to learn to function comfortably and enjoyably, not in some fantasized tranquility that is never going to happen.

My cyberholism also manifests itself in caretaking and responsibility-taking, and continually gets me into trouble. I am forever anticipating some need I think a person is going to have and then taking action to meet that need before they even realize they have it. It is natural for parents to anticipate things their child is going to need, but among adults it amounts to doing another person's thinking for him or her —a classic control move, I have come to see. Anticipating another person's needs, carried to an extreme, occurs to allay the anxiety I often feel over what is going to transpire between me and other persons, how our relationship is going to develop, what we are going to come to mean to each other in some emerging situation.

Permanent white water is full of such unstructured emerging situations where everyone is off balance and unsure of just how things are going to play out, of what objectives are going to be pursued, and of how tasks and responsibilities are going to be allocated. Cyberholic caretaking often leads me to suppress the stressed feelings I and others are having and to grasp for actions that will supposedly cope with the problem. If I or others feel discombobulated (or in a state of *koyaanisqatsi,* as Robert Rabbin calls it in Chapter 6), no matter—I'll just come up with some insightful analysis of the situation that others find credible and soothing, and then volunteer to carry more than my share of responsibility to deal with the situation. For years and years I've been holding myself responsible for calming other people's white water.

Recovery for me from such cyberholic behavior means learning just to *be* in chaotic, unstructured situations, just to sit in them, to be careful about what I volunteer for, about whose needs I decide to anticipate and address. If I am going to heed Kipling's advice about keeping my head while all about me are losing theirs, I need to remember that keeping my head should not consist of a lot of high-powered analysis, for this only removes me from contact with reality. Letting go in white water for me involves pausing before I activate all the analytical and anticipatory powers I possess. The pause creates space for other energies in the situation to arise, for natural processes of evolving order to occur. It gives me time to feel the cyberholic urge within, to take a step back from it, to learn more about it. It gives me space to ask what I really want to do in the situation, how I can be truly helpful. It gives me space to pay attention to the growth that others in the situation need and want, not just to what I compulsively think they should need and want so I can busily set about getting it for them.

I have learned that letting go means becoming more willing to be surprised. The essence of permanent white water is surprise and novelty: One never dreamed that whatever crazy thing has happened would or even could actually happen. Yet in my unrecovered state I have been one of those folks who does not like surprises. The world Scott and Hart have critiqued so powerfully, governed by the organizational imperative, is thoroughly a world of no surprises. It is virtually an article of religion in modern control-oriented management that a subordinate must never, never let the boss be surprised. Permanent white water has been teaching me a different lesson—that, far from trying to avoid surprise, I need to learn to embrace it, take pleasure in it, dwell in the feelings it generates.

Letting go has forced me to rethink a perfectionist streak in myself, a desire for everything to be just right, and a tendency to be miserable when it is not. Perfectionism, I was actually shocked to discover, is not some noble desire in me for high quality and to be the best. Rather, it can be based on a profound negativism and pessimism. As Plato discussed centuries ago in his *Ideals*, nothing is ever perfect, least of all in permanent white water; so letting go entails reflecting on what can realistically be accomplished. A mantra about perfection does not help.

I have learned to think of letting go as itself a kind of learning process. The phrase by itself implies that either one lets go or one doesn't. In fact, recovering from cyberholism has not been an all at once, "cold turkey" kind of process for me. In particular, the everchanging world of permanent white water is continually presenting new challenges to one's ability to let go. Progress on one topic is no guarantee of progress on the next. Fortunately, I have found that letting go is a reflexive process: I learn more and more about it as I do it more and more.

Basically, I am learning that letting go means to stop denying. In permanent white water, the urge to control is frequently an urge to deny: denial of unexpected realities one had not perceived; denial of energies that have suddenly appeared; denial of other people's points of view in the situation; denial that one could have been on the wrong track in the first place; denial that other approaches might work better; denial that one can let go and flow with the system rather that keep trying to ride herd on it.

Working Spiritually Smarter

Permanent white water disturbs meanings. It has caused me to reflect on how I and others around me make sense of the world in which we live. I have found that we do this by deciding, often unconsciously, what is the meaning of various elements in our situation—elements like the objectives we are pursuing, the authority we have to do what we are doing, our qualifications and the qualifications of others, the larger mission our work serves, and so on; an orderly house, as it were, that we have worked hard to construct and maintain and that we worry about when it comes under attack. The white water of continual change calls into question many of our most cherished sources of meaning and stability.

Permanent white water forces me to rethink what I am doing, including the basic foundations that give my life and work meaning. Values that I hold dear can no longer be taken for granted. The white water I find myself in is a stream of continual reflection on values, often under extremely stressful and confusing conditions. I have come to speak of learning to work spiritually smarter, by which I mean becoming more conscious of the spiritual foundations of my life and work, and more willing to have major new learning experiences about these foundations.

I have, in other words, come to the same conclusion that the addiction recovery movement came to many years ago—that giving up the various props and crutches we use to try to control our lives must be a spiritual process, not merely a physical and intellectual one. I cannot just think my way out of cyberholism, because it is a disease of my thinking in the first place!

I have written at greater length about this process elsewhere. For the moment let me simply note that the most important change-as-growth so far in my spiritual learning as been the idea of a *program* of recovery and growth. Somehow I did not get this aspect of spirituality in my church-related experiences. Religious and spiritual events were things you did, actions you performed, but actually feeling oneself growing spiritually was not something I expected to happen. In later years I have found myself in permanent white water with a bad case of wanting to control everything and no resources that seemed to be of much help except Twelve Step principles and other insights from the addiction recovery movement. Working spiritually smarter is not just a catchy phrase for me; it has become a program for life.

Ms. Murphy's Law

Murphy's Law—"Whatever can go wrong, will go wrong—is not a calm philosophical observation. It is a cry of anguish by someone who's just had a budget blown, or a timeline aborted, or key people transferred, or a kid arrested, or vacation reservations canceled, or a tax appeal denied, or all of the above.

But there is also a Ms. Murphy who has been getting concerned about Murphy lately. He brings two attachés home, hardly talks or listens during dinner, then falls asleep right after dinner. He has always gone to work on Saturdays but is now going in on Sundays as well, leaves the house before sunup to beat the traffic, and talks about installing a couch in his office. Of course he never gets to the things he said he would do around the house. The kids have figured out that he would just like them to stay out of his way. Ms. Murphy sees all this and can only say to herself, "Murphy's got to lighten up!"

Many readers and I can certainly see ourselves in this little sketch. It is the basis for the third major kind of growth.

The original Murphy had his insight in the early 1960s when disruptive change was not regarded as continual. If Murphy could take things less seriously, how might he phrase his law for today?

The Law of Continuous Disimprovement

The performance level of any complex system is a result of a set of unknown size of "Things That Could Have Gone Wrong (but

Didn't)." Attempts to improve the performance of the system inevitably increase the number of Things That Can Go Wrong, resulting in an increase in the probability that something *will* go wrong and undercut the intended improvements .

The Role of Humor

Can Murphy and I lighten up a little, have some fun with all the strange things that happen in permanent white water, see growth possibilities as well as scary challenges in odd, unexpected happenings? Can I learn to enjoy the novelties of this fragilely interconnected world, even when my own projects and cherished values are the objects of chaotic change?

Much of our humor today about white water is bitter, ironic, divisive, and sarcastic. Who would want to work in Dilbert's office environment? I am talking about a different role for humor, for it is one of the oldest bonding devices the human species has. Humor can be loving and caring. It can recognize our interdependence and our common powerlessness. It can playfully stimulate our creativity, and it can help us mourn. Humor can be the vehicle and expression of our spiritual development. Those in recovery from various addictions know these lessons well. There are no human sins or desperations that cannot, by the grace of a spiritual fellowship, be transformed into the relief and healing of profound laughter.

Peter Vaill

Peter Vaill holds the Distinguished Chair in Management Education at the Graduate School of Business, University of St. Thomas. He was Professor of Human Systems and Director of the Ph.D. program at George Washington University's School of Business and Public Management and is a former Dean of this school. He holds a Bachelors degree from the University of Minnesota, and MBA and DBA degrees from the Harvard Business School.

Dr. Vaill is known for his innovative approaches to managerial leadership and organizational behavior. He designed and taught one of the first courses in cross-cultural management offered in a U.S. management school. He has pioneered in speaking and writing about the spiritual problems of business leaders. He is well known for his ideas about what he calls "permanent white water" the extremely turbulent conditions in organizations and society that managerial leaders are coping with today.

He has worked with many well-known corporations and with most major U.S. government agencies. He has also published many articles in academic and professional literature. A book of essays, *Managing as a Performing Art: New Ideas for a World of Chaotic Change*, was published by Jossey-Bass in 1989. In 1996 Jossey-Bass published his new theory of managerial learning in a book titled *Learning as a Way of Being: Strategies for Survival in a World of Permanent White Water*. A new book, *Spirited Leading and Learning: Process Wisdom for a New Age*, was published by Jossey-Bass in 1998.

CHAPTER ELEVEN

In this, the final chapter, Margaret expands the vision of how business may be conducted in the future. What is required in the new millenium, she argues, is a quantum leap in systems thinking, in how we view our selves, our business, and our world. Capitalism, itself a revolution in human existence when it was first introduced and applied, will give way to a new economy. This "new economy" will have a higher purpose and will stress the common good, the interconnectedness of all life on this planet, and the need to embrace the principles of sustainability. Leaders will be more philosophical in nature and, in addition to more traditional roles, will advocate qualities of the spirit that transcend money or self-aggrandizement. Margaret in fact offers a twelve-step model that incorporates these qualities and that is based on the Twelve Steps. The chapter ends with an overview of four new operational business systems that embody the holistic system that will support change and transformation.

—Editor

Transformation:
An Economy with a
Higher Purpose

Margaret Lulic

$\mathcal{C}\!\ell$s we enter the new millennium, we are embarking on a journey to create a new world order. Another system has been gestating and is moving through the birthing process. What is needed today are more people who can think beyond themselves and their own lifetime. Further, we need a fundamental rethinking of our economic system and its impact on life on earth.

Significant players in the transformation will be our business organizations and economic systems. Many leaders are trying to hold on to old worldviews. They do this by denying the weaknesses of the old order or by working around the dis-ease it is causing. It is as if they know they are addicted but are seeking only a partial recovery. A critical mass, however, is breaking through the bulwarks to champion a new corporate life inspired by soul and vision. This bold initiative represents the last step in the transformational Twelve Step model.

Marilyn Mason in Chapter 5 of this book describes the experience of moving beyond recovery into transformation as both agonizing and exhilarating. An executive client of mine, a Vietnam veteran, incorrectly assumed he had recovered from his wartime experiences. Becoming depressed after a layoff, he sought therapy. He discovered then how much the Vietnam experience was still haunting him. He told me, "Life was in black and white" before therapy, "and then, suddenly, there was Technicolor" (transformation). It was only through the process of therapy that he was able to wash the horrors of the war from his body and soul and celebrate true recovery.

Feelings of elation and expectation are normal when moving to a more transformational purpose. I remember one of my first such experiences. My classmates and I were busy memorizing the letters of the alphabet. For what seemed like endless hours we practiced all the associated sounds and the formation of the letters. One day I discovered the big secret: The order of the letters, spaces, and sounds actually mattered. I had discovered words and sentences! A new level of understanding and meaning had appeared behind the agony of individual memorization and practice drills. That revelation was exciting; but what was transformational was the realization that I could now become not only an avid reader but also an author.

Einstein noted this phenomenon when he said, "You cannot solve problems with the same level of thinking that created them. There comes a time when the mind assumes a higher plane of knowledge without full understanding of how it got there. All great discoveries have involved such a leap." The transformed business and the transformed economy will be new examples of such forward leaps.

In the course of history we creative beings have solved many problems and social issues in ways that have made them even more complex. What our global society needs in the new millennium is a quantum leap in systems thinking, in how we view our business, our world, and ourselves.

As Robert Radin notes in Chapter 6, Vaclav Havel, president of Czechoslovakia, is one of several world leaders who have warned that this higher leap is exactly what the world must have now.

> The salvation of this human world lies nowhere else than in the human heart, in the human power to reflect. Without a global revolution in the sphere of human consciousness, nothing will change for the better. The catastrophe toward which this world is headed—be it ecological, social, demographic, or a general break-down of civilization—will be inevitable.

In an earlier chapter Daniel Hanson quoted a friend of his. "The bad news is that my life is falling apart. The good news is that my life is falling apart, which means that I now have an opportunity to put it back together again, only better this time." Many people acknowledge that they could say the same about their own lives. Few, however, are confident that they can really do anything about it. The truth is, they can. Each of us can choose to be part of the problem or part of the solution. Not choosing is by default choosing to be part of the problem.

We have created a powerful collective tool for this next leap. The global economic system in which we live was a revolution in human existence. There was a specific intent of the consciousness that created the system we have today. The intent was wealth creation. It included giving control to the individual to become as successful in this life as possible, bringing more goods and services to larger numbers of people, raising the material standard of living, and flexing our technological muscle to create wealth. To harness the resources to do this, we established a system designed to control both nature and humans. It is called capitalism. It has done its job as well as was possible without another leap in consciousness.

Today, industry and commerce have become the most powerful forces on earth. Already in this millennium these forces have been summoned to underwrite the next major systemic revolution of life on earth, one that embraces a more complex view of human and spiritual purpose. If these forces can be moved to a higher level, we can create significant and sustainable benefits for the global village.

This new purpose will focus on the "common good," or well-being of the whole, with each of us representing an integral and vital part. In his videotape and book *The Global Brain*, Peter Russell, the English mystic, scientist, and researcher, discusses how one characteristic of the new millennium we are entering is larger and larger-scale integration—political, social, economic, and technological. We as individuals, companies, and countries are no longer islands. Increasingly, the whole planet is merging as one global community. To carry this initiative forward, new leadership and new roles are needed in our corporations and institutions.

Visions of the Common Good

Business, community leaders, and the average person are working to redefine the core purpose of our economic system. While we will want to continue to extend the benefits of the current system, we will add more complexity to that purpose. A conscious economy will seek the "good society," and businesses, if they truly understand their own self-interest, will become actively involved. Doing good works will increasingly be viewed as serving stakeholder interests.

Charles Handy in *The Hungry Spirit* describes the current situation. "Capitalism," he writes,

> which was suppose to set us free, may be enslaving us in its turn, with its insistence on the dominance of the economic imperative . . . If capitalism is to be our servant rather than our master, it will be because our belief systems want it that way.

The new agenda asks that we use our hearts and spiritual cores to create a higher purpose for the economy and its organizations.

We will have what Willis Harman, past president of the Institute of Noetic Sciences, called "a quiet change of mind." We will decide the economy should serve as an instrument for holistic responsibility and as an agent of social change. New questions are already being asked: Do human beings exist to serve the economy and the company? Or do the economy and the company exist to serve us? Our practices have suggested the former. That perception, however, is gradually changing. To release the potential of organizations to undertake this new work, the rules of the larger economic system must also change.

This new millennium system will necessarily be philosophical in nature because it will have to ask and answer some of the most basic questions of life. These questions will concern purpose, justice, truth, compassion, balance, and more. Some people will claim these are spiritual questions. If by *spiritual* is meant the larger philosophical reflections as to meaning, purpose, and transcendence, I concur. What I am not referring to are various formal religious dogmas.

According to Plato, the good society can exist only when it is founded on justice. All other foundations eventually manufacture greed, hate, and violence—and eventually their own demise. He goes on to write in *The Republic:*

The society we have described can never grow into a reality or see the light of day, and there will be no end to the troubles of states, . . . or humanity itself, till philosophers become kings in this world, or till those we now call kings and rulers really and truly become philosophers.

Today this means, "Until philosophers become governmental and corporate leaders or until those leaders learn to become philosophers."

The fundamental characteristics of philosophers include a passion for truth and wisdom. Most philosophers are primarily interested in those qualities of the spirit that transcend money or self-aggrandizement. Only through truth and wisdom, they say, and with absolute freedom from self-interest will come an understanding of justice. Peter Senge writes in *The Fifth Discipline*, "We must look into the underlying structures which shape individual actions...Structures of which we are unaware hold us prisoner." Since these structures often have benefited current leaders, the passion for truth must become so prevalent that self-aggrandizement is diminished. Breton and Largent describe this shift eloquently in their book, *The Paradigm Conspiracy*. To them, only one force is powerful enough to right the world: "the internal guidance system of our souls."

How will this new structure be designed? William McDonough, dean of the Virginia School of Architecture and head of his own consulting firm, is one who is implementing new system designs to help us answer this question. In an October 1998 *Atlantic Monthly* article entitled "The Next Industrial Revolution," he summarizes the negatives of our current state of affairs as a design issue. He writes:

> If someone were to present the Industrial Revolution as a retroactive design assignment, it might sound like this:
>
> Design a system of production that
>
> - puts billions of pounds of toxic material into the air, water and soil every year;
> - measures prosperity by activity, not legacy;
> - requires thousands of complex regulations to keep people and natural systems from being poisoned too quickly;
> - produces materials so dangerous that they will require constant vigilance by future generations;
> - results in gigantic amounts of waste; and
> - erodes the diversity of biological species and cultural practices.

McDonough continues with his vision of the next revolution. In the future, he states:

The design assignment might be to create a system of social justice, market viability and environmental intelligence that

- introduces no hazardous materials into the air, water, or soil;

- measures prosperity by how much natural capital we can accrue in productive ways;

- measures productivity by how many people are gainfully and meaningfully employed;

- does not require vigilance by future generations; and

- celebrates biological and cultural diversity and solar income."

The new system will be conscious of the interconnectedness of all life. McDonough and others now understand we must view nature as our teacher. The relationship of trees to the forest and to the earth is more complex than anything humans have designed. No longer will we separate a person into mind, body, heart and soul and pick and choose different pieces to come to work or to heal of physical and emotional problems. We will understand that the economy must focus on justice and the common good, not just shareholder wealth. We will know that what happens to children is a manifestation of the larger system. We will know that we cannot have 20 percent of the world depleting 70 percent of global resources. We will understand that we must create human systems that are sustainable.

In the new millennium, the economic system will therefore have a higher purpose, be philosophical in tone, learn from nature, and be systemically oriented. What that means and how it may manifest itself is already being defined around the world. Leading-edge organizations and philosophical leaders have begun experimenting, testing, and learning. We are not starting from scratch.

Getting to the Next System

The transformational Twelve Step model provides insights about how we might create this new framework. Many of these Steps require both individual and collective work. A variety of collective models are also available. Pathfinding has been initiated by the Institute for Noetic Sciences. Another process is available from the Foundation for Conscious Evolution initiated by futurist Barbara Marx Hubbard. The following steps could be melded within these or used as an independent framework.

- *Step One.* Give up the limiting core belief that we are powerless victims of today's economic rules. Neither Wall Street, nor the company, nor my mortgage, nor human nature truly controls my life or my organization.

- *Step Two.* Collectively agree, at least in theory, that an improved system based on values and higher principals can create a better life for everyone and everything on Earth. For many people, this will mean including their souls and hearts as legitimate players in this drama—whether these be supported by God, Yahweh, Buddha, a Higher Power, or a humanitarian commitment.

- *Step Three.* Commit to the creation of the vision. Faith and trust will precede logic and facts. Let go of old assumptions and beliefs to accept new possibilities.

- *Step Four.* Make a fearless and thorough inventory of the strengths and weaknesses of current systems. In particular, we must look through the eyes of the architect to see the fundamental design problems of the system.

- *Step Five.* Compassionately share the truths about these findings with all stakeholders to gather support for change and transformation.

- *Steps Six through Nine.* These Steps must take us into specifics of how to empower those in each organization to make new and improved systems a reality in our daily work. (In the next section I provide a framework for the organization's four new systems.)

- *Step Ten.* Practice continuous improvement at the highest levels of national and international business policy. Such improvement includes altering monitoring systems such as the gross domestic product that consider the creation of waste a productive activity.

- *Steps Eleven and Twelve.* Practice an ongoing philosophy of creativity and spiritual development through global service. The motto of the Rotary Clubs, "Service Before Self," is an apt descriptor for the work ahead.

The critical outcome of this process is a commitment to a new and larger purpose. That which does not relate to the common good will no longer apply. Leaders and followers alike will assume responsibility for creating a more principled system capable of responding to the added complexities of this new purpose.

A precursor to this effort is the Caux Round Table Principles for Business. This document contains seven principles for ethical global business and complimentary principles for each of six stakeholder groups. The principles, which have garnered considerable global interest, were initially put forward by members of the Minnesota Center for Corporate Responsibility. Subsequently they were integrated with the Japanese *kyosei* principles that Ryuzaburo Kaku, chief executive of Canon, suggested. *Kyosei* means "living together for the common good." Ryuzaburo Kaku has preached and lived this doctrine for his entire professional life. He has been called a "philosopher king and a great businessman."

Such wisdom will help define a larger purpose as we work on Step One, as previously defined. While the early charters that established corporations as legal entities contained the belief that such corporations were created to serve the people and the country, many CEOs either ignored or misunderstood that original intent. Instead, shareholder wealth became the one and only goal of most organizations. Economist Milton Friedman would still argue that this should be the primary corporate goal of any business.

But viewpoints such as Friedman's are increasingly seen as being out of step with today's realities. In the future, making money will be an insufficient answer to these questions: What are you here for? What purpose do you serve? What is your contribution?

More acceptable answers will incorporate elements related to the common good at all levels of the scale—local to global. As a result, organizations will need to confront the difficult issues of what goods and services they should provide, and for whom.

Framebreak, by Ian Mitroff, lays out the design of a total ethical management philosophy. He contends that business has lost sight of its fundamental purpose: "to make products and to deliver quality service that satisfies the *ethical* desires and needs of humankind, not merely that which sells." Recent court cases involving the tobacco industry would seem to support this contention. The right to exist must be balanced with the responsibility to promote the common welfare. Each company must both accept this principle and find its own way to sustain it.

One area that will require adjustment is the stock market and its emphasis on quarterly earnings. Another area is the very basis for equity investments. Recently, as Craig Neal posits in Chapter 9, a new type of investor has emerged. Often referred to as "socially responsible" investors, these financiers seek to invest their funds in companies that are aligned with their own ethics and values, even if such investments may not maximize total investor returns. Today, over $45 billion is invested in socially responsible mutual funds. These funds are established with a screening process that considers types of products and services developed by the company in question, its treatment of employees, its environmental record, and its commitment to social justice issues. Individuals, foundations and venture capital firms have invested many additional billions of dollars in similar ways and on similar conditions.

These trends are converging with a great spiritual longing in the workplace to work in organizations where integrity and commitment to the common good are paramount. According to the *Wall Street Journal*, in the past decade there has been an 800 percent increase in numbers of books relating to spirituality and values in the workplace. Men and women alike are spending a larger portion of their lives at work, and they want that portion to feel meaningful.

I have written and spoken about finding our sense of calling and then sculpting new careers. Often, this effort requires a return to the roots of a profession and then reaching out to a new vision of what the world needs. Frederick Buechner captures it well: "A calling is when a deep gladness in your heart meets a deep need in the world."

A number of international conferences and seminars have espoused the principles outlined in this chapter. More and more professions are forming organizations to help further define them. Several decades ago the concept of holistic medicine was viewed as almost heretical. Today, it is gaining respect and momentum and helping heath care professionals return to a sense of calling.

What is happening in the medical field will soon happen in many other professions. One of my clients, a partner in an accounting firm, learned one day that the historical mission of the finance profession was "to bring integrity to commerce." This came as a revelation to him and provided a new sense of purpose to his professional life. He finds it much more stimulating to think of himself as an instrument of integrity than as someone who crunches numbers and helps people make a buck. Similarly, in the legal profession, three lawyers who are members of the Institute for Noetic Sciences have teamed with the Fetzer Institute to initiate the Healing and Law Project to help lawyers return to their roots as peacekeepers.

Visions of the Emerging Organization

Already on-line are organizations and practices that suggest the vision of a new type of business organization. The vision is large enough to house considerable diversity within a common framework.

The emerging organization will not discard all that business has learned and established. It will in fact build on that foundation through a fundamental reordering and re-creation process. Returning to the analogy of a child understanding letters versus meaning, we can see what could happen in an organization. Our functional and operational expertise will find new meaning and creative powers. Like the child, we can build on our innate ability to author new practices, processes, products, and behaviors that are meaningful and contribute more positively to life on Earth and in the workplace. The holistic system that will support this change consists of four new operational business systems.

These four systems provide the higher framework that will influence all subordinate functions and operations within the enterprise, to infuse it with new meaning, order, and integrity. Each system answers a fundamental question and provides daily guidance. Implementation tools to support these systems have been emerging over the last several decades, and more will follow. Many companies have at least experienced these systems, though few have yet to exploit them. Most have dealt just with the surface manifestation of the program without tackling the more difficult philosophical work that must precede fundamental change.

The Meaning Making System

The first system, "meaning making," has been evolving for several decades but with a noticeable increase in the last decade. Meaning making addresses the question of what purpose we as individuals and as corporate entities serve in the big picture. Why are we really here? Explorations into vision, purpose, mission, values, philosophy, and worldviews all support this system. Total quality management (TQM) systems reintroduced these questions into the organization in the late 1980s.

Several major trends are currently coalescing to put the question of purpose on corporate agendas. Demographic trends are contributing to changes in employees' expectations. As more and more people achieve higher levels of learning, they expect more freedom, responsibility, respect and meaning. Baby boomers today are contemplating retirement and are concerned about the legacy they are leaving. Those individuals associated with Generation X have seen the effects of the old paradigm on their parents and family life and often are not interested in following that path. This "system question" has already profoundly taxed businesses' human resource function in its ability to attract, support, and retain people. In addition, it could lead to totally different requirements in leadership, decision-making, rewards, and recognition.

Bill George, chairman and CEO of Medtronic in Minneapolis, provides an example. He observed that asking employees to develop new products or improve the quality of existing ones to increase shareholder value did not generate much positive energy. However, when these same employees were asked to do the same thing "to alleviate pain, restore health, and extend life," there is a very different response. These were goals that appealed to the employees' sense of personal and corporate mission.

A successful client company of mine, Reell Precision Manufacturing Company, defines its main reason for existence as "the growth of people." Meeting customer needs at high levels of quality must happen, of course, and financial analysis and reporting must serve to measure progress and success. But according to senior management this is not why the company exists. "It's analogous to food," one executive told me. "People don't live to eat; they eat to live. We don't exist as a company to make money; we make money to exist and nurture our people." This philosophy is imbued in virtually all of Reell's business practices, not just in human resources (or "coworker services" as it is called there). As one might expect, turnover in this company is extremely low.

Such trends also affect consumers. Many people today demand more meaningful products from more socially responsible companies. This trend will increasingly influence how marketing professionals view their target markets. Key questions will include not only how to efficiently reach diverse market segments, but also how to package the products and services to appeal to more complex indicators of value. In the future, customer philosophy will be based less on "Make me the best product at the lowest price" and more on, "If you want my money and loyalty, you must first prove you deserve them."

The Relational Responsibility System

This second system relates specifically to the issue of relational responsibility. To whom is the organization responsible and for what purpose? To whom is each function and individual responsible? Am I, the employee, responsible to the larger community or only to the company? Or only to my boss?

Consumer trends related to the environment are also putting pressure on business organizations. Futurist Faith Popcorn, has identified a consumer group called S.O.S. that is concerned with saving our society. This group demands socially responsible behavior from companies in addition to more sustainable products, and they use their collective buying power as an instrument for change. In another example, Paul Ray has identified a fundamental change that is taking root and growing among American consumers. In *The Integral Culture Survey* he describes a group he calls the Cultural Creatives. This group represents about 24 percent of Americans whose concerns include the environment, social change, and spiritual growth. Other data on voluntary downsizing, investments in social responsibility venture funds, et al, confirm this data. The "80/20" rule applies to social change just as it does to many other issues: When 20 percent of a populace shifts, momentum is created to motivate the other 80 percent.

This trend is also captured in the word *stakeholders* as opposed to the more traditional *stockholders*. Many companies today understand the concept of five groups of stakeholders: owners, customers, employees, suppliers, and community. In the future two additional stakeholders will be added: the Earth and future generations. The Native American concept of "do no harm to the seventh generation" would be a good model to consider here.

Relational issues rise to the surface for executives, owners, and stockholders in the form of questions related to justice and fairness. How much is enough? What is enough compensation, return, and growth? Are there limits to growth? Should there be limits? At the same time, employees are questioning their balance among work, family, and community volunteering. What is enough responsibility at work? What is enough salary to provide for my family while still affording me a life outside of work?

Corporations receive many benefits from the community, including clean air, water, natural resources, infrastructure, and tax credits. In return, corporations create jobs, donate money to local charities, and even provide day-care services. Today, the relationship between a large corporation and the community it serves begs the larger question: What is a responsible relationship between an organization and all its stakeholders?

Many newer business organizations such as the World Business Academy, The High Tor Alliance, The Greenleaf Center for Servant Leadership, and Business for Social Responsibility are leading the way in exploring new business relationships.

Each of us, for example, has a stake in the advertising industry due to its power to influence our entire culture. Kevin Lynch, a partner in the firm of Lynch, Jarvis and Jones, personally leads a national campaign to eliminate what he terms "toxic advertising." Rather than produce a commercial trying to convince people they need a product, his firm produces a creative and *informative* message that is associated with the potential purchase. The message in fact has value apart from the product. Imagine if even a small percentage of the $202 billion spent in 1998 on advertising in this country alone were redirected in this fashion.

We will need to transform our monitoring and feedback systems into one integrated system that studies the organization's impact on all stakeholders. Separate financial reports that do not address the environmental costs of doing business and are not connected to marketing and sales reports of customer satisfaction will not be sufficient in the new system. Market research, finance, employee satisfaction, and environmental monitoring must all tell a story together and be interrelated. Moreover, this is one story that must be told over time—past, present, and future—and not just in quarterly reports. Most companies have experience with certain of these components, but few companies view them as a systems report. Therefore, companies make decisions to address one problem without realizing the effects and costs such decisions may cause elsewhere within the system.

A few leading-edge companies have begun to tie such comprehensive reporting into corporate Annual Reports. Scandic Hotels; IKEA, the world's largest furniture retailer; and Interface, the world's largest carpet manufacturer, are examples of companies that have become proactive in both monitoring and reporting their impact on the world. Such efforts must be applauded, learned from, and emulated by other companies in other industries.

The Responsible Creation System

This third system concerns a company taking responsibility for all its business processes. Once a company is clear on its purpose and mission and on who its stakeholders are and what their needs may be, it is time to review how the company can realize its strategic objectives in a responsible manner.

This system concerns the underlying support systems of most organizations: manufacturing, quality control, operations, maintenance, building, and disposal. One priority for the future will be ecological sustainability. Every company will need to review the use of all materials it takes from the Earth and what impact this has on the environment. Another top priority will be to study the "soft" systems we create, many of which concern social justice, and ask if we are being responsible in those areas as well. We will need to both understand and respond appropriately to the impact our employment systems have on human beings, families, and communities at large.

A catalyst for change will be the increasing costs of doing business within old paradigms. Regulatory controls, environmental destruction, and the increased healthcare costs associated with pollution are already increasing business costs, especially for manufacturing companies. Tax implications of not addressing social ills at their root causes will give bottom-line-oriented organizations the incentives they need to re-examine their core beliefs. Pressure from consumer and investing groups will also provide momentum.

Manufacturing and engineering will be challenged to design and produce quality products that preserve Earth's vital resources. Such products will not only please consumers, they also will be innovative products that are easily repaired, upgraded, and recycled into new products. "Throwaway" designs or built-in obsolescence will no longer be acceptable. As in nature where there is no waste and everything becomes food for something else, consumers no longer will consume most nondisposable products. Instead, they will lease the product and return it to the manufacturer once its functionality and utility have been consumed. Interface is one company that is already proceeding in this direction. As its CEO, Ray Anderson, points out:

> People who buy carpets aren't necessarily looking to own a carpet. What they want are warmth, comfort, and beauty. When the carpet they buy no longer affords these attributes, we'll take it back and re-cycle it. Better that than simply throwing it away and possibly harming the environment.

Horst Rechelbacher, CEO of Aveda Corporation, describes responsible creation in his organization:

> Our raw materials come from around the world. We are currently using about 1,500 flowers and plants in the products we develop. Our goal is to produce 100 percent of our resources organically.

> We focus on beauty, health and a sustainable lifestyle in everything we do. When we work with our foreign suppliers, we want to help them preserve their wisdom, their way of life and their intellectual property rights. At the same time we want to provide our employees with a healthy environment and supportive atmosphere. We have a wonderful facility on sixty-five acres of beautiful grounds. This facility has exercise rooms, racquetball and basketball courts, walking trails, and bicycles. We have natural sunlight in every work area, including the factory. We provide mothers with cribs in their offices and a Waldorf-inspired child-care center on site.

> We have a cafeteria called Organica. It's a natural foods restaurant, featuring a wide selection of delicious, healthy meals. Most restaurants of its size produce

about fifty pounds of waste per day, but Organica only generates about five pounds per day. We also send food waste to a pig farmer. We use soy inks, double siding everything, and recycle throughout the facility. We also have a recycling program for our plastics through our 25,000 salons, schools, esthetiques and spas. As you can see, the principles of sustainable living pervade everything we do.

Examples of the "soft" systems we create and the social justice issues they raise are whole employment, underemployment and unemployment situations, by themselves and also how such issues relate to a livable wage. The current system demands that some people work sixty to eighty hours per week, while others are unemployed or underemployed. Correlated with such discrepancies are increased health care costs, family violence, and divorce, in addition to increased teen pregnancy, drug use, and suicide. In the emerging organization we will work fewer hours, live more simply, and devote more time to such issues as family and volunteer work. Some of these issues can be influenced by individual organizations; others will require a collaborative effort across the economy. One client has developed its own livable wage standard. Others participate in collaborative efforts to share employees in down times to avoid any employee being laid off.

Joel Hodroff, founder and director of Commonweal Inc., has conceived of a new approach to wealth creation and sustainable development, which he calls "dual-currency commerce." Hodroff asserts that a second currency can complement the dollar and build a bridge between cash and noncash economies. Commonweal's patented transaction system allows people to volunteer for work in the community and earn community service dollars (CSDs). Participating merchants accept CSDs, with cash, to apply toward goods and services that might otherwise be underutilized—from empty restaurant tables and movie theaters to unsold inventories of every description. This model is already in a pilot phase in Minneapolis and includes stakeholders such as the Mall of America, National City Bank, Hennepin County, and the United Way.

Hodroff maintains that the inspiration for this concept came in part from the dynamics of Twelve Step groups. Recovery achieved through the implementation of Twelve Step philosophy and principles proved to be as valuable as anything hospitals and clinics provided. At the same time, he studied the utility of non-cash economies based on volunteerism, barter, the Internet, family finances, and such corporate scrip as frequent flyer miles. He is today more convinced than ever that such creative designs can emanate from within larger American corporations to serve as paragons for smaller and emerging companies.

The Leadership and Capacity Building System

Companies get nervous when they contemplate long lists of proposed changes. Few have yet mastered the art of balancing the five stakeholder groups effectively. To add two more while promoting internal transformation can appear expensive, time consuming and threatening. It is indeed an enormous challenge, but it can be done if we plan for it effectively. Before most of us take on something significantly new, we usually add capacity and learning. Before we launch a career, we attend classes or otherwise gain understanding of how we are going to realize personal objectives. Before one enters a marathon, one works out to build muscle and endurance. Before a company adds significantly to the product mix, it first does exhaustive market research in addition to internal analysis of manufacturing systems and capacity. Likewise, companies will enhance their competitiveness by first engaging in organizational capacity building.

Just as with other systems introduced in this chapter, companies may have unconsciously been building resources and expertise to undertake the work of capacity building. Systems thinking skills must nonetheless be more consciously developed if a senior executive, for example, is to consider the needs of the seven types of stakeholders from an integrative perspective, rather than as seven separate groups with separate agendas. The new organizations mentioned previously can provide insights and models for others. The increase in books and business consultancy in the areas of spirituality and transformation, the long history of the Twelve Step model, and the insights of quantum physicist Fritjof Capra and psychoneuroimmunology researcher Candace Pert, all provide examples of advanced systems thinking. Such examples also provide clues to the path that many organizations will be following in the next millennium.

When the four systems shown below become operational, American business will achieve great leverage with less investment.

Table 1: Four Operational Systems for Emerging Organizations

System Name	System Questions	Implementation Tools
• Meaning making system	• Why are we here? Why do we exist?	• Purpose, vision, values clarification, philosophy, total quality management (TQM)
• Relational responsibility system	• To whom are we responsible and for what? How do we monitor this?	• Seven Stakeholders, TQM, Chapter 4 in this book
• Responsible creation system	• How do we responsibly do what we are here to do?	• Natural Step, Commonweal, ecological systems
• Leadership and organizational system	• What do we need in place to create and support the first three systems?	• Spiral dynamics, global knowledge, servant leadership

Hodroff's dual-currency system is a good example of integrative systems thinking and the leverage it provides. The effects of this one system are multidimensional: Individuals gain new purchasing power; businesses gain new customers; wasted inventory is reduced; the community benefits from volunteer work; and it is all self-funding by transaction fees from a simple credit-like card. This is a quintessential win-win-win scenario.

A client of mine recently experienced this type of leveraged result. This company has made a laudatory commitment to the principles espoused in this chapter: balancing stakeholder needs, offering products that do well and do good, and being fair to and supportive of its employees. Nonetheless, the company had retained the typical agenda of strategic and operational initiatives—all separate, all demanding time, attention, and resources, and all competing with one another. That agenda included, among other items, an employee motivation initiative, a marketing effort to increase customer satisfaction, another marketing initiative to increase market share, and a cost reduction project.

I brought a systems consciousness to the table by asking this one question: What is one thing you could do that would affect each of these objectives? As a result of the discussions that followed, we created what was, in essence, a new paradigm for the company. This paradigm saved the company money, increased its market share, increased employee and customer satisfaction, and created a team learning experience across five functional groups. And all this happened from working off one leverage point.

At the beginning of this chapter, I noted that the emerging organization will have a higher purpose, be philosophical in nature, be sensitive to Earth's limited resources, and be systemically oriented. Such a system will also require a new type of leader, one who is philosophical in matters of mind, body, and spirit and who is both willing and able to accommodate change.

In his book *Mid-Course Correction*, Ray Anderson describes how Hawkin's book *The Ecology of Commerce* came to him through a series of synchronistic events and what it meant to him. He wrote, "It hit me right between the eyes. It was an epiphany. I wasn't halfway through it before I had the vision I was seeking for ... the company, and a powerful sense of urgency to do something to begin to correct the mistakes of the first industrial revolution. Hawkin's message was a spear in my chest." Anderson has gone on to initiate changes that are environmental windfalls and that inspire employees. At the same time they are serving to change the basis of competition in the industry. The end result, not surprising to the new generation of systems thinkers, has been significant financial gains for the company.

A large body of research has been built on the evolution of consciousness through the work of the Institute of Noetic Sciences and the ongoing psychological research started by Clare Graves. This research will help us understand more about the evolution of consciousness. It explains developmentally what the system requirements are for change to the next, more complex level of thinking. Since continuous change will be a key basis of competition for organizations and critical to their ability to address these four system issues, leaders of organizations will need to become well versed in such knowledge. Building on existing intelligence systems, corporations must also have ongoing access to new models, tools, and insights to implement the emerging organization. As with the continuous improvement espoused by TQM, and as with the recovery model espoused by the Twelve Steps, this process is a journey without a clearly defined end, but with critical milestones along the way.

The most ethical thing each of us can do now is to evolve our own consciousness and that of those we can influence.

If this principle is followed, it will create leaders at all levels of our society who are spiritual, philosophical, and systems thinkers. These leaders will view every business function to be within a system, one that is connected to functions, departments, organizations, communities, and the global common good. To paraphrase renowned photographer John Muir, when these leaders look closely enough at anything, they will find it is hitched to everything else in the universe.

When we talk about spiritual and transformational leadership in the context of an organization, we are talking about the opportunity to create business systems that actually help heal the world. There is a common quest, already begun and reaching to all corners of the Earth, that envisions a different kind of world filled with more wholeness and more soul. As the most powerful creative institution on Earth, affecting more lives per day than any other, the workplace has become the leverage point for the creation of this New Order. Together we are poised on the brink of a more purposeful economic system and business organization. Together—with commitment, resolve and a common purpose—we can produce the best of what humanity has to offer.

Margaret A. Lulic, M.A.

Margaret Lulic is an organizational and management consultant, human systems architect, author, and national speaker. Her business assists individuals and organizations explore a better future by solving concrete problems in unique ways. Clients include 3M, ADC Telecommunications, Boise Cascade, DataCard, Dupont, Allina Health Systems, and Norwest Corporation.

She also has worked for organizational, social and educational change as an MBA adjunct faculty member at the University of St. Thomas, as an active member of the Citizen's League, the Minnesota Council for Quality, the World Business Academy, Business for Social Responsibility and the Minnesota High Technology Council. In addition, she is a Board member of Reell Precision Manufacturing Company.

Margaret has published a number of articles and two books— one a book of thought provoking quotations entitled *Working As*

If Life Mattered and the other entitled *Who We Could Be At Work*. The latter book, published in hardcover by Blue Edge Publishing (1998) and in paperback by Butterworth Heinemann (1996), demonstrates her ideas about the transformation of the workplace through the stories of real companies.

POSTSCRIPT

Twelve Steps for Business: Beyond AA?

Krista Weedman Tippett

"*A*A," confessed Bill Wilson, one of its founders, in 1943, "is utter simplicity which encases a complete mystery." Alcoholics Anonymous was a successful, global, flat organization before such a concept was thinkable in the business world; it represented a model of lifelong learning before the phrase was coined. This book offers a multi-faceted and provocative reflection on how the philosophy and foundation of AA—namely, the Twelve Steps—might transform the unfolding realities of the global marketplace.

My own research into addiction awareness and treatment confirms the astonishing adaptability of Twelve Step principles around the world. These Steps transcend cultural, national, and religious differences. They disregard hierarchy, class, wealth, and poverty, and demonstrate the capacity to reach people in every condition and at every stage of life. Yet how rarely we pause to consider the confidence we place in AA's effectiveness, even its existence in our society. It is enlightening to speak with people in countries in which AA is a newer force, where still in living memory alcoholism was an utterly destructive and untreatable affliction, and all too often a lethal one.

Proximity to the Twelve Steps, and to people whose lives have been changed by them, is often in itself a transforming experience. My own professional view of the Twelve Steps is by now mingled richly with my own personal insights as a strategic analyst, planner and communicator, theologian, and erstwhile journalist and diplomat. I appreciate how AA has stood the test of time. I am particularly aware of how the inner logic of the Twelve Steps is increasingly validated by cutting-edge modern disciplines. Why, then, are the Twelve Steps not more widely admired, embraced, studied, and applied by individuals and businesses?

The answer to this enigma must lie, at least in part, in the fact that the Twelve Steps are inevitably linked with the enduring stigma around alcoholism and other addictions. Like the Twelve Steps, this stigma is fluid across cultural, demographic, and religious lines.

Throughout the remarkable process that led to this book, the authors frankly addressed their own questions and misgivings. For example, can we live with the traditional language of the Twelve Steps, as crafted by AA? Should we rework them to reflect new sensibilities? Early on, several authors expressed serious discomfort with key words in the AA/Twelve Step vocabulary—words such as *Higher Power, powerlessness,* and *disease.* AA jargon can feel exclusive, even cult-like, to people who have no firsthand experience with Twelve Step groups. By the same token, the underpinning of faith in a *Higher Power* can seem awkward when Twelve Step addiction treatment professionals advocate for their cause in the political arena.

AA itself, interestingly, has never advocated for its cause but relies on cumulative "marketing"—one life at a time. At this stage in my own thinking, I believe that tapping the wisdom of

AA also means accepting the wisdom and vocabulary of the spare statements which have transformed so many lives. We have no choice but to take Bill Wilson's advice that we are dealing with "mystery," and we should not tamper lightly with this reality.

I would rather underscore a fascinating observation implicit in these pages: At the beginning of the twenty-first century, the word "mystery" is in fact much more palatable, even in a book designed for business audiences, than it was in 1943. The unusual phrase *Higher Power* may be jarring, but collectively we are more comfortable with the language and concepts of "spirituality" than ever before in modern history. The Enlightenment doctrine of reason has proven too narrow a foundation for our civic institutions. Science itself is developing a vocabulary of wonder. *Powerlessness* and *disease* may offend our modern impulse towards self-actualization, and may challenge our boundless confidence in the human capacity for healing and change. But the insights of modern psychology, on which we also often rely, teach that we all carry wounds that we can never fully heal or outgrow. Our burgeoning understanding of the human genome confirms the existence of a physical propensity for addiction, while at the same time enlightening us on the delicate, multifarious interplay between biology and behavior. By insisting that recovery is a lifelong process rather than a cure, the Twelve Steps create an ongoing spiritual discipline that is at once exacting and miraculous, less a method than a way of life.

This insight begs another compelling question, however. Is the full integrity of the Twelve Steps available to people who are not in the throes of some form of addiction? Profound hopelessness led AA's founders to forge and follow the exacting miracle of the Twelve Steps. Despair has mostly characterized those who have found their way to the Twelve Steps ever since. Can we access the mystery of recovery unless we first hit bottom?

This book's authors suggest an intriguing new paradigm, if not perhaps an answer. While the new millennium may not hav

witnessed a higher state of being for humankind, human consciousness has continued undeniably to evolve. Technology
trumps the impossible at a virtually addictive pace. The same
overwhelming pace has brought us to new crises in our personal
and corporate lives, and paradoxically has led many of us to a new
and deepened appreciation for what is human and relational. The
field of "emotional intelligence" is producing stunning data on
effective business development and employee performance and
retention. Like the Twelve Steps, it honors the health of the
whole person and the personal and corporate good sense of nurturing ongoing growth. Similarly, relationships are at the essence
of Twelve Step recovery—a searchingly honest relationship with
all of the aspects of one's own life, including how that life inter-
acts with others.

Personal relationships are also at the core of global business, representing the only bond powerful enough to bridge vast expanses
of distance, differences, and time. The Twelve Steps bring such
practical truths, and many more, into realistic, sustainable, and
creative synergy.

Perhaps our own distinctive twenty-first century experiences
and perspectives allow us the proper humility (another counter-
cultural AA term) to meet the Twelve Steps halfway, and to tap
into AA's simplicity and mystery for new purposes within new
contexts. If so, we may find the culture and language of AA
redefining our vision rather than the other way around. We may
experience serenity amid the increasingly frantic pace of our
lives, culture, and business. We may find courage in the irony
that the "information age" only intensifies our need of comple-
mentary tools for discernment, wisdom, and meaning. We may
find wisdom inside the insidious reality in which work is engulf-
ing more of life. It is forcing us, out of a new despair, to reinvent
business to nurture the fullness of our humanity.